JUST PASSING THROUGH

INTERACTIONS WITH THE WORLD 1938–2021

Also by Daniel Snowman:

USA: The Twenties to Vietnam

Eleanor Roosevelt

Kissing Cousins: An Interpretation of British and American Culture, 1945–1975

If I Had Been ... Ten Historical Fantasies (ed)

The Amadeus Quartet: The Men and the Music

The World of Plácido Domingo

Beyond the Tunnel of History: the 1989 BBC Reith Lectures (ed, with Jacques Darras)

Pole Positions: The Polar Regions and the Future of the Planet

Plácido Domingo's Tales From the Opera

Fins de Siècle (with Asa Briggs; ed)

PastMasters: The Best of 'History Today' (ed)

The Hitler Emigrés: The Cultural impact on Britain of Refugees from Nazism

Historians

Hallelujah! An informal history of the London Philharmonic Choir

The Gilded Stage: A Social History of Opera

Giuseppe Verdi

JUST PASSING THROUGH

INTERACTIONS WITH THE WORLD 1938–2021

DANIEL SNOWMAN

BROWN DOG BOOKS

First published 2021

Published under licence by Brown Dog Books and
The Self-Publishing Partnership, Office 10b, Greenway Farm,
Bath Rd, Wick, Bristol BS30 5RL

www.selfpublishingpartnership.co.uk

ISBN printed book: 978-1-83952-286-4
ISBN e-book: 978-1-83952-287-1

Cover design by Kevin Rylands
Internal design by Tim Jollands

Printed and bound in the UK

This book is printed on FSC certified paper

Contents

In the office.

Introduction

I first started drafting the text of this book in the late 1970s, encouraged to do so by my then agent and principal publisher. The idea was soon dropped as more immediate concerns took over. By chance, I came across the text in 2013 and have periodically added to it over the years that followed. It is not just a 'memoir' recounting one personal experience after another; rather, an attempt to say something about the world in which I have lived via a series of more or less personal vignettes: what it looked like while I was 'passing through'. I write about a Jewish/British child's memories of the war and after, and of life and love in the Cambridge of Denis Brogan, CP Snow and Noel Annan where I watched Churchill delivering one of his last speeches. I recall my time in and across JFK's America, at the new University of Sussex, a year in California in the early 1970s and what I think back to as the high noon of the BBC. I write of extended visits to the Arctic and Antarctic and also to some of the hottest places on the planet, of history and historians, of opera around the world from Gigli to Domingo and of encounters with many of the most memorable of the 'Hitler émigrés'. Do not look in this book for intimate details of personal relationships, except for those that represented important developments in my early life and concern people long departed from it.

If there is a predominant theme running throughout these pages, it is the constant attempt to pass through traditionally accepted boundaries. I used to joke that I was a 'jack of all trades and master of none', or note sardonically that snooty academics doubtless found my writings (and lectures) too 'popular' while some BBC colleagues probably thought me too 'highbrow'. All that was fine with me. Again and again, from the secure base of a happy and fulfilling childhood, I seem to have felt the urge to stake out new territory, often going further afield – both physically and psychologically – than many more conventional 'rebels'.

It wasn't rebelliousness in the traditional sense. Yes, I went on marches, opposing America's involvement in the Vietnam War, Britain's decision to quit the European Union and much in between. But primarily I think it arose from something more positive: a tireless (and to some who had to put up with it, tiresome!) form of intellectual curiosity. A Jewish lad brought up during and after the War in suburban Edgware, I yearned to find out what it was like not being Jewish. Maybe Cambridge would open the gates to the wider world I aspired to inhabit. I wanted to find out what it was like being German. Or a 'Negro' in the American South at a time when the civil rights movement sought inspiration from JFK's 'new frontier'.

At Sussex, Asa Briggs and his senior colleagues gave primacy to the idea of cross-disciplinary studies, unthinkable in the previously almost exclusively mono-disciplinary academic world of Britain, while the BBC in its heyday enabled me – positively encouraged me – to reassess the very nature of what had previously been understood as 'history', to produce projects that sought links between history and the arts, to explore on air a range of largely unquestioned philosophical concepts and to investigate some of the hottest and coldest places on earth. In later years, I relished the chance to lead tours to the great cultural centres of Europe while writing books that attempted to place in their widest historical context such topics as the history of opera and the cultural impact of the refugees from Nazism. Everything I produced – lectures, books, articles, BBC programmes – had a central aim: to create something that, while thoroughly researched, could reach the widest potential audience.

Today, as I write, the world is being overrun by Coronavirus: the deadliest epidemic since the Spanish flu of 1918–19. It is quite likely that, as an 82-year-old with a heart pacemaker, I will not survive for long. Yet I seem to retain the insatiable intellectual curiosity of yore, reading the news on my iPad, clicking on every potentially interesting link and seeking out, for example, what Pepys and Defoe had to say about the Plague of 1665. Why do I need to know all this? Or to be reminded of things I once knew but had meanwhile forgotten? The older I get (as Aristotle nearly said), the more I know I don't know. I might add that the older one gets the more it seems one also tries to recapture the more colourful details of long ago. You want to know about VE Day, the civil rights movement in the old American South, what Churchill or Harry Truman (or Isaiah Berlin or Plácido Domingo) were like up close – or the polar scientists who first identified global warming? Read on!

I may have aspired during my life to break through certain kinds of boundaries. But the aim has always been to create not to destroy, to understand rather than to judge. My lifetime motto or personal cliché was that two plus two could, if carefully amalgamated, make five!

Daniel Snowman, May 2021

Book 1

The War and After

1938–58

Chapter 1
Legacies

My mother used to tell me with a laugh that I was born while she was cooking the fried fish. That is, I was born on a Friday morning at about 11.30am, just around the time she would traditionally have been preparing the 'Friday night' family dinner.

We were Jewish, and Friday night was sacrosanct. When I was eight or nine I sometimes used to think of myself, with much pride and a little self-congratulation, as 'The-Chief-Rabbi's-Grandson'. My mother's father, Harris M. Lazarus (1878–1962), was, in fact, Deputy Chief Rabbi, a stop-gap appointment between 1946 and 1948 when a younger man was chosen for the job, though I contrived to hide this from people. I was once walking in Edgware with a couple of older boys and one of them, mishearing something I had said, asked 'Eh?' The other, only half in fun, turned on his companion and told him that, in addressing me, he should be more polite and say 'I beg your pardon?'. I was, it was explained, the CR's-G.

To me, Grandpa was the Jewish equivalent of the King or the Pope; like the King, his writ ran throughout the British Empire and like the Pope he had the additional advantage of a special relationship with God. You couldn't have a better grandfather than that! However, this also created its problems: when Gandhi was assassinated, in January 1948, I lay awake at night worrying whether they were going to go for Grandpa next.

Gandhi and Grandpa: the two were often compared in our household. Grandpa was the mildest, gentlest, most tolerant of men, as naïve as a child when it came to practical matters such as money, and passionate in his devotion to his God and his family. A man with a rich sense of humour, he also had a strong streak of irritability. In his later years, when he became absorbed in a somewhat obscure study of the correct intonation with which the Jewish scriptures were to be recited, his wrath against those who transgressed in these arcane matters was unbounded, though usually held in reserve until the wrongdoers were out of earshot. He was a purist, a perfectionist, a scholar so painstaking that he was almost incapable of committing anything to print. All his humanity and all his frustrations

Archbishop of Canterbury Geoffrey Fisher (left) and Deputy Chief Rabbi Dayan Harris M. Lazarus (right), c.1947.

were expressed in the intensity with which he tried to communicate the things he loved to the people he loved.

Grandpa was a British patriot and his love for his adopted country and its traditional pomp and ceremony knew no bounds. As 'CR', he met the Archbishop of Canterbury (Geoffrey Fisher) and, with Grandma, attended the wedding of Princess Elizabeth and Philip Duke of Edinburgh in 1947. Almost any general conversational point, whether about language, history, music, the function of law or whatever, would as often as not be illustrated by reference to – and a beautifully reverend rendition of – 'God Save the King'. Politically, he was second to none in his admiration for British democracy, but he voted wherever he thought that the Jews would benefit (which, because the Balfour Declaration had been issued under a Liberal Prime Minister, probably meant a general allegiance to the faltering Liberal party). In his later years, he lived in a block of flats in West Hampstead just opposite the chauffeur of Ernest Bevin, the Labour Foreign Secretary until 1951 and certainly no friend of the Jews. I remember feeling very much part of the clan as we all made anti-Bevin cracks looking out at the Foreign Secretary's limousine from Grandpa's bedroom window.

Grandpa was our moral weather-vane. Many of the awkward day-to-day decisions of life would be resolved by reference to the question: 'What would Grandpa do in this situation?' And, after he died, 'What would Grandpa have done?' In the mid-1960s, when I married my non-Jewish girlfriend Alice and, thereby, caused much heartbreak, one or two wise members of the family said that if Grandpa had still been alive he would no doubt have treated the whole matter with magisterial tolerance and understanding, if only for the sake of poor Alice, and the rest of the family would have fallen into line.

Born in Riga, then part of Tsarist Russia, Grandpa had come to England in his late teens in 1897 (just in time for Queen Victoria's Diamond Jubilee). My other three grandparents were British born, though all eight great-grandparents presumably came from somewhere within the greater Russian 'Pale' (alas, I have no idea from where or how my strange surname emanated, and never thought to ask when there were still people alive who might have known). Grandpa Lazarus's education had been little more than rudimentary, yet within a year or so of arriving in England he had mastered the English language sufficiently to enrol in London University where, in due course, he was awarded an MA degree. His large collection of books, many of them dating back to those first years in England, attested to the most varied tastes; in addition to a large body of Judaica there were Greek and Latin texts in the original, volumes of English, European and Arabic history, philosophy and literature, lots on music and linguistics, a variety of what we would nowadays call do-it-yourself books, and an assortment of heavier volumes on the natural sciences. Grandpa loved his books and his study. He was at his most characteristic pottering around his bookshelves, looking up a point here, checking a reference there, singing quietly to himself in his clear tenor voice or whistling little tunes through his teeth as he did so. In such moods, nothing could disturb him and he lost all sense of time. He was a reader, a browser, the eternal student. For most of his professional life, he was the rabbi of a bustling Jewish congregation and in due course a judge (or 'Dayan') in the highest Jewish Court, the 'Beth Din'. As a public figure, he was conscientious to a degree, a kind man, a person who touched with warmth all who came into contact with him. And yet his work died with him. He left no lasting monument, no important published work, no major administrative reforms. His book

The Ways of Her Household soon looked fussy and dated. That on the correct intonation of the Bible – written in classical Hebrew – lies in manuscript in (I believe) the archives of the Hebrew University in Jerusalem. Grandpa influenced a whole generation of Anglo-Jewry, but fast became a faded memory.

Most patriarchs are recalled as figures to be regarded with awe and even fear rather than unalloyed affection. But the patriarch I remember was a sweet old man, widely admired for his humanity and warmth, slightly patronised for his inability to polish up his thoughts for public consumption or impose all the right worldly routines upon himself, and acknowledged by all who knew him as a genuinely good man. He was important to me as representing the apex of two different hierarchies: the familial and the Jewish.

* * *

Both of my parents came from girl-boy-girl families. My father, Arthur Snowman (1913–82), had an older and a younger sister, my aunts Freda and Diana, while my mother, Bertha (1915–97), had two considerably older siblings, my Aunt Vivienne and Uncle Cecil. I remember thinking impishly that she must have been something of an afterthought to her parents (or one that 'got away'!). Arthur was a handsome young man with blue eyes which he focused exclusively on pretty, dark-haired Bertha Lazarus from the time they were both young teenagers. Bertha was flirtier, flightier, playing tennis with sundry young men until, when she was twenty, she accepted his proposal of marriage. Arthur adored her, the more so as he also revered her universally loved and admired father, Rabbi Dr Lazarus. Bertha had some doubts at first, but was reassured by her parents that Arthur was a good young man who loved her and came from a highly respected Jewish family and that, in time, she would come to love him. They married in May 1937 and went off to honeymoon in Nice; I was born on 4 November 1938.

A few months later, Arthur, Bertha and their baby boy moved into their newly built semi-detached Tudorbethan house at 17 Hillersdon Avenue, Edgware (just behind the Leather Bottle pub, as I later learned to tell people).

Arthur the Soldier, with Bertha.

Chapter 2
The War

Five days after I was born, the Nazi regime in Germany and Austria embarked upon what came to be labelled *Kristallnacht*. Far more than a 'night of broken glass', this was an unprecedented orgy of anti-Semitic cruelty and destruction in the course of which, Jewish homes and shops throughout the Reich were smashed, Jews everywhere humiliated and forced to clear up the mess and many of the men carted off to camps. I have often wondered what it must have been like for Bertha and Arthur, then 23 and 25, as they learned of this appalling near-massacre and cradled their new-born infant. Less than a year later, war was declared and Arthur volunteered to do his bit for King and country. First, he joined the Auxiliary Fire Service helping to put out the flames of the blitz, then he went on to join the army on the Kent coast as an anti-aircraft gunner, leaving Bertha and baby Daniel at home in Edgware. Here we were joined by Kitty Braun, a teenage Jewish refugee from Vienna, and it was essentially by these two young women that I was raised.

My earliest memories are of wartime London. One afternoon I woke up from a little sleep and my mother took me over to the window of the breakfast room and showed me our broken windows and the remains of a nearby house that had been bombed that afternoon. 'Damage,' I mumbled (one of the few words I knew by that stage), blissfully unaware of the fate I had just been spared. At night, I would go to sleep in my nursery and wake up to find myself in the 'shelter' downstairs: our (reinforced) garage. Later on, I became aware of the swooping air-raid sirens and what they told us, and of the single-note 'all clear' which meant we could carry on cheerfully with whatever that earlier call had interrupted. By 1944, I remember my mother taking me into the front garden of a morning and pointing out the overhead fighter squadrons as they flew off on their bombing missions, and then, in the evening, watching them return, often with a poignant gap or two in the formation. And I recall the drone – and then the ominous silence followed by a distant explosion – of the 'flying bombs' as we huddled together in our makeshift shelter. My father, meanwhile, would return on leave from time to time and then, in the morning, return to his

Daniel on the shoulders of Arthur.

'ack-ack' duties on the Kent coast. As he left, dapper in his army uniform, he would smile at my mother and me and tell me to 'look after Mummy while I'm away', at which I would salute and, trying to look as grown up as I could, promise to do my best.

I don't recall any sense of deprivation during the war. My mother, a keen adherent to the latest theories of child-rearing, kept or checked every toenail or hair her baby sprouted, marked my height on every birthday with a carefully drawn line on the nursery wall and kept a loving Record Book of memories, photos, statistics and the like as I grew and (in time) grew up. She would take me in my pram on a walk to the shops or through nearby Stonegrove Park, or perhaps to see her parents, my adoring Lazarus grandparents, who had moved into a house in Old Rectory Gardens (a great name for the residence of a rabbi!) just behind Edgware's Ritz cinema. Rationing was in force, but I had no idea what I was not able

Daniel the Soldier.

to eat. Indeed, I ate well and healthily, almost entirely from domestically produced food, including an extra egg every now and then from our genteel next-door neighbours who had turned part of their back garden into an allotment and part into a chicken coop. Occasionally, my mother or Kitty would give me a soft-boiled egg for breakfast, with bread fingers, and I would draw the face of Hitler on the shell ('Higlerbone', I would call him) and then smash it open joyously with my spoon. I listened to 'the BBC' with my mother and imitated the news broadcasts as I lay in bed at night ('The Russian tanks are approaching the River so-and-so…') and, as the war neared its end, asked her in all innocence whether, once it was concluded, the 'news' would cease. After all, there would be nothing to report. I listened to Churchill's broadcasts by her side and remember celebrating the news of Hitler's death. A few weeks later, I danced around the street bonfire on what we learned to call 'VE Night'. And what a night it was! Everyone up and down the avenue was as warm and welcoming as could be, all doors were open and I was as happy as the proverbial sandboy.

* * *

We had not been without our trials. In October 1944, presumably nine months after one of my father's home leaves, my brother Julian was born in London's Elizabeth Garrett Anderson hospital. At eight days, he was circumcised by our uncle Jack (Dr Jacob Snowman, the leading practitioner in the field). Alas for Julian, the wound did not heal properly and he contracted septicaemia. It seems that wartime hygiene standards at the hospital may have been lacking, or maybe my mother had had rubella while pregnant. Whatever the causes, Julian's life was clearly in danger and he was moved to the Great Ormond Street Hospital for Children. Here he became one of the first civilian patients to be given penicillin. This saved his life. During Julian's illness and slow recovery my mother moved into the hospital to be near him and it was there that I first set eyes on my infant brother. He was in an oxygen tent, his little body studded with spots and markings and tubes of various kinds. I cannot begin to imagine the limitations this severe early illness must have had on his subsequent mental, intellectual and emotional life. He did, however, achieve brief celebrity when Great Ormond Street issued a special pamphlet about their 'miracle baby' and their early, successful use of penicillin. Many decades later, I took Julian over the Alexander Fleming lab in St Mary's Hospital (Paddington) where penicillin had first been developed.

During Julian's illness, I moved in with my Lazarus grandparents and remember reflecting for the first time about the inevitability and finality of death and the very brief time during which we were likely to be alive. The Pharaohs in the Bible were around some 3000 years or more ago, but Grandpa Lazarus would probably die soon and I myself probably had only another 70 years or so to go. I was quite distraught. But 'Auntie Lily' (Mirrie, who had 'done' for the family since she was a teenager in the 1920s) tried to comfort me by giving me a pair of Grandpa's slippers to play with. My mother, meanwhile, was tortured by more painful reflections. Having produced a 'perfect' first baby, she was all the more disturbed by the illness of her second. Was his suffering her fault in some way? At times, as she watched its infantile agony, she even found herself thinking that, if only for its own sake, it might have been better had her poor baby passed away peacefully rather than survive and live a painfully inadequate life. Years later, this thought continued to haunt her, that (like Medea or Norma) she had contemplated the death of her own child: a topic she returned to during the detailed and daily psychoanalysis she underwent in the early 1950s.

Many years later, as I found myself moving away from some of the values and expectations of my childhood and wondering about my (possibly excessive) independent-mindedness, I would hark back to that early period in my life. I thought of the standard sibling rivalry I saw between my own two children and, having been brought up as the adored only child of a loving mother, reflected that I could hardly have failed to have some inner feelings of suppressed resentment when not only did a younger brother come along but he immediately claimed virtually all my mother's attention. Then, just a few months later, my father was de-mobbed so that whatever remaining emotional space she retained was directed in his direction. Crudely, you could say that, having been the total focus of my mother's love for six years, I was suddenly supplanted within a very short time by two other male claims on her love and attention. It didn't of course feel like that at the time and I never consciously resented either my loving father or my poor brother. But perhaps all this helped push me towards a subconscious sense of independence, of having to do my own thing and make and implement my own decisions, that was increasingly to surface in later life.

Chapter 3

Cricket – and Opera

Julian survived, my father was de-mobbed and, as the war receded, family life took over. My father resumed work with his father, the insurance company becoming S. Snowman & Son with offices in Manstone Road in Cricklewood, and my Snowman grandparents moved to a flat up the road in a block called Vernon Court by the crossroads of Hendon Way and the Finchley Road. As for Grandpa Lazarus, on becoming Acting Chief Rabbi in 1946 he and Grandma moved to the official residence in Hamilton Terrace in St Johns Wood and then, from 1948, to Cholmley Gardens, not far from the synagogue in Dennington Park Road where, for the rest of his life, people pointed him out as something of a celebrity. I saw a great deal of both sets of grandparents and it was always a treat when I was able to stay with one or other pair over a weekend and (of course) attend 'Shul' at Dennington Park Road. Grandpa Lazarus trained me for my Bar-Mitzvah, which was held at his synagogue. Indeed, under his tutelage I read the entire 'Sedra', or portion of the Torah, to the assembled congregation – an unusual feat for a 13-year-old – and did so, moreover, in what was then the trendy new 'Sephardi', or Israeli, accent. And it was Grandpa, not the local Minister (Dr Isaac Levy, himself something of a star in the Jewish world at the time) who gave the sermon.

But for all this, home was in Edgware. That is where I lived, where I went to school (Edgware Primary School), had my friends and, under the affectionate eye of my parents, developed my early interests. Two, in particular, which my father loved, enthusiasms he passed on to me: cricket and opera.

Cricket was what jolly good chaps did at the weekend. But it was more than that. My father had learned to love cricket as a boy and talked of the great players of the 1930s he had seen. During the winter of 1946/7 he would often put the wireless on in the early hours of the morning to catch the close-of-play BBC commentary (by crackly telephone) from Australia of the first post-war Ashes series. 'We' lost to the Aussies; but one day, Dad assured me, the Ashes would be ours once more.

As my father taught me the rudiments of cricket in our back garden, I learned to keep a straight bat – in life as well as in cricket. Also, that when

The Cricketer.

you know you are 'out' you should start walking even before being given out by the umpire, and that you should always wish the other side well and hope the best team will win. It was no disgrace to lose honourably; hadn't our boys in the Light Brigade done so, and Scott of the Antarctic (a lesson I also learned from the 1948 film starring John Mills)? What *was* dishonourable was to try and win by any means possible, fair or foul – as Amundsen had done when beating Scott to the South Pole. Cricket was like saying the Prayer for the Royal Family in synagogue. It was a way of showing that you cared for more than the merely transient, that your heart was in the right place: that you were British. As I bowled at my dad in the back garden, he would boast cheekily that 'no one has ever got me out yet!' All that made me do was laugh – and try to bowl even better! As I got older, I often went to Stonegrove Park on a Sunday to play cricket with the other boys and, with my dad and later without him, I would take the 113 bus to Lord's where I would vociferously support Middlesex against all rivals (and come back with as many autographs as I was able to muster).

On 27 August 1948, I went with a friend to Lord's where the invincible visiting Australians under Don Bradman were playing one of the last matches of their legendary tour. It was Bradman's 40th birthday and I remember being almost ecstatic as I watched 'the Don' take a catch in the outfield. Nearly forty years later, while planning a visit to Australia, I wrote to him about the possibility of a BBC interview to mark his forthcoming 80th. He sent me a courteous home-typed letter (he was then living in Adelaide) explaining that he was already committed to a series of interviews for the ABC but that I might want to contact them about the idea. The old man's signature was almost indistinguishable from the autograph I had from nearly forty years earlier: yet another sign of the extraordinarily consistent self-discipline of this great but modest man. Once in Sydney, I spoke to him on the phone but, sadly, it proved impossible for me to visit him. Then, in March 2006 while on a lecture tour of Australia, I made a pilgrimage to the Bradman Museum (now the International Cricket Hall of Fame) in the town of Bowral in New South Wales.

The last time I went to Lord's was in 2021 on 8 January 2021 and again on 26 February. Not for cricket. But because it was being used by the National Health Service as a site at which to administer vaccinations to the over-80s against Coronavirus (Covid-19), the pandemic that was by then killing large numbers of people across the world.

* * *

As for opera, this too was something deep in my father's soul. He would tell me how, back in the late 1930s after a busy day in his father's insurance office, he would trundle off to Sadler's Wells Theatre and enjoy (wallow in) a probably not especially good performance of *Trovatore, Traviata, Carmen, Bohème* or whatever. He loved these works and their eye-watering arias and love duets, and had a treasured collection of early gramophone records (78 rpm) of Caruso, Melba, Tetrazzini, Galli-Curci, Gigli and others singing some of his favourite operatic excerpts. I lapped these up much as I lapped up all there was to learn about cricket.

There was not much opera in post-war London. But the entrepreneur Jay Pomeroy set up what he called his 'New London Opera Company' at the Cambridge Theatre, starring singers including Mariano Stabile, Marko Rothmüller, the young Russian soprano Daria Bayan and others, often with conductor Alberto Erede at the helm. Another of Pomeroy's stalwarts was the British (Jewish, communist) bass Martin Lawrence, and he and Stabile would regularly bring down the house in the patter duet from *Don Pasquale*. In a letter to *OPERA Magazine* (April 2005), the Australian music critic and broadcaster John Cargher wrote: 'Why is the New London Opera Company missing from the reference books? It saved London's operatic life when at its nadir.'

On 27 October 1947, the opera was *Rigoletto* (with Martin Lawrence as Sparafucile and I believe Rothmüller in the title role and Bayan as Gilda). Perhaps it was a charity evening. At any rate, my Lazarus grandparents were due to attend and my father offered to take me. Excited, I prepared myself by listening to his records of 'La donna è mobile' and the famous quartet. On the night itself, however, I nearly didn't make it. The plan was that I would be taken by bus (by our Irish 'maid' Kathleen) to an agreed stop where I would meet my father, who would then take me off to the theatre. As Kathleen and I sailed on obliviously past the appointed stop, my father came rushing up the stairs of the bus; he'd spotted us and leapt on! I'm glad he did. The evening that followed was one of the most memorable of my life.

The first scene of *Rigoletto* lasts 20 minutes or so, after which my dad turned to me benignly and asked if I had had enough and did I want him to take me home? I still remember my mock resentment. 'No!' I replied emphatically. 'I *don't* want to go home. We haven't even got to the bits I know from *your* gramophone records!' And we both laughed. We stayed to the end, and I was overwhelmed at the power of this wonderful multimedia performance pouring across to me from stage and pit. Afterwards, we went home by taxi with my grandparents. On the way, no doubt to humour me, my grandma Lazarus said, laughing, 'Oh well, I suppose Rigoletto wriggled out of it in the end!' To which I, still wrapped up in the great theatrical tragedy to which I had just been exposed, was at pains to put her right and explain at length that, on the contrary, poor Rigoletto (and on and on I went...)!

A couple of years later (5 April 1949), my father took me to the Royal Albert Hall to see Gigli. The great Italian tenor was my father's idol – and was about to become mine. As I knew from Dad's records, Gigli had the most mellifluous voice, capable of floating up and above the stave with a honeyed lyricism that, in the tenor aria from *The Pearl Fishers* for example, was utterly irresistible. In earlier days, he had also been capable of a more stentorian sound, though never with quite the macho 'heft' of Caruso, Martinelli or (later) Domingo. By now approaching 60, it was the lyrical Gigli we went to see and hear. Before we did so, I wrote to the great man asking for his autograph and received in the post a signed photo on which he had written 'To Master Daniel Snowman, Best Regards, Beniamino Gigli'. I later discovered that during the war Gigli had sung for Mussolini and Hitler. But so far as I have been able to find out, these activities were never seriously held against him and, if mentioned at all, were attributed to political naivety rather than active enthusiasm for fascism.

On the night of the concert, my father and I had inexpensive seats alongside the organ above and behind the platform (from where I was later to sing countless concerts as a member of the London Philharmonic Choir). We looked out at a packed Albert Hall as 7.30 approached: six thousand excited, expectant fans. There was no amplification. No orchestra. No warm-up act from someone else. Just Gigli and his pianist. Out he came, a chubby old man with a warm smile. He bowed, turned his back towards where we were sitting – and the music began. The programme started with the aria 'O Paradiso' from the Meyerbeer opera I learned to call *L'Africana*. In those days, Italians normally sang all operas in Italian, Germans in German, the French in French and British singers in English. Gigli's programme on this evening included Liszt's *Liebestraum* ('Amor che a me splendé soavamente') though not, I was sorry to note, 'Mi par d'udir ancora' from Bizet's *I pescatori di perle.*

Over the next few years, Gigli made a number of tours around the UK, always with London's RAH appearance as the highlight. Altogether,

Gigli: autographed photo to 'Master Daniel Snowman'.

I heard him on half a dozen occasions, initially with my father and later with my equally opera-loving schoolfriend, and budding would-be tenor, Anthony Goldberg (with whom I soon learned to sing the famous *Pearl Fishers* duet). Just before the interval, and certainly after the official programme had been completed, Gigli would sing a few encores, popular pieces such as 'La donna è mobile' for which he'd turn and face those of us sitting behind him. People would call out what they wanted him to sing. '*Pagliacci!*' someone would yell from the upper reaches of the vast hall, or '*Sorrento!*'. Gigli would pretend to reel from the verbal onslaught and then launch into yet another favourite. I adored him.

* * *

Gigli's was not my only valued (and possibly valuable) autograph. During my early teens, there was scarcely a celebrity to whom I did not dispatch an obsequious letter, with an enclosed stamped addressed envelope, requesting a signature. Most complied, often sending a signed photograph, and my albums came to be packed with the autographs of sports heroes (particularly cricketers of earlier times), the great stage and screen stars of the day (Noel Coward, Olivier etc.), writers and intellectuals (T.S.

Eliot, Bertrand Russell), politicians (Herbert Hoover, Harry Truman, Eden, Attlee) and countless musicians (Menuhin, Klemperer, Toscanini, Stravinsky, Sibelius). Britten and Vaughan Williams each wrote me a letter. Britten's said:

> Dear Daniel Snowman,
> I don't usually like answering autographs – but you wrote such a nice letter that I send you my signature with great pleasure. I hope you go on hearing and liking operas.
> With every good wish,
> Benjamin Britten

As for wonderful, crusty old VW, he wrote back to say:

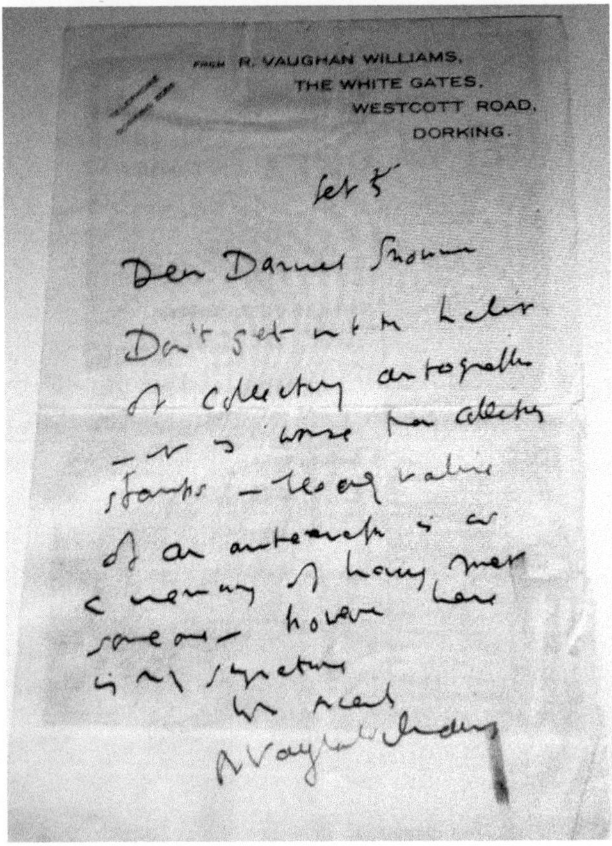

FROM R. VAUGHAN WILLIAMS,
THE WHITE GATES,
WESTCOTT ROAD,
DORKING.

Sept 5

Dear Daniel Snowman
Don't get into the habit of collecting autographs – it is worse than collecting stamps – the only value of an autograph is as a memory of having met someone – however here is my signature with best wishes
R Vaughan Williams

Letter from Ralph Vaughan Williams.

Dear Daniel Snowman,
Don't get into the habit of collecting autographs – it is worse than collecting stamps – the only value of an autograph is as the memory of having met someone – however here is my signature.
Yours sincerely,
R Vaughan Williams

* * *

During the late 1940s and early '50s, I went to a score or more of operas, mostly with my father at the treasured theatre of his own adolescence, Sadler's Wells, and it was here that I was introduced to my first *Bohème, Fledermaus, Carmen, Barber, Tosca, Trovatore, Faust, Cav-&-Pag* and the rest.

Covent Garden had to wait until, in autumn 1952, Anthony Goldberg and I took advantage of the half-term holiday to mooch around the great opera house and wondered how we might obtain a glance of its legendary interior. There, guarding the portals, was the stolid, top-hatted and be-gowned figure of Sergeant Martin, door-keeper extraordinaire. Was there anything we young boys wanted? Well, yes there was, we answered with all the chutzpah of intrepid not-yet-14-year-olds, and told him we loved opera, sang it together, and would give anything to see inside his great theatre. Sergeant Martin took pity on us and said that, yes, he could sneak us into the theatre. But there was a rehearsal going on so we must promise to sit very quietly and keep out of everybody's way.

On stage, wearing a wide, full-length rehearsal dress, was a pleasantly rotund young lady with rich red hair, and a small, older lady all in black. They were evidently working on a succession of duets, to piano accompaniment, while getting used to the basic moves: through a doorway ('la porta?', I heard the redhead ask at one point), across to the other side of the stage or wherever they were instructed to go. The opera was *Norma* and the man in charge, beating time from the pit, was the conductor Vittorio Gui. The dark-clothed lady, I learned, was the famed Italian mezzo Ebe Stignani and the plump young redhead a Greek American soprano about to make her Covent Garden debut. Her name was Maria Meneghini Callas.

For a couple of hours or more, Anthony and I sat enthralled, close to the stage, as Callas and Stignani, working cooperatively together under guidance from Gui, sang and re-sang one of the most powerful duet scenes in all opera. Callas's debut at Covent Garden was still a few days away; this morning was mine.

A year later, when Callas returned to Covent Garden, I added Maria Meneghini Callas to my autograph collection. By now, she had slimmed down almost beyond recognition. And a few years after that, she was no longer Meneghini. The legend had begun.

Chapter 4
Family Values

'Family', like 'democracy' or 'cricket' or 'Hebrew classes', was a moral concept that could brook no criticism when I was a child. To me, 'the family' was a tightly knit structure of four grandparents, two parents, my brother Julian and myself. And, on special occasions like weddings and funerals, a plethora of more or less distant cousins (since each of my four grandparents had come from a family of eight or ten children). This was the way our family was, and this was how families were supposed to be. Outside our little clan there were, I knew, other sorts of families: husbands and wives who got divorced, youngsters whose parents died, parents who beat their kids, kids who ran away from home. Cases such as these one knew about, naturally, and even sympathised with in a mature and distant fashion. But their way was not our way. Our family was the standard against which all others were assessed.

Both pairs of grandparents included a strong-willed female. Grandma Lazarus, an organiser and hostess to her fingertips, saw it as her duty to protect Grandpa from the mundane things in life so that his energies could be kept for higher matters. Grandma knew how to throw a gracious tea party, how to speak to the mighty, and how to manage her husband's affairs so that he gave the appearance of having mastered these same skills. If it had not been for her ambitions for him, he might well have remained just a humble rabbi and scholar in the best *Shtetl* tradition. Grandma was sometimes called 'The Duchess' behind her back, and her airs and graces could undoubtedly be hurtful. Mirrie constantly felt demeaned by Grandma's imperiousness and it was only after Grandma's death in 1951 that she was able to develop to the full her own formidable capacity to organise both Grandpa and his home.

* * *

The contrast between Grandpa and Grandma was even stronger on the Snowman side. My paternal grandmother was the daughter of a Jewish immigrant, Morris Wartski, who had settled in North Wales, founded a jewellery business that later came to include royalty among its clientele, helped the young Carnarvon politician David Lloyd George over some of his early hurdles, and ruled over a large and idolising family. Two of his daughters, Harriet and Rosa, married two Snowman brothers from London, Emanuel and Samuel ('Mannie' and 'Sam'). Mannie entered the Wartski business and built up the branch in London's Regent Street, became a prominent local politician (Tory Mayor of Hampstead in the early 1950s) and he and Harriet maintained a splendid lifestyle full of grand sociability for half a century. When our new Queen Elizabeth II had her Coronation, on 2nd June 1953, I was invited to join members of the family and watch the procession from the window of the Wartski jewellers in Regent Street. We had to arrive early to get through security, and I recall sitting alongside my second cousin and almost exact contemporary, Rosemary Alexander (whose maternal grandmother, Sara, was a Wartski) and watching the horse-drawn Royal coach as it passed below us, the Queen waving to the packed crowds. Also as part of the procession was another coach containing a beaming Winston Churchill and, further along among leaders from the Empire and the wider world, the much-publicised Queen Salote of Tonga, at that time a British protectorate.

For a proud young British lad like me, that summer of 1953 saw one cause for celebration after another. On 29th May, just a few days before the Coronation, news reached Britain that 'we' had conquered Everest. That is to say that for the first time men had climbed to the peak of Mount Everest in the Himalayas, the world's highest mountain, and that the 'conquest' had been achieved by Edmund Hillary, aided by Tenzing Norgay. Never mind that Hillary was from New Zealand and Tenzing a local Sherpa. It was 'we', a British team, who had done it. Many years later, when visiting Delhi for the BBC, I had a delightful meeting with Hillary (who shortly thereafter was appointed New Zealand's High Commissioner to India).

Then there was sport. Just four days after the Coronation, the Derby was won by the greatest of all British jockeys, Gordon Richards. And, to me, a cricket fan, the most celebratory event of all that summer was that, for the first time since the disreputable 'bodyline' series of 1932–3, 'we' beat the Aussies and won back the Ashes. After four successive draws, the final Test took place in August at the Kennington Oval. I managed to get into the ground on the last two days of the match, and was forefront among the crowd of ecstatic onlookers who, as Denis Compton scored the winning run, poured across the sacred turf to cheer our victors.

* * *

Victory at the Oval, 19 August, 1953.

There was a strong artistic element among many members of both the Wartskis and the Snowmen and their kin. Some were practitioners, others energetic entrepreneurs and consumers of the arts. Kenneth, the son of Mannie and Harriet, was a talented and enthusiastic painter. He inherited the management of Warstki, had many friends in the artistic community and wrote eloquently about the Russian court jeweller Carl Fabergé whose richly bejewelled eggs the company had obtained in the wake of the Russian Revolution. Kenneth's son, my second cousin and fellow opera lover Nicholas, founded the Cambridge University Opera Society and, with David Atherton, the London Sinfonietta, went on to work with Pierre Boulez in Paris and later ran London's South Bank, Glyndebourne and subsequently the Opéra National du Rhin based in Strasbourg. Another of my second cousins, Jeremy Robson, became an admired poet (and one of the founders of the poetry-and-jazz movement of the 1960s) as well as a successful publisher, while yet another of my Mannie-and-Harriet related cousins, Colin Snowman, was, from his youth, a brilliant if sometimes provocative painter. Back between the wars, Leonard Snowman (the son of Dr Jacob Snowman, the eldest of the Snowman brothers) and himself a doctor, produced English translations of the works of such pioneers of Hebrew poetry as Bialik and Tchernikovsy, while another of the brothers of Mannie and Sam Snowman, the painter Isaac ('Icky') Snowman, was commissioned to do portraits of King George V and Queen Mary. A nephew of Sam Snowman's sister Jessie was the multi-talented Jonathan Miller, and the niece of Minnie Snowman, wife of Ezra, the youngest of the Snowman siblings, was a young actress called Claire Bloom.

Sam Snowman and Rosie Wartski, my father's parents, lived a comparatively simple existence. Sam founded a modest insurance brokerage, provided Rosie and their three children with a series of small but comfortable homes in the Brondesbury and Kilburn area of London, and enjoyed a quiet domestic life that was well suited to his fundamentally retiring personality. Like many of the Snowmen of his generation – Jacob ('Jack', the successful doctor and celebrated circumciser), Louis the less successful of the Snowman painters, Ezra the furniture dealer and, above all, Mannie himself – my grandfather had drooping eyes and a sardonic sense of humour. Jokes were mumbled and guffaws muffled but both were plentiful. Emotions were powerful but usually repressed. Occasionally, things would bubble out. Grandpa Sam would suddenly push his way aggressively to the front of a queue, or hit with his umbrella a car that had passed him in the street too close for safety. He was not above letting his aggressions take even more dubious forms; he would, for instance, get an occasional kick out of re-using an unfranked stamp and I even recall him surreptitiously sneaking off with a marrow lifted from someone's wartime allotment. But, in general, Grandpa Snowman kept his resentments and his aggressions, his loves and his hates, firmly bottled up. He was the sort of person who would have sat in the back row at his own wedding.

Not so Grandma Rosie. Carried off from her Welsh hills at the age of 17 to be married to a bright young Londoner and soon plunged into the cares and responsibilities of young motherhood, she probably never knew the full fun and glitter that can accompany mature girlhood: the parties, the gentlemen admirers, the excitement of travel. The lure of London must have been great at first, but the life that ensued was fairly humdrum, particularly in contrast with the wealth and social success of sister Harriet. My grandmother displayed her sense of deprivation not by bitterness or moodiness for she was by nature a bubbly soul. But she seemed to have cultivated a sort of compensatory fantasy life that enabled her to regale

Portrait of 'Rosie Snowman' by her brother-in-law, the painter Isaac ('Icky') Snowman – who was also commissioned to paint portraits of King George V and Queen Mary.

her companions with a torrent of stories about the latest goings-on in high society or about the murkier aspects of some book that she had just read but which of course should be banned. All this did wonders for her morale, enabling her to think herself into the social circles from which she felt herself barred by her husband's shyness and relative impecuniosity. But if she had an exaggerated notion of who was who, she retained to the end of her 85 years a solid grip on what was what. A splendidly down-to-earth woman with an unstoppable flow of language, a slightly whimsical adjustment to the frustrations of life (represented physically by a facial tic that surfaced whenever her oratory was in full flight), Grandma Snowman knew and enjoyed her role as wife and mother, grandmother and, in her last years, great-grandmother, and lived life as fully as her circumstances permitted.

* * *

The thing about them all was that they – we – were Jewish (or at least 'Jew-*ish*' as Jonathan Miller famously put it in the 1960 show *Beyond the Fringe*) and this at first provided one of the principal aspects of my identity. At home, we 'kept' what we called 'Friday night' (prayers – and good food

– to inaugurate the Sabbath), observed the Jewish festivals and, each week, attended Edgware synagogue in a small 1930s building at the north end of Mowbray Road, now used as a Jewish school (in 1957 the synagogue moved to a new building along the Edgware Way). Later, I was to have endless debates with myself and others about precisely what it meant to be Jewish; was Jewishness a question of one's race, one's religion, one's nationality? Or primarily something ascribed to one by others? Before the age of ten such questions scarcely bothered me. I was Jewish in all these respects and more and (as I learned to say, but only in the presence of others who were also Jewish) 'proud of it'.

The pride was strong but semi-secret. At school, when a teacher was being reproachful or supercilious, I would reassure myself with the inner thought that I (unlike the silly old teacher) knew how to read Hebrew. Maybe I didn't come top of the class at school. But at Sunday classes I was often awarded a prize. And, for a while I was the CR's-G! These things were rarely mentioned outside Jewish circles and, if they did come out, one was very defensive and formal about them. But they were a source of great inner pride and comfort to me as a child, especially when the outside world administered one of its occasional buffetings.

Being Jewish, therefore, brought a lot of benefits and, in particular, gave me a feeling of being an integral part of a powerful and vibrant community that treated me as though I were something special. People told me I had all the makings of a future Chief Rabbi. Nobody ever said equivalent things in the 'Christian' world of school; there, I was but a ragamuffin among ragamuffins. But in the Jewish community I was marked out for great things.

There were other by-products of this intensely Jewish identity. For instance, a rigid differentiation between the way in which I learned to treat our Jewish and non-Jewish neighbours in Edgware. I always felt I had freer access to the Jewish homes than to what I thought of, with exaggerated courtesy, as the 'Christian' ones. I could shout and giggle and run across barefoot and raid the larder in many of the Jewish homes, but felt I had to be on my best behaviour in the non-Jewish ones. Those Christian homes were so clean, so respectable, so lacking in oomph. I couldn't eat in those homes (what forbidden 'trefah' food might they offer me?) and I couldn't marry one of their daughters. And, I supposed, they were probably not terribly interested in us and would only see and hear things they wouldn't understand if they became too close to us. So there was no real point in getting too friendly. Or so I grew up believing. Even when I became pals with some of our non-Jewish neighbours I knew without being told that, for all the street cricket or tennis we might play together, an essential division nonetheless remained.

When I was first assimilating these attitudes our house at No. 17 was an oasis of Jewishness in a desert of Christianity, a somewhat beleaguered outpost of our secret Empire. There were other Jewish households up and down the avenue to be sure, but still far too many un-breached fortresses for comfort. Our neighbours on both sides and opposite were all so good, so nice, so correct. Then the fortresses began to fall. First to go was No. 19 (where Cyril Stein and his family moved in); then an East End jeweller (Kutchinsky) and his family took over at No. 16, across the road. The Judaification of our stretch of the avenue was completed when a gown-trade designer and his family became our semi-detached neighbours at No. 15. As this process unfolded, and was paralleled further down the road, more and more doors were open to me, increasingly uninhibited conversation could take place over more and more garden gates and fences, and more and more children in the street became my potential playmates and intimates. The few bastions of Christian respectability that remained no doubt observed this gradual erosion of their power and may even have resented it. If so, they would not have been either the first or the last denizens to have regretted the changing character of their neighbourhood. But they were far too polite ever to say or even imply anything derogatory to us. Indeed, I received nothing but unfailing courtesy from all our non-Jewish neighbours whenever we would meet in the street. 'Good morning. Lovely day today.' Or whatever. Did they feel what I felt? Did they experience the Big Divide as acutely as I did? I don't know. I doubt it. I hope not.

Chapter 5
Schooldays

I must have been five when taken to Edgware Primary for my first day at school. I was not quite sure why I was being sent there. After all, I could read and write and count, thanks to my mother's earnest and assiduous pursuit of all the latest and most fashionable theories of child development. She knew about Montessori and Rudolph Steiner and Froebel, and I knew my ABC, how to spell difficult words and no doubt how to count from nought to a hundred and more. On a tube back to Edgware one day, I had looked out at the sign indicating the name of the penultimate station, Burnt Oak, and amused my fellow passengers by reading slowly, out loud: '**BURR... N'T... O-ACK**'. What more was there to learn?

Lots, as I soon came to discover under the kind and conscientious attention of Miss Rebould, Miss Robinson, Miss Arnold, Miss Scutt, Miss Minty, and of the older Mrs Harmer under whose benign guidance we listened to the BBC's regular 'Music and Movement' programmes. All of them were presided over by the headmaster Mr Byrd (who got himself into the local paper by 'stealing' school milk, i.e. taking home some that would otherwise have remained unconsumed). I was probably something of a 'good boy', setting off on the mile or so to school at 8.10 every morning, satchel on back, and home again in the mid-afternoon. I had firm instructions from my mother not to talk to anyone along the way if I didn't know them, particularly if some man tried to persuade me to go home with him for tea. I found this something of a mystery, failing to understand how anyone could get me to follow them if I didn't want to. Nothing untoward ever happened. But one day a friend and I stopped on the way home to cram our satchels with fallen conkers from beneath an overripe horse chestnut tree. When I eventually got home, my mother, clearly anxious, asked where I had been and coolly decided to punish me by taking two handfuls of conkers from the pile and throwing them away. After which the incident was closed.

By autumn 1948, after some four or five years of primary school and with the 11-plus exam beginning to loom, my parents decided I was a clever little boy, at least potentially, and I transferred to the Junior (or preparatory) branch of Haberdasher's Aske's, an outstanding day school for boys. In due course, I moved on from the prep school (in Page Street) to the main school, then in Westbere Road on the edges of Cricklewood and West Hampstead. Education at 'Habs' required payment (£19 per term, as I recall) which my parents were willing to pay. But Julian, by now growing into an angry, frustrated and mentally retarded child, clearly needed special schooling, and my parents were keen to send him as a weekly border to a Rudolph Steiner school in King's Langley. In order to pay for this, they would have to withdraw me from Habs and send me instead to an ordinary (free) grammar school such as Christ's College, Finchley, which (for a 'mere' grammar school) apparently had an excellent reputation. Would this be acceptable to me, they asked, to which I reassured them that I would be happy to do anything I could to help my poor brother. They consulted my grandfather (Lazarus) who, they told me later, had reassured them that Daniel would 'do well' wherever he was sent. So off I went to CCF, initially into Class 1B as I hadn't excelled in the 11-plus exam.

I soon moved up the ranks (into the A stream) and, working my way into, through and beyond puberty, gradually learned the challenges and fulfilments of serious study. Christ's College, on the southern edges of Finchley near the confluence of Hendon Lane and Regent's Park Road, was an old Victorian Gothic pile dominated by a great tower which, with its pointed top, provided generations of post-pubic schoolboys with opportunities for suppressed giggles. It was a good school in which, despite its name, many of the pupils were from local Jewish families. At CCF, I was happy to start learning French from the genial Mr Oliver and to love French literature under the watchful eye and ear of Mr Rhys, to read Shakespeare and Keats with the ageing Mr Tallis and later his talented replacements Messrs Whitworth and Carey, and to learn Geography from Mr Daines, Latin from the shy Mr Barber and, above all, History from Mr Felsenstein. Perhaps in his case 'happy' is not quite the word. Denis Felsenstein, a young man in his mid-twenties, could be intimidating as he stepped into a noisy classroom and would frown at the class and demand to know 'What's going on in here?' Silence was instantly restored as 'Felsey' got on to the job of instructing us methodically about the Crimean War, Gladstone and Disraeli or whatever.

Our 'Phys Ed' instructor was at first the rotund and ageing Mr Pumphrey and later on George Robb, talented celebrity weekend footballer

CCF Boys: Sense (and Insensibility) 'On the Road'.

for Finchley United and, on one famous occasion in 1953, outside left in the England team that played (and lost to) Hungary at Wembley. Then there was Mr Chamberlain, memorable for a deeply booming voice, especially when giving out notice at morning Assembly or ordering the boys *not* to run along the corridors. At the top of the pile was the CCF headmaster, Mr Pegrum, a diminutive, ageing gentleman who also took it upon himself to teach Religious Instruction. Pegrum and the school secretary, the severe, grey-headed, preternaturally virginal Miss Beal, made a genteel, old-fashioned pair, much respected but all too easy to make secret fun of.

* * *

In addition to work, life at school for us 'Finchleians' included sports days, prize days, school plays and the like. A number of us became particularly friendly: mostly young Jewish lads with lively minds and a sense of adventure. We would arrange parties, perhaps inviting girls one or other of us knew from good local schools (in the hope that an innocent afternoon might turn into a 'necking party'). And we'd go hitchhiking abroad over the school holidays. I liked to think of myself as an experienced foreign traveller, having been sent by my parents to stay with a friend of my mother's in Paris when I was 14. I travelled by propellered aeroplane from an aerodrome (Croydon? Northolt?) and, on arrival at Le Bourget, was asked by the obsequious man who had carried my case for 'Service' (a term that had to be explained to me). A couple of years later, I was one of six Finchleians who hitchhiked in pairs across France, Belgium and Luxembourg, meeting by prior agreement at various youth hostels along the way. Amazing as it may sound in these modern, dangerous but digitally linked days, everything worked out perfectly. We even, when in Basle, made a brief foray across the border into Germany, something I was keen to do but of which my parents would probably have disapproved.

As I climbed up the greasy pole of adolescence, I took on fewer subjects and concentrated for my A Levels on just three: English, French and History. The day I entered the Sixth Form, I made a decision to stop collecting autographs. What had started as a pre-adolescent hobby, a childhood way of feeling some control over the big outside world, had become an all-consuming obsession. Everyone of consequence had to be signed up. There was only one way of dealing with this if I was to have any hope of scholarly success, and that was to bring the whole enterprise to a halt. Which I did. Henceforth, no new autographs. It was time to get on with real life. And that meant, above all, to do well at History.

Mr Felsenstein could be a hard taskmaster, especially towards a lad he thought showed genuine promise. Jonathan Frankel, one of his recent pupils and a distant cousin of mine, had recently obtained an Open Scholarship in history to Jesus College, Cambridge, and Felsenstein thought I had the potential to follow suit. He pushed me, marked my essays a little on the harsh side, pointing out minor deficiencies or illogicalities, and somehow never quite gave me the 'A' I hoped they might merit. 'Good in a lackadaisical sort of way,' he wrote in one of my termly school reports (forcing my father and me to check what was meant by that unusual adjective). The pressure became painful and at times I became so self-conscious about the need to read this or that set book that, rather than take in the content of what was before me, I found myself checking the page numbers and involuntarily counting how many I still had to complete before reaching the end of that week's assignment. I could have wilted under the pressure, and my parents went to have a word with Felsenstein. But he reassured them of my abilities and potential and clearly knew what he was doing and why. For me, it was a test of personality as well as intellect. But I managed to struggle on, deeply aware that a brilliant history teacher had faith in my abilities.

Many decades later, during my later 70s and early 80s, I came to know Denis again and, frequently taking coffee with him at his flat just north of London's Henlys Corner, I obtained great pleasure from being able to tell this wonderfully alert nonagenarian what a huge and beneficial affect he had had on my life.

* * *

Early on during my time at CCF, the school produced Shakespeare's *Julius Caesar* and I was one of the crowd who turned out to hear Mark Anthony's 'Friends, Romans, countrymen' speech. I was even assigned a solo line: 'Live Brutus, Live!' But the big event was *Hamlet*, produced in the school's centenary year of 1957. Many of my close friends were involved, among them Jack Gaist as Hamlet and the richly creative Neil Hornick as Claudius, while I played the part of Laertes, Hamlet's old schoolfriend, son of Polonius and brother to Ophelia. All of us were duly made up and costumed (and struggled with what Neil dubbed 'the curse of the wrinkled tights'). My part involved considerable athleticism,

Hamlet, *1957.*
Daniel (left, as Laertes) and Neil Hornick (Claudius).

including a sword fight with Hamlet (for which Jack Gaist and I were trained by old Mr Pumphrey). Ophelia, incidentally, was played by the youngest, and by far the most brilliant, of our schoolboy colleagues, John F.C. Kingman. A slightly diffident lad, Kingman went on to become a professor of mathematics in his twenties and later acquired a knighthood and became Vice-Chancellor of the University of Bristol.

There was another 'big event' in 1957, one that almost put an end to my future ambitions and those of several of my schoolboy colleagues: our parody of the School Song. Christ's College had been the creation of one Thomas Reader White, a high-minded Victorian cleric no doubt keen to raise the moral and intellectual standards of young Christian manhood. The School Song was in the form of a typically Victorian hymn, a Luther-cum-Bach-style chorale each verse of which ended with the name of CCF's revered founder. In this, the school's centenary year, it was due to be sung as a prominent feature of the Centenary Speech Day. How could a number of clever latter-day Finchleians, many of them Jewish, fail to compose their own cheeky new version? The result, with primary input from the intrepid and ever-imaginative Neil Hornick, was (I thought at the time) a masterpiece of parody. A five-verse chorale that began thus:

Now stand we here in terror
Of one who wields the power
And gives the head his sexual thrill
Each day behind the tower.
We know how much he likes her,
He thinks of her at night:
If he but knew who had her first,
'Twas Thomas Reader White...

This was pinned up in full a few days before the great event, inside the upper reaches of the Tower (where else!).

On the morning of the day itself, Mr Pegrum summoned all in the Sixth Form to a special meeting. Grim-faced, he held up the piece of paper and, slowly and quietly, read out the poem. Apparently, it had been seen by the school's caretaker, who had handed it in. 'When I read this filth,' Pegrum told us with infinite sadness, 'I felt that all I had tried to achieve during more than thirty years as a teacher had been rendered null and void.' Would any of us who knew about this please step forward. It was impossible not to feel sorry for this honest old man. After some hesitation, Neil led the way and we all, slowly, followed. Pegrum and his colleagues duly conferred about how to react. Without doubt, some of us could have been expelled. On the other hand, the wrongdoers included among their ranks a bunch of boys who were likely to obtain good university places and thereby bring further glory to the school. In the event, Pegrum, good Christian that he was, decided to do nothing. But we all came to the Centenary Speech Day in somewhat sombre mood, attending with duly reverend mien to the wise words uttered by our elders and betters.

Chapter 6
Being Jew-ish

In my early years my Jewishness was all gain. But as I approached my teens and my horizons began to widen, it also began to produce occasional problems. At first, these were largely logistical, and they usually had to do with the two great loves of my life – opera and cricket. Take Friday nights. 'Friday night' was a ritual with us. If ever the familial and the Jewish came together it was here. Friday night, the inauguration of 'Shabbos', the Sabbath. This lasted from nightfall on Friday until just after nightfall on Saturday, and during this 25-hour period all activities associated with the world of work were forbidden. In those days we did not even put lights on and off or use the telephone or radio during the Sabbath period. And Friday night was especially sacrosanct. Late one Friday night when I was about ten, there was a Gigli concert on the radio. I went to bed early that evening, full of food and love and purity, waited wide awake until the appointed hour arrived, and then, with the most razor-sharp calculation, listened to the concert on the little wireless next to my bed from a distance of half an inch or less, turning it as loud as I dared consistent with the requirement that the noise must on no account reach my parents' bedroom next door. I didn't hear it very clearly. But I heard it!

Then there was the vexed question of playing cricket on the Sabbath. My cricket captain at school, when I was about 14, a superbly athletic Indian boy, a Brahmin gentleman to his leonine fingertips, wanted me to play in some class or house match on a Saturday and I just didn't have it in me to explain to this paragon of Briticised culture why my religion wouldn't let me. If I wasn't allowed to go in buses or trains on a Saturday, why couldn't I walk to the ground? Sadly, I put him on the phone to Father who explained to him all about the tradition and forbears and the sanctity of the family and that seemed to settle it. You win some and you lose others.

In time, I found myself challenging the dictates of my Jewishness with increasing virulence. *Why* couldn't I put on a light on Saturday? Because it represented work, I was told; in the old days you had to rub two sticks together and that was real toil. But, said I, the harnessing of gas (let alone the discovery of electricity) had long since taken away any work from the process of putting on a light… My arguments were not without effect. By the time I was in my teens, my parents had succumbed to my superior powers of logic (or, perhaps, to my tireless and arrogant assertiveness) and we put on lights on the Sabbath and – on Saturday but not Friday night – the radio. This little victory did not satisfy me. Why couldn't we have milk after meat, I asked? Because, replied my father, in the Bible it says: 'Thou shalt not seethe a kid in its mother's milk'. But what chance could there possibly have been of the milk in this piece of chocolate I wanted to consume coming from precisely the cow that provided the beef dinner I had just eaten? Unlikely, my father would concede (as my mother looked on, worried only about family harmony), but the rule was a useful fence around the law. OK, said I, but why no milk after chicken? Chickens don't produce any milk for their kids to be seethed in. My father would again resort to the 'fence-around-the-law' argument and I would become obstreperous and wonder sarcastically why the fence stopped at chickens and didn't also forbid milk after fish. If the dietary laws were defended as 'a useful discipline' ('You never know,' said Dad ingeniously, 'when you might experience severe deprivation'), I countered by saying that, in that case, we should all practise the long jump every day since we could never be sure that we wouldn't one day come up against a wide fissure in the ground.

Then there was Yom Kippur, the Day of Atonement, the most important day in the Jewish calendar. On this day, the Bible commanded you to afflict your soul as you repented of your sins, and the time-honoured way of administering self-affliction was by fasting. But as a strapping young lad of 14 or 15, I found a 25-hour fast no burden, let alone an affliction. Indeed, I even made a point of taking home my young brother Julian from synagogue in mid-Yom Kippur, giving him (but only him!) his lunch, and cheerily returning with him for the rest of the day's services. Since fasting was no affliction, I began to ask cockily, surely by doing so I wasn't fully obeying the biblical injunction? Fasting should surely only be incumbent upon those who suffer thereby. In which case, I concluded triumphantly, there was no point in my fasting!

I had a further Yom Kippur twist up my sleeve. All the important Jewish festivals were celebrated over two days in order to be sure (said the ancient rabbis in their wisdom) that the correctly designated period was covered even in far-flung corners of the earth – a sensible precaution in the days before telegraph and telephone. Then how come, I would ask with the arrogance of a soldier brandishing a new weapon, how come Yom Kippur too is not celebrated for two days and nights instead of just one?

With arguments such as these I grated away at my father's nerves, convinced that, since my freshly discovered powers of logic were no doubt greater than his, I was therefore 'right' merely by virtue of having won a verbal argument. I had all the aggressive confidence of one whose precocious talent was bolstered by a secure and reinforcing home. My parents lovingly nurtured my talents and it was no doubt ungracious of me to sharpen my intellectual teeth against the fragile skin with which my father clothed his instinctive attachment to a religion more cherished than understood. But every elk battles with whatever antlers it manages to sprout, and no society (they used to say) has ever refrained from putting to practical use whatever technological innovations are available to it. If I was learning at school how to think straight and fast, I had to try out this new skill at home as well. So, Dad:

> How do we know the Bible was divinely inspired?
>
> How can we be against racism and yet proclaim ourselves a 'chosen people'?
>
> How can we believe in a heaven for good people after death but hold no belief about the destination of bad people?
>
> How can we have faith in a God that permitted the Nazi gas chambers?
>
> How can God be omnipotent if He gives us free will?
>
> Why are we selective about which biblical laws to obey (e.g. those on diet) and which to ignore (e.g. about stoning adulterers or witches)?

It was tough on my father. The greatest minds have tackled questions such as these and failed to come up with adequate answers. But these general shafts were fuelled by more immediate concerns:

> By what logic was a bus ride to the cinema on a Saturday considered work whereas getting all togged up in suit and tie – and hat – and sitting through a 3-hour synagogue service was not?
>
> Why were even the gestures of conformity to the wider Christian culture taboo? If I had uttered the forbidden word ('Christ') while singing a Bach chorale or had knelt down with the other boys at a school service, would my allegiance to Judaism really have been one whit the weaker?

And, in time, the big one:

> Why shouldn't I befriend non-Jewish girls?

Chapter 7
The Girl Problem

This was the nub of the matter. The whole point of 'Friday night', Sunday classes, my Bar-Mitzvah, the dietary laws and of everything else was to generate a sufficiently strong Jewish identity in me that I would never commit the ultimate, unforgivable transgression. There had been a mere 18 million Jews in the world when I was born and a third of these had been massacred by the time I was six-and-a-half. To be Jewish was to be part of a small and excessively vulnerable group. I heard much talk, in the most scathing and moralistic tones, of 'marrying out' and every self-respecting Jewish household I knew erected a massive fence around even the possibility of this dreaded event ever occurring.

Virtually my entire active social circle was composed of Jewish people. At school, where most friendships were made at meals and during breaktime, I would spend the lunch period in a special classroom with the other Jewish boys who, like me, would bring sandwiches rather than eat un-kosher school dinners. At weekends, I would go to synagogue on Saturday morning, Hebrew classes on Sunday morning and, in my teens, off to the Edgware – or the larger, livelier Golders Green – branch of Jewish Youth Study Groups on Sunday evenings. JYSG was a wonderful organisation, perfect for serious-minded Jewish adolescents keen to meet others and to learn about their shared legacy. I found myself on the national committee, learned to chair a meeting and to speak in public, and particularly enjoyed the residential winter and summer schools I attended where, in addition to having lectures and outings, we sang Israeli songs together, danced '*rikkudim*' and, with a little luck, we boys might actually have a chance to snog the '*Havera*' of our dormitory dreams. One with whom I became (respectably) friendly was Pamela Howard, from Birmingham. Many decades later, when Pamela was an internationally respected theatre scenographer (and opera lover), we re-met from time to time. Another with whom I became close was my fellow Edgwarean, Naomi Silverstone (later Nomi Sharon): actor, novelist, playwright and lifelong seeker after spiritual truth with whom I lived for a few years in the later 1960s and with whom I remained a close friend until her death in 2019.

One way and another, there was little chance of my becoming closely acquainted with non-Jewish people and virtually none of knowing any non-Jewish girls. Well into my early teens I found this closed social system perfectly congenial. Individual non-Jews may have been a source of amazement or amusement to me and my schoolfriends; they were, by and large, granted respect but not intimacy. As for non-Jewish girls, they might figure in our jokes, our fantasies and our night-time longings or we might dismiss them as mere '*shiksas*'. But none of us really knew any. Not properly, anyway. *Shiksas* were a fruit both forbidden and unavailable. Exciting to contemplate but no more attainable than a national sweepstake jackpot.

'Do you know the one about Yankele who is brought up before the rabbinate accused of sleeping with his fiancée before marrying her?' someone would ask in the boys' dormitory at a JYSG summer school.

'No. Go on.'

'"Yankele," says the rabbi sternly, "do you realise the seriousness of your sin? Why, sleeping with a fiancée is as good as sleeping with a shiksa!"

'"Excuse me," replies Yankele with a smirk, "but nothing is as good as sleeping with a shiksa!"'

As I grew into my mid-teens, I made two discoveries and they proved to be disturbingly interrelated. The first was that I seemed to be able to administer what I thought to be devastating blows to the brand of Judaism in which I had been raised, simply by applying to it the logical and analytical mode of thought that I was being taught at school. Maybe (I began to think) I should expose myself more openly to all that the wider non-Jewish world had to offer. At the time, we had a succession of Italian *au pairs*, notably 'Tina' (real name Concetta), a bright, feisty Neapolitan in early middle age who had come to London in part to keep a sororal eye on her glamorous younger sister 'Assia' (r.n. Assunta) who, having gone through who-knows-what conjugal problems, was *au pairing* half a mile down the road from us. My father always had a soft spot for all things Italian, especially earthy women in the Mangano/Lollobrigida/Loren mode, and I, like him, enjoyed trying out a phrase or two of my embryonically operatic Italian on Tina. Tina also spoke French, which I had also been learning, so she and I were able to talk conspiratorially to one another from time to time, always with a good hearty laugh. What was it like being a Catholic, I would ask her? Did she and others like her actually believe the things the priests told them? One evening, I joined the sisters at a social evening at a nearby Catholic church and was introduced to the priest. I don't think I learned much about theology that evening; but I remember enjoying myself hugely: a Jewish lad among a throng of Catholic girls from France, Spain, Italy and elsewhere. For reasons I couldn't fathom, I was always trying to imagine what it must be like being someone else, striving to find out what it was like living in another place or time. I went on to take a postal course in Roman Catholicism, not – I had to explain to my anxious parents – because I was thinking of converting but because I was curious to understand what it was like being a Catholic.

The second discovery was that, at the very stage at which I began to assert my newly discovered intellectual prowess, I also found myself periodically in the grip of an even more powerful force, one which paid scant allegiance to either Judaism or logical thought or anything else I was supposed to care about: sex. The physical demands of puberty gradually pushed themselves with ruthless insistence to the forefront of my consciousness and there were moments in my mid-teens when I could scarcely concentrate on much else. At the very time that my Judaism was being undermined by my logic, my logic was being undermined by my emerging romantic urges. Thus, a natural convergence began to develop in my mind between the two new areas of concentration upon which I had alighted, and 'the wider world' and 'girls' came, at first separately and then together, to dominate my thoughts and feelings.

'The wider world' meant Tom Paine on the *Rights of Man*, Verdi and the Risorgimento, here a touch of Indian philosophy, there a smidgeon of French existentialism. It meant that black and brown and yellow people the world over should be treated equally with whites and that every culture had things it could learn from every other. As though to compensate for a rich but narrowly blinkered childhood, I began to grope for a new ethic, 'humanism' perhaps, of global scope. I learned French with assiduity and picked up scattered phrases and a passable accent in several other European languages. I sought out the latest films by Godard or Truffaut, Vittorio De Sica or Satyajit Ray, and read (or read about) Kierkegaard, Goethe and Cervantes. And I hitchhiked with friends during school holidays to Copenhagen, Brussels, Basle and Paris. I went to coffee bars and learned to eat baklava and something called 'pizza' and to drink cappuccino and espresso, and to be especially charming to any Indians and Africans I ever met. And in time, I learned to chat up that inexhaustible supply of human material on which to practise my new intercultural theories: the *air pair* girls who graced many of the Jewish homes in our neighbourhood with their delectable presence.

I found them utterly captivating and enjoyed entering into every sort of subterfuge in order to get to know them better. These kitchen flirtations were harmless enough. But their legacy was that I now knew for certain that 'they' were no different from 'us'. I had broken through the Great Divide and, like the Bear who Climbed Over the Mountain (not to mention Keats's Naughty Little Boy who Ran Away to Scotland), had discovered that things on the far side were much like things on my own. Non-Jewish girls ate and drank and talked and laughed and cried just as Jewish girls were wont to do. They neither smelled nor felt different (nor even tasted different) from Jewish ones. However, this knowledge was so sacred and the manner of its discovery so secret that I was not able to communicate it to anybody. I was in the privileged but frustrating position of one of the great mystical prophets of old who is vouchsafed some special revelation but only on the condition that he keeps it strictly to himself.

* * *

For the next year or so the non-sexual aspects of my quest for the 'wider world' took precedence over the romantic and most of my energies went into my schoolwork as exams loomed. So I studied my Corneille and my Flaubert, my Chaucer and my Dickens, and memorised all the facts and theories about Henry VIII and Bismarck and Lloyd George, and successfully negotiated my A Level and State Scholarship exams.

It was decided that I would stay on at school for a third year in the Sixth Form in order to try for an Open Scholarship to Cambridge. Up I went in December 1957, with my particular sights set on Jesus College (by now the home of Jonny Frankel). I was in residence for nearly a week during which I had to submit to a succession of demanding exams and interviews. The only way to deal with the inevitable strain, I decided, was not to spend the evenings desperately revising for the next day's ordeal but, on the contrary, to find ways to relax and get a good night's sleep. One evening, I went round to the Arts Cinema (then in Market Passage) where they were showing a film of *Aida* in which actors mouthed the parts pre-recorded by leading singers. The name part was sung by Renata Tebaldi, but what I most remembered was the heaving bosom of the actress who played the part, the glorious Sophia Loren.

During the course of my stay in Cambridge, I had to undergo several

History exams, of course, each offering a wide range of questions from which to choose, plus an exam inviting the candidate to expatiate at length on a single topic. Against all advice, I tended to leap straight into writing and, only after completing my essay or essays, go back over what I had written, make corrections – and, crucially, write out on another sheet of paper a somewhat pseudo 'structure', full of sections and subsections, 'moreovers' and 'howevers' and affix it (flimsily crossed through) to the top of the main text so that, with luck, the examiners would be impressed by the orderly mind with which I had seemed to pre-plan all that I had gone on to write.

I also had to do a language exam, translating into English both a 'modern' and an 'ancient' text. My French was excellent, and the only word I did not know was *nénuphar* (which, I have never forgotten since, is a water lily). My Latin, however, was abysmal since I and my CCF friends had spent most of our time with poor Mr Barber trying to humiliate or trick rather than to learn from him. Were we correct, we'd ask Barber, that the Latin for 'yesterday a cow' was 'heri vacca' (hairy whacker – get it?); yes, he'd confirm, and we boys would all collapse in helpless laughter. So when I was confronted with a Latin text to translate for my Cambridge Open Scholarship, a new plan of campaign was urgently required. I decided that if I couldn't satisfy my examiners I could at least entertain them. So I wrote as witty and elegant a piece of prose as I could, drawing on the meaning, or apparent meaning, of any Latin words I happened to recognise. I like to think my sheer bravado may have drawn a smile from whoever had to mark this particular paper.

My father had driven me to Jesus College the day before the Scholarship exams began. When we arrived, we asked the Head Porter at Jesus if he could kindly arrange for me to have vegetarian meals while I was in residence. Ten months later, when I returned to the college to take up the Open Scholarship I had been awarded, the Head Porter remembered me and offered to arrange vegetarian meals for me. 'No thanks,' I said. 'That won't be necessary.'

I had entered my wider world at last.

Book 2

Cambridge

1958–61

Chapter 8

Israel – and Brussels

When the telegram arrived at our home in Edgware in December 1957 that I had won an Open Scholarship to Cambridge, my mother was ecstatic; I still recall her scream of delirious delight at the news. My father (who always, I think, regretted never having had a university education himself) was equally congratulatory. But I remember him quoting, amiably enough and with a mock Jewish accent, some distant, older cousin of his to the effect that 'educatio' is the curse of religio'. When young people went off to study the wider world, in other words, there was always a danger that they would forget, or at least downgrade, the world that had first nurtured them.

Perhaps I was already doing that to some extent. There were ten months between achievement of my Scholarship and going up to Cambridge. Part of the time was spent reading *War and Peace*. But in the summer of 1958, I undertook a period of extensive travel. My parents encouraged me to go on a visit to Israel. The state was now ten years old and, by and large, well-received around the world: a democracy amid dictatorships, an entrepreneurial society that watered the deserts and produced outstanding scientists, a modern state led by a man (Ben-Gurion) who looked like an Old Testament prophet, and a country in which many idealistic inhabitants lived on collective communities called *Kibbutzim* where all resources were amicably and equally shared. I was no ideological Zionist, nor was I by now any kind of observant Jew. But I was open-minded, prepared to try any experience that others recommended, and off I went on a six-week tour sponsored by a Jewish organisation keen to recruit new young settlers. After a sleepless rail journey down to Marseilles, I joined the ship, the *Artsa*, and off we sailed across the Mediterranean towards Haifa.

I enjoyed the six weeks that followed and, with the rest of my group, picked grapes on a Kibbutz, sat on the Dead Sea, took tea with a Druze community, saw Ben-Gurion at a 10th anniversary event atop Mount Carmel and was taken by friendly and informative guides to every major centre from Jerusalem, down through the desert to Eilat and up to Galilee, the Golan Heights and the Syrian and Lebanese borders. What a beautiful country this was! Did I want to make '*Aliyah*' and live there? No way. But I was perfectly at ease with those who had.

At the end of the summer I returned to Marseilles and took the train to Paris. But I was not yet ready to return to Edgware. I made instead for Brussels, in effect the capital of the recently established European Coal and Steel Community (ECSC) and, throughout the summer and autumn of 1958, home of the World Exposition. At the time, I had very little knowledge of the great movement towards unity and interdependence that had been developing on the continent of Europe. If my instincts and inclinations were cosmopolitan and international – I spoke good French and had travelled extensively around north-western Europe – my ignorance about the European Community was almost total. At the Brussels Exposition I wandered from one pavilion to the next, enjoyed this, hated that, and relaxed by sitting for hours in the Austrian pavilion in a deep armchair through the head section of which was wafted sweet music by Haydn, Mozart, Beethoven and Schubert.

But the greatest impact upon me was made by the pavilion representing the ECSC. I was distressed that this section of the Exposition was tucked away behind the Belgian Congo and thought it should have been the centrepiece. Although the pavilion was ostensibly about coal and steel (and featured a coalmine), the literature accompanying it spelled out clearly that the eventual aim of the Community was far broader and included the possibility of ultimate political federation. The Brussels Exposition left a profound impression upon my imagination. A year later I joined the Cambridge University European Group and the following year became its Chairman.

Chapter 9

Up to Cambridge

In the event, Cambridge proved to be not quite the wider world I had expected but the substitution of one largely exclusive world for another. Life was just as privileged, protected and immured from the great outside as anything my supposedly blinkered childhood had provided. At Cambridge, everything was laid on. There was literally nothing I had to worry about if I didn't choose to do so, except – only in the run-up to exams and even then only if I wanted to get a good degree – my work. If I wanted to spend my entire time studying, this was perfectly acceptable. If I wanted to play squash or rugger or act or play in a jazz band or become a minor politico, that too was fine. At Jesus College, all the practical, material things were looked after. As a Scholar, I was given rooms in College, just off the central tower facing the main square (or 'Lawn'). I never had to give a thought to the provenance or content of the next meal, nor to how my room or corridor or toilet would be cleaned. Even my bed was made by a lady especially employed for the purpose. I was one of the 'gentlemen', was addressed as 'sir' by the 'college servants' and had personal access – at Jesus and throughout the wider university community – to some of the most brilliant and civilised men and women on the planet.

* * *

This was in many ways the tail end of an era. I remember thinking this on 17 October 1959 when watching Winston Churchill, then nearly 85, as he made one of his last public speeches. By now a bent and somewhat flabby old man, he had come to Cambridge to dedicate the ground on which Churchill College was to be built. He nevertheless stood for some time in the breeze and read a prepared text in which he acknowledged those who had helped make the new college possible, and he emphasised the importance it would attach to science and 'technology' (savouring, and slightly stumbling over, that relatively unfamiliar word). The man primarily associated in every mind with victory in the Second World War concluded his oration with an inspirational vision of world peace. 'I trust and believe,' he said with conviction, 'that this College, this seed

Churchill at Cambridge, 17 October 1959.
(Photograph, and text of speech, courtesy of the
Churchill Archives Centre, Churchill College, Cambridge)

that we have sown, will grow to shelter and nurture generations who may add most notably to the strength and happiness of our people, and to the knowledge and peaceful progress of the world.' Having helped plant and water the sapling on the site that would grow into Churchill College, he ended with a poem:

> The mighty oak from an acorn towers;
> A tiny seed can fill a field with flowers.

When the ceremony was over, Churchill's car drove slowly past me. For a fleeting moment, those once fierce eyes looked out benignly into mine, and into those of a young German girl who was accompanying me. I fancied that I had been present at possibly the final page in one of the most remarkable chapters of British history.

* * *

In other ways, the end-of-era atmosphere was not so obvious. Things may have been about to change, but few fully realised it yet. Undergraduates were still normally expected to wear gowns at lectures and supervisions and also in the evenings in the college refectory or in the streets outside college, and nobody seriously challenged a custom that seemed likely to remain in force in perpetuity. All colleges were single-sex residences (and the Cambridge Union still an all-male preserve) and members of the opposite sex were not generally allowed into college rooms before noon or after 11 pm, a ruling that made for a certain amount of surreptitious, spike-ridden 'climbing in' and 'climbing out'. The majority of undergraduates seemed to me to have been recruited from Britain's wealthy and privileged public schools, many of which enjoyed special relationships and even closed scholarships with particular Cambridge colleges. Throughout the university, one encountered smooth and self-consciously superior styles of dress and speech that seemed so deeply entrenched as to be almost part of the topography; nobody could have imagined these things giving way within a few short years to the long hair and jeans and affected working-class vowels so common among the student body by the later 1960s. The social atmosphere at Cambridge in my time is brought vividly to mind by an abiding memory I have of an evening in 1960 at the height of the Congo catastrophe when I slipped into the rooms of a friend before evening hall. One or two other men were there and we all, wearing our gowns and sipping our sherry, discussed the appalling carnage in the Congo with all the blasé sophistication and detachment we could muster.

Detachment was the watchword. One had to be, or appear to be, what a later generation would describe as 'cool'. '*Surtout pas trop de zèle*,' said Talleyrand. This quality of restraint, so characteristic of British elite culture ever since the days of Wellington, was something I had to learn the hard way just at a time when, ironically, it was about to come under considerable attack. Unlike so many of the men and women at Cambridge, I had not been tempered in the blue flames of the English public-school tradition. It is true that my parents had tried to display an emotional mastery of most situations and my background was by no means as wildly expressive as some. But the upper-class cool I encountered at Cambridge, the almost imperceptible cock of the head and instant frozen smile from a passing acquaintance, the calculated and easily withdrawn mealtime bonhomie, the tense and controlled back-of-the-throat enunciation – these things were not easy to get used to.

Why couldn't people wave and smile and laugh and pout and talk with their hands and their eyes just as people had done at school, in family gatherings and at Study Group summer schools? Why did they take their sports (and their drinking) so seriously? I was simply dumbfounded as I tried to understand the routines of this public-school culture, which I was encountering *en masse* for the first time. I wasn't part of it, tended to be a little intimidated and had few aspirations to join it. But I knew that I had to make some adjustment to it if I were not to have an excruciatingly uncomfortable three years.

* * *

One afternoon, early in 1959, I sat by the Jesus College sports field with one of my few college friends. He was of an even more cynical disposition than I was and he painted with a few acid strokes the futility of everything that all the people around us – and we ourselves – were doing in life. The chap who talked endlessly about cricket, rugger and the respectable ladies of Newnham and Girton colleges, the mechanical genius who actually cared about the inside of car engines, the big noise in the Union, the Footlights type, the 7-days-a-week swot: where would they all be in a few years' time? And with what effect upon humanity at large?

My friend worked himself up into a bitter lather of nihilism. I was

Jesus College lawn.

reminded of the philosophical position that held that, since inertia was a natural state of affairs, one should never get out of bed in the morning as one's reasons for doing so were bound to be inconsistent with first principles. But my friend had a point. Why lift a finger? Why bother to learn how to converse with the 'rugger buggers' or how to throw a successful sherry party? Why bother to chat up the bevy of boring bluestockings? Why work hard to master the intricacies of the Tudor economy or the Cluniac reforms? What difference would any of this activity make? Indeed, what difference to the wider world, my friend asked with a sigh of disgust, if he or I were to die? Or had never existed?

This passionate nihilism held a certain attraction for me and it undoubtedly corresponded with the mood with which I regarded many of the cool smoothies who surrounded me at Jesus College. But it was also brimming with dangers, the most obvious of which, if extreme, was suicide. Temperamentally, I was not given to the sort of absolute self-abnegation that could lead to suicide, however, and tended to enjoy my fair share of ego fulfilments, aware as I was of the petty inconsequentiality of them. I told my friend that, meaningless though it undoubtedly was, I intended to pass my time on this earth (and more immediately here at Cambridge) busying myself with pastimes that lived up to their name and successfully passed the time. I acknowledged that rowing and drinking and the social rituals associated with them could be unbearably tedious. My college, furthermore, was little more to me than a hotel and I shared my friend's distaste for anything so parochial as a college-based society or club.

However, Cambridge as a whole provided many opportunities for one to invest one's time and talent in various acceptable 'public' activities with a reasonable expectation of being able to enjoy a gratifying yield of private fulfilments. Thus: I enjoyed music so I would join an opera group or choir. I thought that Britain should be part of a wider grouping of nations so I would join the Cambridge Federalists – and get to know the foreign girls in town. And I enjoyed reading History (and doing well in exams) so would keep up with my studies. It was all very calculated and it was, I admitted from the start, no more than an insurance policy against the discomforts of cynicism and nihilism. But it worked. I pursued this formula throughout my remaining two-and-a-half years at Cambridge and found that my time and attention and emotional energies were fully stretched. Time really did pass. My poor friend, incapable of making so practical a compromise with the world, retained the melancholy logic of his original vision and landed up, a year or two later, in hospital suffering from severe depression.

The adjustment I had made was characteristic. Although I had branded the super-cool public-school ethic as the polar opposite of the Jewish suburban life from which I had come, there was in truth a common element to my perception of each. For I saw them both as exclusive and privileged systems while what I was searching for was something *in*clusive, all-embracing, universalistic. Just as I had hoped that, by leaving Edgware and going off to the wider world of Cambridge, I would tear off the blinkers of my childhood so, as I sat talking to my cynical friend by the sports field that afternoon in early 1959, I found myself laying down plans for transcending the provincialism of college life and incorporating as my realm all that Cambridge as a whole had to offer. Before Cambridge, I had read Corneille, hitchhiked around the continent of Europe and, back home, tried to befriend its beautiful envoys. At Cambridge, I sang Verdi and Bach and Beethoven, learned about Pericles, Canossa, the Fronde, the Vendée and the Zollverein, became chairman of the Cambridge University European Group ('CUEG') that wanted Britain to join Europe and had a succession of continental friends (especially German). The wider world was forever beckoning. Any new experience was there to be savoured; those that I liked I would repeat and those that I did not would at least have been enriching.

* * *

Like Raskolnikov in Dostoyevsky's *Crime and Punishment*, I knew that everything I did, however outré, would have to have its own intellectual rationale. Thus, I became the only person I had ever known who, from a thoroughly observant orthodox Jewish background, decided to take a calculatedly intellectual decision to drop everything. There were to be no halfway measures. Not for me the residual taboos that some Jewish friends retained against pork or shrimp, nor would I regard Friday night or Saturday – or Passover or even Yom Kippur – as something special. People told me that I would miss Friday nights, the candles, the warm communality, the sense that one was safely distanced from the hurry and bustle of everyday life. Others, more insistently, assured me that, although I might think that I could dispense with things spiritual while temporal things were going so well, I would one day return to Judaism and that I could be assured that my God and my coreligionists would never desert me in my time of need. My response was not haughty. I was not 'anti' and had no desire to shock or offend. Rather, my aim was to achieve a position from which my decisions about what to eat or refrain from eating or what to do or avoid doing on an any particular day were the product of my own preferences rather than those of a social group into which I happened to have been born.

One day, all these fine sentiments were put severely to the test with the Incident of the Blood Sausage. I sometimes used to share a sandwich lunch with a friend, a diplomat's son, who had somewhat exotic tastes. His contribution might be a particularly rare and ravishing cheese or, on another day, some darker-than-dark bread. One lunchtime it was a blood sausage. Blithely, I took a bite, pretended to myself that there was nothing unusual about such a step – and spat it out instantly as the cloying and half-clotted blood refused to slither down my gullet. Was I retching in response to ancestral prejudice? Did my new policy oblige me to eat – and to enjoy – every variety of formerly forbidden food? No; this would have been an even greater enslavement than that from which I thought I was freeing myself. I decided that real liberation from the restrictions of my childhood consisted in being able to avoid some particular foods, not because they were forbidden but because I just didn't like them! Henceforth, I would never eat blood sausage again; my reasons for not doing so proclaimed not my thraldom to atavistic rituals but my liberation from them. A man is genuinely free, explained Marx, not when he shakes off the forces by which he is driven but when he is fully cognisant of them.

* * *

The Raskolnikov syndrome fell well short of murder and did not touch on even the outer fringes of crime. But my predisposition to try out and analyse new experiences led me quite a distance from the world of home and school. In my early days at Cambridge, I sometimes used to go to Dr Alice Roughton's regular Sunday evening Open House. Here, one was guaranteed a huge open log fire, a massive stilton and some wine and the presence of an occasional intellectual or artistic giant – plus, of course, a horde of undergraduates and sundry young ladies from across the map of Europe. It was on such an occasion that I met Gabor Cossa, the first of a series of charming, talented and maddening Hungarians whose paths would cross with mine, and the result was that I took a small part (a member of Macheath's gang) in his Christmas 1958 production at the

The Threepenny Opera *(Daniel second on right).*

ADC theatre of *The Threepenny Opera* by Bertolt Brecht and composer Kurt Weill. The conductor was Guy Woolfenden.

In the run-up to the production I grew a beard. One evening, Gabor and members of the cast went to London where (along with the young Shirley Bassey) we participated in a live arts programme on television. After it was over, I went to Edgware to spend the night with my parents before returning to Cambridge. They had watched the TV performance and stayed awake to welcome me. When I entered their bedroom, around midnight, they exclaimed, with much amusement, that I had forgotten to take off my beard! To which I responded with a cheeky (or chinny) grin as they gradually realised it was real. I retained a beard for the rest of my life.

The following term I sang an even tinier part (alongside Michael Rippon, later a distinguished classical soloist) in Peter Tranchell's opera *The Mayor of Casterbridge*, again conducted by Woolfenden. I loved singing and acting. But the thankless and tiring exertions of two stage productions were enough to convince me that I wanted to put in less and take out more. It was with something like this in mind that I decided to devote my spare aesthetic energies to the Cambridge University Music Society.

Chapter 10

Music in Cambridge and London

CUMS under the baton of David Willcocks of King's unlocked a new world to me. My first concert, in June 1959, was a performance in King's College chapel of Verdi's *Requiem*, an event my parents were able to attend. As the sun faded outside that austere Tudor building and I poured out my heart in the 'Dies Irae', I felt that I had found the only form of religious ritual that was ever likely to stir my heart. During my second and third years at Cambridge we performed *Gerontius*, Beethoven's Ninth

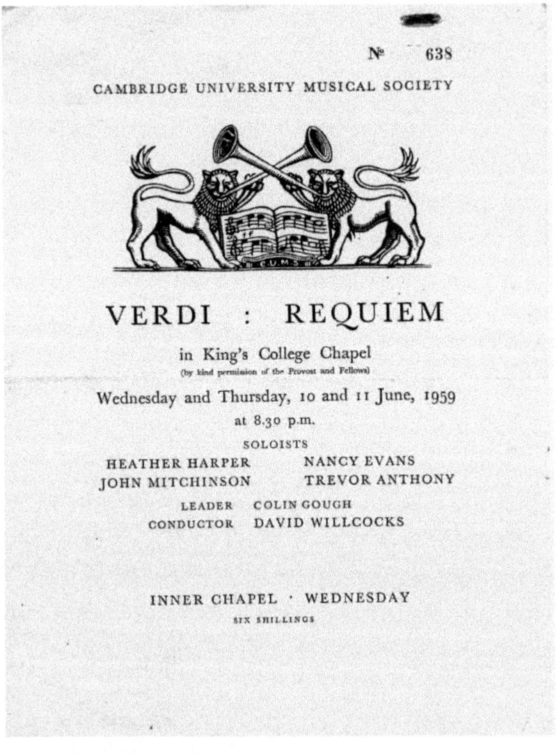

№ 638

CAMBRIDGE UNIVERSITY MUSICAL SOCIETY

CUMS

VERDI : REQUIEM

in King's College Chapel

(by kind permission of the Provost and Fellows)

Wednesday and Thursday, 10 and 11 June, 1959

at 8.30 p.m.

SOLOISTS

HEATHER HARPER NANCY EVANS

JOHN MITCHINSON TREVOR ANTHONY

LEADER COLIN GOUGH

CONDUCTOR DAVID WILLCOCKS

INNER CHAPEL · WEDNESDAY

SIX SHILLINGS

Verdi Requiem, *Cambridge, June 1959.*

Symphony, Berlioz's *Damnation of Faust* (complete with costumed stage chorus and lantern slides), Mozart's *Coronation* Mass and the Tallis 40-part motet *Spem in Alium*.

But the greatest occasion was the first British performance, in November 1960 under the composer's direction, of Benjamin Britten's *Cantata Academica*, a piece commissioned a few months earlier by Paul Sacher to mark the 500th anniversary of the University of Basel. Britten had recently received an Honorary Doctorate from Cambridge, and I was bowled over by the clarity with which 'Dr Britten', on paper and in person, communicated his intentions to his performers, the total authority with which he would conduct rehearsals, and the deft mixture of seriousness and wit with which he would coax a chorus of amateurs and persuade them to enter his strange but enchanting world of sound. As its name implies, the Cantata is full of academic tricks, such as lines that are repeated backwards and/or upside down, and the words are in Latin. At one point during

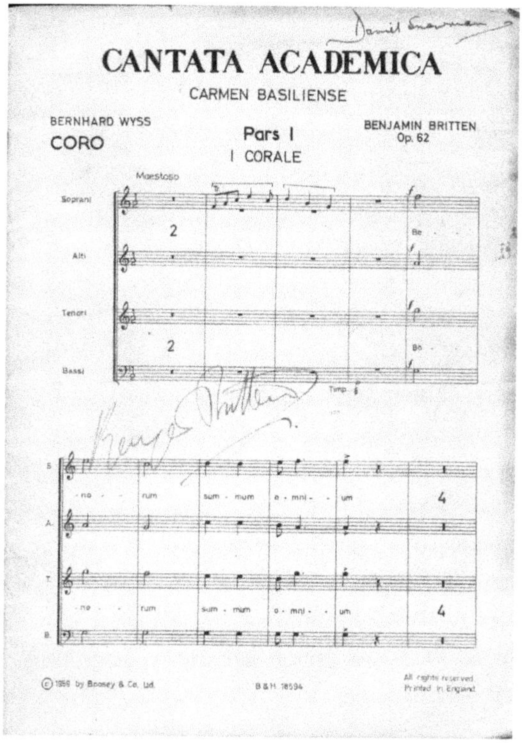

Benjamin Britten: Cantata Academica *score.*

rehearsals, as we giggled nervously at some startling musical effect, Britten looked up reprovingly, stopped the orchestra, and then smiled at us, threw his hands up in the air, and asked impishly: 'Well, what would *you* have written if you had had to set these words?'

After the performance, many of the chorus members asked the composer and soloists to sign our scores. When it came to my moment with Britten, I told him how he'd once written to me to say how he hated people asking for autographs, which he cheerfully acknowledged while signing my copy with a friendly grin.

In addition to the performances in which I sang, I also went to listen to a great deal of music while at Cambridge, notably the regular performances of the Chelsea Opera Group under the baton of an exceptionally dynamic young man called Colin Davis. I exulted with him at his great night of glory in London in October 1959 when he was suddenly called upon to conduct a star-studded concert performance of *Don Giovanni* at the Royal Festival Hall in place of the perennially ailing Otto Klemperer.

London was inevitably the scene of the most memorable performances. I went to one of Klemperer's legendary Beethoven cycles at the Royal Festival Hall and for most of the concerts sat in the choir seats behind the orchestra, gazing into the deep, gaunt eyes of the massively crippled maestro in front of me who seemed by sheer force of will to be recreating Beethoven's vision of the universe. I watched Beecham from close up, too, at one of his last concerts. In a little speech from the podium at the end he apologised for the heavy (Wagnerian) first half, which he compared with a gruelling cricket series then underway in Australia. Then there were the early Sutherland triumphs at Covent Garden (*Lucia, Traviata* and *Sonnambula*), the first night of the zestful Berganza–Alva–Giulini *Barbiere*, and a potent plea for liberty in the Klemperer production of *Fidelio* with soprano Sena Jurinac and the spine-chilling, steel-throated tenor Jon Vickers. I recall wondering whether Beethoven might not have brought Florestan into Act I of *Fidelio* (and dispensed with some of that domestic nonsense early in the score) if only he had had Vickers in the part.

Opera can be sublime when it works well, but the stakes are high and it can be dire when it doesn't. In December 1959 an Italian company starring Ferruccio Tagliavini gave a 'Gala Week' at the Adelphi Theatre in London. I was in the front of the stalls on the opening night of *L'elisir d'amore* with Tagliavini as the lovesick village idiot Nemorino ('little nobody') and an attractive young blonde named Rosalina Neri as the proud and coquettish Adina. Neri, out of her class and obviously nervous, was a catastrophe. Her acting was limited to alternate grins and pouts and her singing, when it could be heard, was consistently flat. As the evening progressed and the boos grew in volume, Tagliavini visibly assumed the role of Neri's protective father-figure; never before had Nemorino shouldered heavier responsibilities or Adina been more in need of comfort. By the time of 'Una furtiva lagrima' (there was in fact nothing furtive about poor Neri's lagrimes), Tagliavini was in such a state of shock that he launched into the coda of his second verse while the orchestra was embarking on that of the first. Everything came to a scrunching halt – and Tagliavini was treated to the most thunderous ovation of his career by an overwhelmingly sympathetic audience. He bowed modestly and then sang the entire aria again with a poignant intensity that was unforgettable. At the end of the evening, Neri and the conductor were hissed mercilessly off the stage, the impresario (Jack Hylton) for whom the catcalls were really intended did not show his face, and the curtain came speedily down and stayed down. Never before or since have I experienced an audience in so uncontrolledly venomous a mood and, although I shared their view of the proceedings, I did not have it in me to express my sentiments in the form favoured by most of the people around me. I was sitting fairly near the stage and after a while it was almost as if the boos and hisses were addressed at me for not joining in. I remember wondering at the time what it would have been like to have been a secret Jew at a Nuremberg Rally.

Three months later, I went to one of Jussi Björling's performances of *Bohème* at Covent Garden, his first appearances there since 1939. I had heard him in concert at the Royal Albert Hall, but a stage appearance was bound to be something special. It was. I was in the lower slips and, a minute before curtain-up, the Queen Mother appeared and had the grace to slip into the box directly across from me. Five minutes elapsed. Then ten. Then came the dreaded spotlight and a distant, dapper figure announced that Mr Jussi Björling (cries of 'ugh' from the assembled multitude) had had a mild heart attack that very day, that he craved our indulgence and that it was touch and go whether he would be able to sing. Would we be patient? Björling was reputed to have a drinking problem and I wondered uncharitably whether that was the real cause of the delay. We all, Queen Mum included, continued to wait.

Finally, Covent Garden's General Administrator David Webster appeared and apologised to 'Your Majesty, my Lords, Ladies and Gentlemen' for the delay. Mr Björling, anxious not to disappoint so distinguished an audience, had decided, against doctors' orders, that he would sing. The curtain would go up shortly. Björling sang (though little else; he didn't even pretend to search for Mimi's key), looked a ghastly shade of green throughout the evening, and died a few months later at the age of 49. I have often wondered since whether to be grateful to the Queen Mother, without whose august presence Björling would surely not have performed that evening, or to hold Her Majesty inadvertently responsible for his early death.

* * *

Music provided many of the most indelible memories of my undergraduate years. Britain was just then in the early stages of a phenomenal musical renaissance and the feast of good music available was on a scale that daunted older connoisseurs accustomed to the lean pickings of the interwar years. To a 20-year-old, there was nothing especially significant in the fact that Covent Garden could mount an immaculate *Don Carlos* with the world's Number One cast in a production by Luchino Visconti. This was the heyday of Schwarzkopf and Fischer-Dieskau and I came to consider as normal fare their infinitely and precisely prepared recitals. Fischer-Dieskau gave a performance of Schubert's *Die Winterreise* to a packed Royal Festival Hall and I sat totally rapt as this giant, baby-faced wonder-boy wove an uninterrupted spell of the most intricate gold. I even took for granted London's unique benefaction of five top-level symphony orchestras, never thinking that most of the world's great cities had one at most. There were not yet as many British musicians of the top rank as a few years later. The great days of Janet Baker and Neville Marriner, John Ogdon and Peter Maxwell Davies, Gwyneth Jones and Colin Davis were still to come. But the path had been well laid by Tippett and Britten, by Beecham and Boult, and above all by the BBC which, by taking seriously its role as the major patron of music in the country, was helping to generate, among composers, interpreters and listeners alike, an insistence upon standards of a level undreamed of before.

Chapter 11

Europe (and Fräulein Renate)

Alice Roughton was not only the *châtelaine extraordinaire* of a regular Open House at which the talented, the quaint and the exotic would mix on easy terms but was also one of the Vice-Presidents of the Cambridge Federal Union. This was a group that believed in the idea of world government along federal lines and which advocated, as a practical step, that Britain should join the newly formed European Economic Community.

The idea of European unity had been around since at least the time of Charlemagne. But it had been given new impetus by the ghastly destructiveness of World War II. In the wake of that bloodbath, men of vision in many of the lands of Western Europe began to consider the possibility of establishing mutually interdependent economic links between the formerly warring nations – particularly France and Germany – in the hope that this would make less likely any future conflagration between them. Some people advocated more than merely economic links and talked of eventual political union, a sort of United States of Europe, though this was anathema to statesmen from many of the larger countries involved in the early discussions. As the Cold War became increasingly tense, some advocates of unity saw their work as contributing to the efforts of western leaders to 'contain' the supposed expansionism of the Soviet Union (NATO was set up in 1949), while others, the true idealists perhaps, thought that any moves towards European unity ought to try and involve Eastern Europe as well, though this likelihood became more and more remote as Stalin tied that part of the world with hoops of steel to the Soviet Union.

By the early 1950s, the arguments for some degree of European unity were beginning to bear fruit, notably in the form of the coal and steel community established between France and Germany and subsequently joined by Italy, Belgium, the Netherlands and Luxembourg. A somewhat premature idea of a pooled European Defence Community was broached (but vetoed by the French who did not relish the idea of their armed forces being placed under international command). In 1955, the six coal and steel countries met in conference at Messina in Sicily and came out advocating the creation of a common market and this, along with a pooling of atomic know-how, was formally signed into being by the 1957 Treaty of Rome.

Throughout this period, Britain adopted a wary attitude. Traditionally somewhat aloof from political developments on the continent and happy to play off one European faction against another, the British governments of Churchill, Eden and Macmillan regarded the movement for European unity with suspicion. However sympathetic these prime ministers might have been towards attempts to integrate the economic systems of France and Germany so as to make it harder for the two to be at loggerheads again, their instincts (and electorates) told them that Britain, physically separate from the continent and not successfully invaded for nearly nine hundred years, might do better to keep out.

The idea of world – or even merely European – federalism was one to which I had devoted very little thought, at least until my 1958 visit to Brussels. But when I went up to Cambridge a few weeks later, I was predisposed to regard with warmth any group, such as the Cambridge Federal Union, that encouraged people to see Britain in a wider context. As it happened, the prime mover and shaker of this organisation, the indefatigably gregarious Diarmid McLaughlin, was in my year in my college doing my subject. Diarmid and I became close friends at Cambridge (he later went on to become a director of the European Commission) and it was largely in response to his prodding that I gradually became caught up in the activities of the Federal Union of Cambridge University (as we liked to call it, in order to joke about its irreverent initials). FUCU was later renamed the Cambridge University European Group, or CUEG, and in the autumn term of 1960 I became its chairman. This enabled me to approach many of my personal heroes in the academic, political and cultural worlds and invite them to come and address the Society.

I learned a lot during that period about how to wine and dine distinguished visitors, to chair public meetings and offer votes of thanks, to get members of a committee to work together and how to organise and publicise a programme of activities. I learned the invaluable lesson that many things wouldn't be done properly or even at all unless I myself saw that they did, and a lifelong neurotic impulse to get things done unnecessarily ahead of deadline was given a powerful boost during this period. When in July 1961 (on board ship bound for the New World) I heard that Macmillan had finally applied for Britain to join the Common

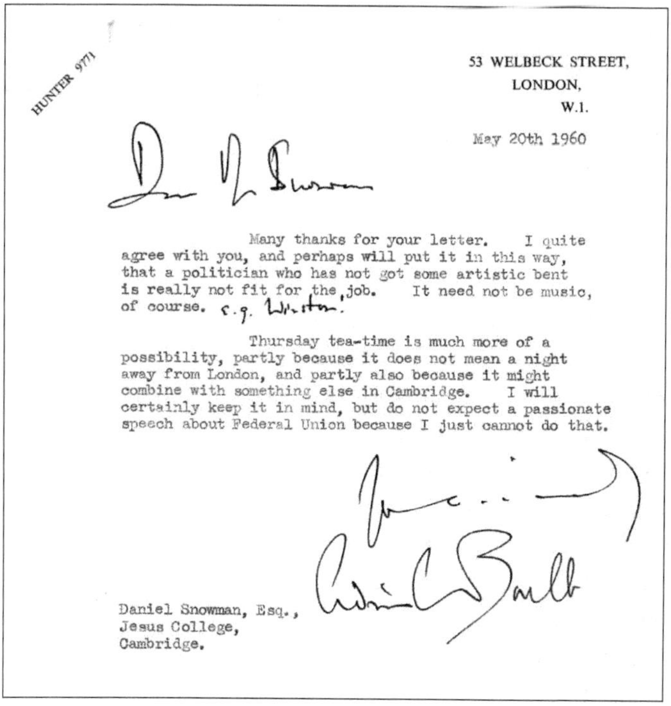

HUNTER 9771

53 WELBECK STREET,
LONDON,
W.1.

May 20th 1960

Dear Mr Snowman

Many thanks for your letter. I quite agree with you, and perhaps will put it in this way, that a politician who has not got some artistic bent is really not fit for the job. It need not be music, of course. e.g. Winston!

Thursday tea-time is much more of a possibility, partly because it does not mean a night away from London, and partly also because it might combine with something else in Cambridge. I will certainly keep it in mind, but do not expect a passionate speech about Federal Union because I just cannot do that.

Yours ...

Adrian C Boult

Daniel Snowman, Esq.,
Jesus College,
Cambridge.

Letter from Sir Adrian Boult.

Market, I felt that our efforts at Cambridge had, in their small way, helped play a part in producing what seemed a momentous result.

* * *

Renate Koring used to turn up at CUEG meetings with a couple of Yugoslav friends and, when I first got to know her a little, I thought she was probably a German spy. Renate was the archetypal blonde German beauty with long, fair hair, deep blue eyes, buxom figure and the most perfect comportment. She could cavort effortlessly with people from the four corners of the earth, talk about clothes and wines and perfumes and show a lively and informed interest in the arts. She gave the impression of a supremely confident, experienced, cosmopolitan woman at the very acme of her powers: every shy young man's fantasy bombshell woman – until he gets taken up by one. Renate reminded me of Goya's proud and beautiful Doña Isabel (of which I had a copy on my wall in college), the woman with the thick, lustrous lips and displaying a most tantalising suggestion of bosom. Such a woman was defying the observer to conquer her, I used to say of the Goya painting. And, in time, of Renate.

She and her Yugoslav friends cultivated me and I was flattered to be cultivated. We went out together, occasionally with others, to concerts and lectures and tea parties. I was admitted as one of their circle. Then, one crisp day in the late autumn of 1959, I found myself alone with Renate who proposed, in terms at once formal and irresistible, that she become my special companion. Her offer was almost like a contract, full of hopes and promises tempered by conditions and warnings. I was filled with excitement and apprehension at being offered something I wasn't sure I could deal with. But, like the sergeant who is offered a generalship, there are things a man doesn't refuse.

For 20 weeks, Renate organised our social and cultural outings, our musical trips (including the Sutherland *Traviata* and the Björling *Bohème*), our walks and cycle rides. She cooked beautiful, rich German meals on my little gas ring and also cooked up fantastic scenarios for our joint future. Renate was too hot to handle. She must have wanted something from me, I figured, for her natural male companion would surely be a rich, cosmopolitan 40-year-old. What could an elegant, sophisticated German spy want with me? I was Jewish. Was that it? Perhaps she was as anxious to show how unprejudiced she was towards Jews as I was towards Germans. Perhaps she needed to display her innocence of the crime of her fathers, just as I needed to disavow vindictiveness towards their children. Certainly, one of the attractions to me was that I was granted intimate access to 'them', and Renate, too, may have felt something of the same. We each enjoyed the taste of forbidden fruit. But, as Renate continued to organise my life and lay down the rules about our relationship, I remained suspicious. When was all going to be revealed? When would I be recruited into the German secret service? Or asked to obtain the Chief Rabbi's unlisted telephone number? Or reveal the names of his principal advisers?

None of these requests came my way and it gradually occurred to me that maybe Renate really cared for me and wanted me all for her own little self. The Goya girl had been successfully conquered. What price all those tight-lipped public-school smoothies now? They might have the money and the cars and the expensive clothes and the social accomplishments. Which of them had ever conquered a Supergirl?

But in time I found the attraction and the excitement beginning to pall. I was not yet ready for a serious, long-lasting relationship and felt trapped by the obvious sincerity with which I watched Renate making plans for the two of us. Eventually, with much sorrow and some bitterness on her side, and a degree of relief on mine, the affair ended and I decided henceforth to take on people of my own size. I garnered whatever pride I could out of an exciting yet challenging episode, let people know that I and not she had ended the relationship, and protected myself from similar incidents by throwing myself into the thick of CUEG politics and agreeing to become its Chairman.

* * *

Chairmanship of CUEG was the acme of my 'public' career at Cambridge and it was both preceded and succeeded by periods of ostensibly quiet and contemplative domesticity. My aspirations in those days alternated wildly between being the academic in slippers quietly absorbed in books, and the smooth, successful public figure. Both had their attractions and, if one mode tended to predominate at any given time, the other would be sure to raise its head and demand attention. Neither the private nor the public life, I was learning, was without its hazards, and by the middle of my final year the liberating wider world that Cambridge had at first seemed to offer was feeling distinctly more restrictive. The Renate episode had taken the edge off romantic adventure by revealing the more brittle and disturbing aspects of proud domesticity, and once the affair was over it was not easy to find new circles of friendship or new walks or new cafés that remained untouched by associations with it. As for CUEG, I felt myself somewhat baffled by its wider vision and yet at the same time gnawed by an inner feeling that it was in essence only a small Cambridge club for clever gentlemen with polished social graces, whom the wider world alternately ignored and indulged. This wider world was still the will-o'-the-wisp for which I craved, but I was beginning to doubt my capacity to make a genuine accommodation to it.

A temporary solution was at hand, one imposed as much by external events as by internal needs. Finals were a few months away and I had before me the possibility of a Double First. Each year only about five per cent of students were awarded a First, and to be placed in that category in both parts of one's degree was a distinction to savour. The Renate traumas and my involvements with CUEG and CUMS had absorbed much of my time and energy, and it was with a sense of both relief and gritty determination that I settled down in the early weeks of 1961 to the run-up to my final exams.

Chapter 12

Dublin and Dev

Third-year History students were offered a choice of a 'special subject'. None of them sounded particularly thrilling and several involved the chore of working one's way through documents in another language. For mainly negative reasons, I chose 'Anglo-Irish relations, 1916–22' and, as so often happens when one studies something in depth, I became enthralled. The tensions between the Irish and the English, the tales of heroism and blackguardry, the romance of the Irish cultural renaissance, the stupendous cleverness and nastiness of Lloyd George: all this came to intrigue me. I had got off to a spectacular start for, in the summer of 1960, anxious to get an early grip on the subject and aware that CUEG was about to absorb an inordinate amount of my time, I went to Ireland, hitchhiked all over the length and breadth of the country, Northern Ireland as well as the Republic, and chatted to anyone who looked 60 or over who might have had memories of the Troubles. Everybody was quite prepared at the drop of a Guinness to tell me what bastards the English had been and I picked up a wealth of amusing and revealing quips and anecdotes. I shook a crusader's hand at St Michan's in Dublin, stayed for a few days down in Cork and Cape Clear Island, kissed the Blarney Stone and made my way round the Ring of Kerry and up the west coast to Galway, after which I headed northeast into the Six Counties where I was shocked by the nonsensical 'Billy of the Boyne' and 'Fuck the Pope' graffiti, and eventually sailed back to England muttering 'Bells and Swastika' and 'Nelson Pillar' smilingly to myself. It was a wonderful introduction to my special subject and, although I can't say I learned a lot that was to be of practical use to me in my exams a year later, I gained an invaluable 'feel' for Ireland and Irish attitudes.

The most illuminating of the over-60s I met was the Founding Father of the Republic, the 78-year-old President Éamon de Valera. I had written to de Valera at his official residence in Phoenix Park asking for an interview but never dreamed that one would be granted. In the event, this tall, austere old man (whom I met on the afternoon of 9 August 1960) was kindness itself. With a physical presence not unlike that of de Gaulle, with his short

Kissing the Blarney Stone.

neck and thick glasses, 'Dev' sat at an almost empty desk, beckoned me to sit down and proceeded to tell me the story, as he saw it, of the founding of the Irish Republic, delving back into the early years of Sinn Féin, the 1916 rebellion, the 'Black-'n-Tans', the 1921 Treaty with England, the Irish civil war that followed and his own triumphant return to power in 1932. He had a reputation for single-minded self-righteousness and so I was pleasantly surprised when he acknowledged at the outset that other people would tell me other versions and that it was my duty as a scholar to expose myself to all interpretations. That said, however, he left me in no doubt that he had always considered the cause of Irish nationhood for which he stood to be right and he added that fortune always favours the side which merits her favours.

Dev told me that, although historians had dubbed his side in the 1920s the 'irregulars', they were in fact the 'regulars' since it was they who risked their all after the 1921 Treaty with England in order to try and maintain the prior status quo (i.e. the Republic of 1919) which the 1921 Treaty had unconstitutionally overridden. He lingered over his great electoral victory of 1932 – the only time in history, he thought, when a party defeated by physical force was returned to power by a majority once the issue was put to a fair vote. The President was almost blind by the time I met him, but his

Éamon de Valera.
(Encyclopaedia Britannica)

mental faculties were immaculate and his memory faultless. Before I left, he told me of his two dreams: that one day his country would be united and that, eventually, the Irish people would speak the Irish language.

This question of language intrigued me. Everybody in Ireland spoke English and few could read Irish, let alone speak it fluently. Street signs, post office documents and the like were printed in Gaelic with an English translation or transliteration for the 99 per cent of the people who needed one. While it might in principle be desirable for the Irish people to speak their own language and not that of a people who had conquered and exploited them, what possible hope was there of that transpiring? De Valera agreed that it was an uphill task, but talked about the example of Israel where the ancient language of Hebrew had successfully been revived and had taken hold as both a practical and a symbolic manifestation of the cultural independence of its people. I suggested that the Israelis, as immigrants from many other places, had had no other single language in common whereas the Irish, maybe regrettably, did all speak English, a point the President acknowledged. But it was still not impossible, he said, that his dream might one day be realised. This stubborn patriot reminded me that all Irish speakers wore – as he proudly did himself – a little golden lapel ring known as a *Fáinne* and when two of them met they would always converse in Gaelic. Perhaps these people would be the wave of the future.

Our debate continued awhile and then, at last, it was time for me to leave. As I walked back through the fresh expanses of Phoenix Park, past the immense Wellington monument, I carried away the memory of a proud and dignified man who had maintained into old age the vision, even some of the illusions, that had sustained him throughout the trials of a momentous and controversial public career. The interview with de Valera and the trip around Ireland left an indelible impression on my mind and enabled me to return to Cambridge determined to work with a will at a special subject that had previously held little allure.

Chapter 13

Up, Down – and Out

History and historians at Cambridge and beyond

The History degree at Cambridge was paced in such a way that it was only in the third year that one was introduced to the opportunity for concentrated research from primary sources, and to the history of philosophy and political theory. The year when I would watch Duncan Forbes, jacketless (though always wearing the statutory gown) and swigging from a hip flask, setting his small but dedicated audience alight with his agonisingly earnest attempts to illuminate the metaphysical abstractions of Hegel. 'Thus,' he'd say, 'the internal contradictions of Spirit are transformed in and of themselves into a new synthesis,' and we would all religiously take notes. It was the year in which I attended the lectures of Denis Brogan on (supposedly) political thought. Brogan, whom Duncan Forbes called 'the personification of the theory of the association of ideas', would pour out an unending flow of facts on the most abstruse subjects, always peppering his talk with astonishingly detailed bibliographical references and scabrous anecdotes, and yet would scarcely structure his thoughts into any memorable or manageable shape. I used to sit near the front in order to catch his quiet Scots burr as the encyclopaedic knowledge would speed by, and was breathless with admiration for Brogan's prodigious learning but could rarely remember the following day exactly what it was that he had been saying. Noel Annan, on the other hand, recently elevated at age 40 to become Provost of King's, gave a series of evening seminars to which I was invited and here, once the sherry and the grand chat about art and politics were over and we were invited to take off our gowns and gather around the blazing fire in the oak-panelled salon, a brilliantly directed discussion would develop on, perhaps, John Stuart Mill and the concept of negative liberty. By the end of the evening, we would all go out into the night feeling refreshed, privileged and convinced that we had learned something of importance.

Brogan was a Fellow of Peterhouse, a college packed at that time with historians of richly varied intellectual talents. The Master of Peterhouse (and university Vice-Chancellor) was Herbert Butterfield who had written (and still occasionally lectured) about the Whig interpretation of history and the history of science, while it was from the young Denis Mack Smith, then a Fellow of Peterhouse, that I first learned something of Italian history from the Risorgimento, Mazzini and Garibaldi to the Fascism of Mussolini.

The medievalist Dom David Knowles, Regius Professor of History at the time, was another of the Peterhouse illuminati. A diminutive ex-monk with a whimsical sense of humour, Dom David told us that Plato and Aristotle may not have answered many of the questions that they had raised but they had, between them, asked virtually all the important questions that there were. And to formulate questions was ultimately a greater contribution than to attempt to answer them. On St Thomas Aquinas he was delightful. He had his class in hysterics with accounts of Thomas's rotundity and how the refectory table in front of the Saint supposedly had a special semi-circle hewn out of it in order to accommodate the fat eater. 'But quite how that enabled St Thomas to get any nearer to his food,' added Knowles wryly, 'I have never quite understood.' The professors at Cambridge all had certain hours each week at which they would be available to any student who wished to visit them ('Office hours,' I learned to call this when I went to the USA, much to my disgust – professors surely had studies, not offices!). One day, I visited Dom David, along with Princess Elizabeth Bagaya of Toro, then a beautiful wide-eyed teenager whom I would occasionally accompany to lectures and society meetings. We must have made an odd threesome, but the chat was jolly enough and Knowles succeeded in stimulating among both of his interlocutors a genuine if temporary interest in medieval philosophy.

One of my minor sacrifices in the pursuit of scholarship was that I made the effort to read documents in the original Latin. I had been taught Latin at school but, as mentioned, had spent much of the time persecuting the timid teacher or helping to organise cruel classroom stunts at his expense. At Cambridge, however, I was so impressed by the magisterial grandeur of Walter Ullmann's lectures on medieval history that I attended a course of special seminars that he was offering and which involved the detailed discussion of selected Latin texts. Ullmann in mid-lecture looked not unlike a great bat as his begowned arms would rise and fall and his alert face and beak-like nose dart energetically hither and thither. To Ullmann, all the great events of the Middle Ages had to do with the ascendancy of the Papacy and the theories governing its relationship with the temporal power. It was from him that I learned to distinguish authority from power and to recognise how papal claims on the former helped to elevate it beyond the reach of generation after generation of Holy Roman Emperors.

Under Ullmann's tutelage I became fascinated by the Investiture Conflict and by the personality of Gregory VII. No subject might have seemed less calculated to excite a bunch of sceptical and empirically minded undergraduates. But Ullmann's ebullient enthusiasm for his subject was infectious and his lectures generally packed. I was to get a lot of mileage out of affectionate imitations. My favourite party trick was to recount, with Ullmann's thick Germanic accent, the story of the medieval forgery known as the Donation of Constantine and to explain, complete with the great man's propensity for unintentional puns, that it was 'thus that the central role of the Medieval Papacy was most dramatically forged!'

Cambridge had the most intense intellectual riches to bestow. But some of the most memorable occasions for me included visits of distinguished scholars from other places, notably 'the' other place, Oxford. It was as an undergraduate at Cambridge, for instance, that I first heard AJP Taylor deliver one of his spell-binding monologues.

Isaiah Berlin, too, would visit us from Oxford from time to time, address the air above his audience, and unravel the intricate interstices between literature and philosophy by the artful device of asking himself, in simple first-person terms, the great questions that had haunted Rousseau or de Maistre or Herzen: 'How can I be certain that this is what I should do?' or 'What would happen if I were to refuse to do thus-and-so?' or 'Suppose everyone were to do as I wish to do – then what?' Every point would be made at a great pace but repeated a number of times with witty variations. Rousseau, said Berlin on one occasion, had written that man was born free but was everywhere in chains; 'this is like saying that sheep are born carnivorous but are everywhere eating nothing but grass!'

In later years, I had the privilege of meeting Isaiah Berlin on a number of occasions. In December 1973, I flew to Israel for the BBC in order to attend a conference in Jerusalem, and record brief interviews with some of the distinguished intellectuals present. Isaiah Berlin was on the same plane, as were Noel Annan and Stuart Hampshire, and later at the conference

Sir Isaiah Berlin lecturing at the Hebrew University, Jerusalem, in 1972.
(My thanks to the Isaiah Berlin archive at Wolfson College, Oxford, and to Berlin's editor Henry Hardy, for their help and advice.)

we joked that we could just as easily have recorded our interviews back home in England. Another of the celebrated conference attendees was the German-born Israeli philosopher and historian Gershom Scholem.

Isaiah Berlin, like my rabbinical grandfather, was born in Riga when it was still part of the Tsarist empire – in Berlin's case in 1909. I always found him a highly-informed yet gently engaging interlocutor, keen to hear your views before expressing his own. More often than not, we would talk about opera (Berlin was a great opera lover and was for some years on the Covent Garden Board of Directors). In 1974, when I was a BBC producer, I invited him to take part in a forthcoming series of Radio 3 programmes in which the political economist John (later Lord) Vaizey would interview intellectuals in a variety of fields about our changing social and political attitudes towards that elusive concept, 'Equality'. Isaiah was known to be a somewhat reluctant broadcaster; his lectures about Romanticism, broadcast a few years earlier, had been widely admired though his verbal and vocal style on air were all too easy to parody. I called him and, as persuasively as I could, explained the nature of the project I had in mind and invited him to be one of the participants. He laughed affably enough and said yes, of course he'd do it but added that I'd have to drag him to the BBC studio 'with hoops of steel'! I promised I would do so and, of course, he was his usual brilliant self.

* * *

In May 1959 I went to the Senate House in Cambridge to hear a special lecture by the scientist, novelist and civil servant CP Snow who unveiled what seemed to me at the time a reasonably self-evident idea – but which made Snow widely famous – about what he dubbed the 'two cultures': the 'sciences' and the 'humanities'. Snow's message was that to solve many of the world's problems these two needed to be bridged by a third, namely the social sciences. The lecture was certainly timely, and today Snow is remembered, if at all, for his lecture about 'The Two Cultures'.

A year later, Sir Oswald Mosley was invited to speak at Cambridge. Mosley, the notoriously anti-Semitic leader of the British Union of Fascists in the 1930s, had been imprisoned during the war and to most was by now a disgraced, marginal figure, an abhorrent relic of an utterly misguided past. But by all accounts he had been a charismatic leader and a brilliant orator, one of a number of Britons who had believed in the mid-1930s that

German Nazism under Hitler could be the one force capable of putting a stop to the threatening brutalities of Stalinist Communism. Mosley was now advocating a broader form of 'Union' than in his fascist days, a kind of Europe-wide nationalism, and I was intrigued to see what this most hateful of figures would have to say on a subject on which, *mutatis mutandis*, I might have been partly inclined to agree with him. How would he argue his case, I wondered as I took my seat? Articulately and intelligently, as I recall, avoiding any reference to his pre-war career. However, what I most vividly remember from the occasion was that partway through his talk someone in the audience chucked a jelly at Mosley, hitting him in the face! I'm glad I went.

It was when I was at Cambridge, too, that the former US Secretary of State Dean Acheson, in town to pick up an honorary degree, gave four lectures about American politics and foreign policy. I knew nothing at the time about the US political system and had never thought to care. But I went along to these talks, was entranced by the evident culture and civility of the elegant Acheson, and concluded that American politics might not be all balloons and ballyhoo. Acheson, still handsome and sounding as detached and aristocratic as a transatlantic Anthony Eden, stroked his moustache and told us that all America's wars had been attempts to solve other people's problems. The great American tradition – mitigated in part by the misguided efforts of fools and partly by the generosity of altruists – was that of isolationism. There was a smugness to this ageing philosopher king, but his talks incorporated a great deal of material, particularly on the American congressional and federal system, that was new to me. Acheson's lectures proved to be a first step in a journey that was to send me many times across to the New World.

* * *

I was not alone in discovering an interest in America at about this time. This was the era of the Eisenhower–Kennedy transition. More and more people in Britain were acquiring television sets for the first time and the Nixon–Kennedy debates were shown in Britain to widespread public interest. In common with many others in the UK, it was around this time that I first came to realise that each US state had two senators, that West Virginia was a separate state in its own right and how the US electoral college system worked.

Each academic year, a distinguished American would be invited to Cambridge as Pitt Professor to give lectures on US history and, in general, make himself accessible to the university community. In 1960–61, the Pitt Professor was Clinton Rossiter of Cornell. Rossiter attracted big crowds to his lectures, shamed his audience by asking if anyone could name Lincoln's successor as President (nobody could, but I recall thinking it an absurdly unreasonable question) and, in a massively theatrical address shortly before the presidential election, publicly debated with himself the pros and cons of voting for Nixon or Kennedy – and then, milking his audience for all it was worth, casting his absentee ballot (for Kennedy) in full view of several hundred onlookers.

I met Rossiter briefly at one or two social gatherings in Cambridge and, as I began to contemplate with some confusion my own future, decided to ask his advice about the possibility of a year in the USA. I knew that I could have stayed on at Jesus College to do post-graduate work if I had wished. But I felt I had 'done' Cambridge by now, that the range of experiences available to me there were limited and that, for better or worse, I had sampled enough of them. Life at Cambridge felt cocooned and I knew it was time to leave. But I had no idea what to do afterwards. In those days, the conventional career options for people in my position lay in advertising or the civil service; but the former sounded too flashy and the latter too subdued for my tastes. During my final year, I went on a short attachment to a civil service department – the Post Office as it happened – and, having signed the Official Secrets Act, was privy to the latest developments in telephone technology which, I learned, would eventually enable a subscriber in London to phone someone in Glasgow or Liverpool directly without having to go through the operator. This was to be known as STD (Subscriber Trunk Dialling), initials that, to a later generation, came to mean a sexually transmitted disease.

On reflection, I thought that perhaps the academic world continued to represent just about the right balance, at least for the time being. But if I was to prolong my studies, I wanted to modernise them. I knew something about ancient consuls and medieval popes and the Tudor economy but next to nothing about the wider 20th-century world in which I lived. Perhaps I should concentrate on the American federal system and its possible application to Western Europe. But where? And how? Maybe Rossiter had the answer.

He was most affable when I went to see him in his rooms in Selwyn

College one afternoon in spring 1961, and he seemed to understand exactly the dilemma I put to him. A year in America, possibly a longer period, would be just the thing he said. I asked about what I took to be the American equivalents of Oxford and Cambridge; which would be better for my purposes, Harvard or Yale? He spluttered with a combination of amusement and indignation. Harvard and Yale were big college-based East Coast snob schools: so similar, in fact, to Oxford and Cambridge that I might as well stay where I was if what I wanted was to perpetuate that kind of existence. No; the place for me was his own Cornell University. Cornell, while its standards of scholarship were among the highest in the country, was also in many ways more typically American. It was campus-based, supported by both private and public funds, and was far enough from the East Coast to have some of the features of the American heartland. When Rossiter told me of the hills and the gorges and the lakes and seemed to display a genuine proprietorial interest in my decision, I became convinced. On his recommendation, I corresponded with Mario Einaudi, head of the Cornell Government Department (and son of the first post-war president of Italy). 'Just the man if you wish to pursue your interest in theories of federalism,' said Rossiter.

My last year at Cambridge was drawing to a close; all that remained was to undergo the final exams. I had already gained a First in the prelim exams, undertaken at the end of my first year, and a (proper) First in Part I of the degree proper, taken at the end of the second. If I could somehow repeat the feat at the end of my final year and leave Cambridge with a Double First this would provide me with a tremendous boost, not only in the academic world but in whatever field I hoped to enter thereafter. I became nervous as finals approached, suffered recurrent colds and sore throats and was even unable on occasion to complete an essay assigned by one of my college tutors. Once I went empty-handed to a tutorial with the conservative historian Maurice Cowling (who was shortly to become yet another of the Peterhouse set). I'm sorry, I mumbled, but I've been feeling… oh, I don't know… erm, inert. Cowling laughed, with a welcome touch of sympathetic bonhomie. 'Well,' he said, 'you'd soon better become ert again!' The Senior Tutor at Jesus College, the medievalist Vivian Fisher, was kindness itself. 'Don't worry,' he reassured me, 'you'll do fine. Once you are in the exam room, however tired or ill you think you feel, you'll be on autopilot and all your knowledge and your ability to write it down clearly will simply take over.'

His reassuring prediction proved self-fulfilling. I left Cambridge with a Double First, and Fisher wrote an extraordinarily generous testimonial. 'Mr Snowman,' he said, 'has a first-class mind, particularly strong in dealing with abstractions. I would rate him in the top five per cent of students.' I was ready for my next break-out into the wider world. The New World...

Graduation, 1961.

Book 3

American Dreams and Realities

Cornell, 1961–63

Daniel and family at Southampton, July 26, 1961.

Chapter 14

Sailing, Driving, Parking

My father's younger sister Diana married a GI. Well, a Canadian soldier, Sidney Barza, who had come over to Europe during the war. Sidney and Diana lived in Montreal and, in the later 1940s and the 1950s, visited England occasionally with their young son Howard. Once it was known I was going to do my post-grad work at Cornell University in Ithaca (in what I learned to call Upstate New York), the Barzas generously invited me to begin my North American sojourn by staying with them for a few weeks. Back in 1961 there were no jet planes nipping back and forth across the Atlantic and, rather than spend many wearying hours flying first to Reykjavik, refuelling, then stopping off in Gander in Newfoundland before reaching my eventual destination, the sensible – and far more enjoyable – thing to do if you were in no great hurry was to cross the pond by ship. That summer, on 26 July, my parents and brother accompanied me to Southampton and waved me off as the *Saxonia* gradually distanced herself from the British coast.

America. Who didn't want to go to America, the New World? Everyone's dream, from the *Mayflower* to the present! By the later decades of the 19th century, many liberal-minded Germans and Scandinavians had followed the traditional path to America, often settling in the newly flourishing Midwestern states, while others arrived on the west coast from China and Japan and sought jobs building factories, roads and railroads. Increasingly, the bulk of 'new' immigrants – the 'poor', the 'huddled masses yearning to breathe free' of Emma Lazarus's poem – came from southern and eastern Europe: Italians who had picked themselves up from the parched fields of Calabria and Puglia or the disease-infested slums of Palermo or Naples, and Jews escaping the pogroms of Tsarist Russia, all of them somehow finding the wherewithal to journey from the old world to the new.

In due course, the bureaucratic shutters came down and restrictions were placed on the number of migrants permitted from any given country. But that did not stop large numbers from trying. In my book about the *Hitler Emigrés* (see Chapter 49), though primarily concerned with Britain, I also noted the huge impact on the USA of the many distinguished artists and architects, musicians, movie directors, historians, philosophers and scientists who managed, against the odds, to escape from Nazism and find a home in America.

I was thrilled to be following in their footsteps. America, I knew, had been through tough times and I read assiduously about the Depression, the War, McCarthyism. But now, with the election of John F. Kennedy to the White House, it seemed the USA was emerging from its darker shadows and repossessing its traditional sense of optimism, its 'can-do!' philosophy: the famed American Dream. America, I knew, was the very embodiment of life, liberty and the pursuit of happiness. Here, you could go anywhere, do anything, if only you put your heart and mind to what it was you hoped to achieve.*

I arrived at a good time, soon after the inauguration of a handsome, intelligent young President (with an academic background and a beautiful wife) who spoke optimistically of Americans aspiring towards a bold 'new frontier'. Together, suggested JFK, we can find a way of reaching the moon and beyond, of bringing the Cold War to an end and, back home, of producing genuine equality between the races a century after the Civil War. In the event, things weren't of course quite like that, and I remember reflecting sadly over the years that followed on the assassination of President Kennedy, the growing ghastliness of the war in Vietnam and the recurrent racial abuse in the American South. But right now, as I looked out from the stern of the *Saxonia*, I was an optimistic young man happily sailing west towards whatever destiny held in store for me.

* * *

I don't remember much about the voyage except that I befriended a group of pleasant if dour Methodists from the Midwest and cheerfully agreed to play the piano to accompany their foursquare hymns at their Sunday service, a venture that somewhat upset my father when I mentioned it to him a long time later.

After a few days at sea, including one or two that were quite rough (I was one of the few defiant passengers to take breakfast on those mornings), we eventually encountered icebergs off the Newfoundland coast and – unlike the *Titanic* half a century earlier – managed to avoid them and entered the mouth of the St Lawrence river. Working our way upstream to

* For more on the 'American Dream' (and the contrast with British attitudes), see Chapter 41.

Quebec City we eventually docked in Montreal, where I was welcomed by the Barzas. They were kindness itself, Diana bonding with me almost like an older sister as I began to absorb a thousand-and-one messages about this New World in which I was about to live: attitudes towards language, food, drink, clothing, sex, age, law, authority and much else. Some of what I learned was of local import; the Anglo-French tensions in the Province of Quebec, for example, and in Francophone Montreal in particular. Others concerned the continent as a whole. I arrived knowing that there were three kinds of ice cream, and rapidly learned that Howard Johnson sold some 24 varieties. Then there were North American attitudes towards distance.

The day before I drove with my Canadian cousins from Montreal to Ithaca I asked them how far it was. Three-hundred-and-something miles. Then where would we stay overnight? Much Canadian laughter. In England, people didn't often undertake a 350-mile drive. In most straight directions, they would have landed in the sea and, in any case, the motorway system had not yet accustomed the Brits to the idea of uninterrupted driving at speed. We, however, drove comfortably from Montreal to Ithaca in a few easy hours – even fewer than my relatives had anticipated because I was at the wheel and, not knowing or believing that the great North American highways had a speed limit, raced cheerily along in their big, airy automatic at 80 or 90 miles per hour. I remember the thrill of island-hopping over Thousand Island Bridge (I'd not yet heard of the salad dressing with the same name) and the sheer exultation, shortly thereafter, of being in the United States. It. America.

My physical image of America had been an uneasy conjunction of various vastnesses with lots of little cosinesses. On the one hand, I knew all the clichés about the stupendous buildings in New York (imagine an office block the size of the Eiffel Tower!), the 'endless prairie rolling as far as the eye could see' (which, owing to the curvature of the earth, my geography teacher at school had said, was actually only about eight miles), the snow-capped Rockies and, at last, mile upon mile of golden coastline in the Far West (epitomised by that wonderful name, later revealed as a brutal misnomer, Long Beach). On the other hand, I also liked to imagine, as perhaps we all do when visualising a place we have never visited, that the whole thing could be comprehended rather as we take in the general detail of a three-dimensional city plan or a relief map laid out before us on a table: there, at one end, my end, would be all those tall New York buildings while, some way inland but well this side of the flatness of the plains and the towering peaks of the Rockies, would nestle my little home-to-be, Cornell University. This fantasy was a telling illustration of how inadequately I had conceived of the sheer size and scale of the United States before I got there.

And even after I got there. I was taken aback by the sheer size of New York State as I drove through it on that first day. It went on forever. And, except for a few places like Watertown and Cortland, nobody much seemed to live there. You could drive for mile after mile in Upstate New York – this was my first impression of the USA – and see virtually no sign of human habitation. You could do that in parts of Scotland or Wales but not in England where you could scarcely drive for five miles without having to slow down as some sizeable village or town turned up to block your way. Americans to whom I reported this early observation were distinctly unimpressed. Just wait until you see Arizona, they shrugged.

* * *

If my physical image of the country as a whole was hopelessly telescoped, my expectations about certain types of people – like the American cop, whom I first experienced within 24 hours of my arrival in the US – were pretty accurate. My Canadian cousins and I had checked into the Collegetown 'Motel' (one of my new words) on the outskirts of Cornell and the next day they went 'downtown' to watch a 'movie' while I went in search of an 'apartment'. Ithaca is not large but it is hilly, so they generously lent me their car. I had a little map and an 'accommodation vacant' list provided by the university. Armed with these, I set out and drove from one location to the next. It was one of those late summer days when the trees are in their last and fullest bloom before the onset of that scarlet autumn (or 'fall') for which Upstate New York and New England are justly famous. The light was dazzling, the sun low and hot, and the 'pavements' (by which Americans meant the road surface) visibly sizzling.

After a tense and tiring day, I had still not come up with the lodgings I needed; everything seemed too expensive, too inaccessible or just plain gone. I sat in the car under the shade of a leafy tree facing down one of Ithaca's precipitous hills, held my foot on the brake pedal and looked yet again at the little map to discern which of my fast-diminishing list of addresses to check out next. And felt the brake pedal gradually declining under the pressure of my foot. The brake touched the carpet and the car began to descend towards the main road far below. There were no gears with which to break the impetus of the car but there was, of course, a handbrake by means of which, in a series of panicky little tugs, I was able to jerk the car to a halt just as it reached the bottom of the hill. Thus, I found myself at the wheel of a brakeless car, a long way from anywhere in town, in the hinterland of a country in which I was about to live but where I had arrived less than 24 hours before. My uncle and aunt, who had to return to Montreal the next day, were currently in a cinema somewhere in Ithaca and I would have to seek them out and tell them the news that (a) I had not found accommodation, and (b) I had wrecked their car.

Even before I undertook those painful tasks, however, I had to move from where I was. Somehow, with only a handbrake, I drove this wreck of a car into Collegetown and stopped near a little café. And that's where the cop comes into the story. I had noticed him earlier, slouching on a bar stool, peaked cap over back of head and holster over back of hips, munching a sandwich too big for even his phenomenally elastic mouth. Like every archetypal movie cop in every Grade B film, this one had left his super-colossal police car outside the café with its engine running. The whole get-up looked potentially dangerous but somehow gave off what would later be called 'vibes' of almost friendly accessibility. He was, in short, a slob. The café in which he habitually sat sold hamburgers and frankfurters, which I took to be two different styles of German sausage; also something mysteriously called cheeseburgers (where in Germany was Cheeseburg, I wondered – or maybe it was Käseburg?). I managed to park my limping car outside this café and dashed in to catch the ever-present cop who, naturally, was not there at the moment. So I ran a mile and a half to Ithaca, caught my relatives as they left the cinema, gasped out my news and taxied back with them to the centre of operations, only to find Sergeant Slob about to ticket the car for facing the wrong direction (which in England was no offence). I told him the whole sad story in my best native accent and he replied unsympathetically in his. Didn't I know that it was illegal to drive a car with no brakes? Well, yes, actually, it had occurred to me, but I considered it best to bring the car back into Collegetown so as to be able to get it attended to as soon as possible. And in any case, I was upset by the experience, it had been a dangerous moment for me, it was a borrowed car, I was new to driving on the right-hand side of the road etc., etc. Sergeant Slob wasn't interested. He was a law-enforcement officer, not a social worker. The job in hand was for him to ticket me for a parking offence, a clear violation of the traffic code. I wondered if I could at least remove the car and park it somewhere legal. Could I, hell! If he saw me driving that brakeless car, he would be constrained to issue a far more serious ticket. Heads he wins, tails I lose. I was Yossarian before his time.*

My uncle Sidney was a psychiatrist and he came to my rescue. All his years of experience came into play at that moment. What would you do, he asked, with all the oozing sincerity he could muster for the occasion, what would you do if you found yourself in this sort of predicament? Haven't you ever travelled to unfamiliar parts? Borrowed a car? Transgressed unknown regulations as a result of genuine ignorance and gross bad luck? What would you do, Officer? Perhaps you have a wife and kids? How would you recommend they act if, heaven forbid, they should ever find themselves in a similar situation?

It worked. My first tussle with the American law ended happily. Sergeant Slob, promoted by my uncle's calculated ooze into Officer Krupke†, gave the erring nephew one more chance to mend his ways. The erring nephew thereupon ran to a nearby garage who towed away the car and did the necessary work first thing the following morning. But every time I saw my Montreal relatives thereafter, Sidney would recall the incident, remember with a chill my 300-odd miles at 80 mph the previous day, and tell me how glad he was to see me still alive.

No such incident occurred again, or at least no more automobile brakes gave way under my foot, though I was to have my fair share of cop confrontations. As I gradually got to know the United States better, it sometimes occurred to me that the whole incident had been a potent symbol, an introduction to a society in which there would be fewer safety nets than I had been used to and in which the rules for survival would generally be more explicit.

* Yossarian was the central character in Joseph Heller's novel *Catch-22* published that same year, 1961. 'Catch 22' is a paradox whereby you are most likely to get your way if you accept a rule you hope won't in fact be applied to you.

† 'Gee, Officer Krupke' is a song from Leonard Bernstein's *West Side Story* in which members of the Jets, one of the street gangs portrayed, poke fun at the gruff Police Sergeant Krupke with a grovelling appeal for clemency.

Chapter 15

Learning the Rules

In a large and (compared with Britain) newly established society composed of a vast and bewildering variety of ingredients, the rule of chance and whim could easily come to predominate unless precise provisions were set up to enshrine in their stead the rule of law. In little, comparatively homogeneous Britain, it seemed to me, social and political traditions had evolved over the centuries, most people knew without being told more or less where they fitted into the order of things, what they could and could not do or get away with, and whom to appeal to – and in what tone – if they felt that there had been a miscarriage of justice. The rules were often not spelled out because everybody was presumed to know them and acquiesce in them. In America, everything seemed less established, less certain, more precarious, more dependent upon local custom, individual whim, personal discretion – and so the rules had to be spelled out all the more explicitly. So, at least, things seemed to a young man straight out of the assured security of Cambridge as he learned the ropes of his new existence.

The explicitness of things American was particularly striking, what with the written Constitution, the rectilinear city plans, the road signs that told you to 'STOP' and the formal injunction on the Cornell exam book that candidates were not to cheat. In Britain things tended to be more often implied, understood, understated. What exactly were the powers of the British monarchy, or the rules and regulations that defined the Commonwealth? Who knew for sure? In the UK, the referee at a football match would decide exactly when time was up and nobody would question his right to this judgement. In American football matches, a huge public clock would enable everybody, including the referee, to share this vital knowledge. At Cambridge, disagreements were likely to be expressed in the form of a polite litotes, as in 'I am not altogether sure I agree with what so-and-so has just said, but…'; at Cornell they said: 'Bullshit!' In the US, a driver trying to enter or exit a car park at the wrong place was likely to face a notice warning bleakly of 'Severe Tire Damage'. What a contrast to the streets of suburban London where a 'Polite Notice' might declare that, for example, the Royal Borough of Kensington and Chelsea 'requests that you curb your dog'!

Overall, I gained the impression that American society and culture were more literal-minded and legalistic than British. Americans enjoyed trying to define and measure what the British preferred to leave vague. Quality in America had, if possible, to be expressed in terms of quantity. I had come to the USA on a Fulbright, a generous form of educational funding named after the Arkansas Senator who had introduced the programme (and arranged through the English-Speaking Union), which paid my transatlantic fare and all initial costs. But once at Cornell, I was a 'graduate assistant', paid to teach small subsections of the vast classes to which the professorial superstars would lecture. The undergraduates assigned to me wanted to be told precisely which pages of which books they had to read and by what date. And I had to administer regular tests, many of them of the multiple choice and true-or-false variety, to which the answers given by my students were either absolutely right or absolutely wrong. One of my fellow postgrads was stopped one day for driving at 28 miles per hour in a 25-mph zone; he was fined an amount that was worked out as a multiple of the three miles per hour of his offence. When a society's rules are that clear and that overt, there is little room for flexibility towards one who has contravened them.

Sergeant Slob had thus been in the mainstream of tradition when he insisted in his literal-minded way that I was guilty of an offence whether I left the car where it was – or drove it away from where it was. The law is the law, and Americans were accustomed to keeping it, or at least invoking it (or maybe breaking it), but not to stretching or bending or adapting it. My visits to America over the years were to spawn a whole population of successors to that officious policeman, like the progeny of Banquo. When I went to California in 1972 to teach for a year, I needed several hundred dollars at the outset in order to put down deposits on a car and an apartment. The college could not advance me any money and, indeed, would only be able to pay my monthly salary cheques (or 'checks'), when they became due, not to me personally but to my Social Security number which, not being a US citizen, I did not have. I went to a bank, armed with a friendly letter from the college that was employing me, opened an account and asked if they could lend me some money for a month or two. Sure, but they would have to have my car insurance form and/or apartment lease as surety. Sorry, but these are the rules… Years later, I tried to persuade Pam ('Hi! Can I help you?') on the toll-free line to Hertz that I needed to rent a car with a baby seat at my next port of call the following day. 'Pam' acknowledged that one could probably be provided but would not put in the requisition on ('in') my behalf since the rules said that baby seats could only be ordered 48 hours or more in advance. If 'Pam' put me down for one, she would be guilty of an 'infraction'. 'Goodbyc, now, and thankyou-for-calling-Hertz.'

To a visiting Englishman, Americans often gave the impression that people were expected to live by constant reference to explicitly stated rules. If you contravened one of them, in however high a cause, you had broken a rule and that was all there was to it. On the other hand, there was much to be gained by close familiarity with all the rules one approved of and playing, up to the hilt, one's superior compliance with them. Thus, the civil rights workers who were at the time embarking upon sit-ins and freedom rides in the South would cite the Fourteenth Amendment of the US Constitution and complain that its provisions were not being fully implemented. So long as you could show that what you were doing was consistent with the rules, you were thought to be well armed against your critics. The thing to do was not to break the rules but to re-define them and adapt their applicability. The greatest illustration of the principle had always been the way the US Supreme Court, even in its most revolutionary utterances, purported not to make new laws but merely to apply old ones to new situations. This was a veneer of social cohesion and stability firmly glued on to a society whose inner conflicts periodically threatened to tear it apart. How unlike Britain, I remember thinking at the time, with its disinclination to enunciate precise rules for all contingencies and its greater disposition to leave well alone in the hope that those in the know will continue to arrange things properly.

Chapter 16

Down to Work

These differences were reflected in the style of the academic work I was expected to produce. At Cambridge, I had been taught to write elegantly, or at least was rewarded if I did so. One of my grammar school teachers had remarked to me many years before that a good British university education was one that taught you to expound with conviction on any topic, whether you knew anything about it or not! There was a kernel of truth in his cynical comment. Style and fluency counted for a great deal at Cambridge. The best scholar was not necessarily the one who knew everything about his or her subject so much as the person who knew exactly where to look things up. The mere remembering of facts was less important than what you did with them. Thus, the assiduous note-taker or the person with the photographic memory was likely to head towards a good second-class degree; the Firsts went to the people who could think, hypothesise and suggest new relationships between hitherto disparate aspects of a field of study. That, at any rate, was the message I had picked up from my years at Cambridge.

A small portent of the change that was soon to hit me occurred in my final year at Cambridge when I took part in a college debate on God or some such inscrutable subject. I made it my business to argue my case, whatever it was, with as much wit, wisdom and oratory as I could muster. Opposing me was an American visitor who, somewhat humourlessly, listed in strict syllogistic order the various steps of his argument. He actually said things like 'firstly', 'secondly' and 'thus we have demonstrated that…'. I don't remember who won, but I do remember the stylistic chasm that opened up between us as the debate unfolded.

At Cornell, such differences were made clear from the outset. I put my name down for a seminar on Russian Government thinking that if I studied the USSR in the USA I might, in a single blow as it were, be able to learn something about both of the nuclear superpowers that dominated the world in which I lived. At Cambridge, I had learned much about ancient Athens, the Holy Roman Empire and the philosophers of the Enlightenment; now I would bring my knowledge of the world up to date. The Russian seminar was taught by the heavily-bejowelled and equally heavy-minded-and-mannered George Fischer (son of the historian Louis Fischer), a man more interested in 'input–output' theories and 'systems analysis' than in such mundane matters as how the USSR was governed. At the opening session, I learned with some misgivings that I would have to type my essays (henceforth to be called 'papers') and not write them, that they would have to be typed, moreover, on stencils and be duplicated and distributed to everyone else in the seminar ahead of time and that every contention and every fact would have to be thoroughly footnoted. I had never before written a footnote in my life and had rarely typed anything. But if this was the world of advanced American scholarship, so be it.

I felt like young Cherubino who (in the aria 'Non più andrai' from Mozart's *Le nozze di Figaro*) is marched off to the army and told by Figaro that all the elegant airs and graces he had so enjoyed are henceforth to be things of the past. Like Cherubino, I found that message hard to take at first. Surely, the cool, sophisticated writing style for which I had been commended at Cambridge was superior to the pretentious jargon which some of my fellow students (and many of the authors recommended by Prof Fischer) seemed constrained to adopt, or the mass of superfluous little references with which a tedious and derivative paper would supposedly be rendered more authoritative. Who would want to write like a Talcott Parsons* if the same point could be made by a Bertrand Russell?

At first, I was reassured in this posture by some of my professors – notably by Clinton Rossiter, my mentor-in-chief. 'Look what I've brought back from Cambridge,' he'd tell his colleagues proudly as, one arm over my shoulder, he would introduce me to them. After I'd undergone an initial semester with the dour George Fischer, I spoke to Rossiter about my ordeal and he kindly suggested I switch from Russian to American Government and become one of his assistants. That meant that, in addition to pursuing my own academic research into aspects of American government preparatory to a postgraduate degree, I would also teach the subject to small undergraduate classes of about 25: 'sections' of the large numbers – often 500 or more – who poured in to hear Rossiter's own lectures. But how, I asked him nervously, could I possibly teach a class of undergraduates a subject with which they had grown up when I had never read so much as a single book on the subject? 'Don't worry Dan,' Rossiter reassured

* Talcott Parsons was an American sociologist associated with the theory of 'structural functionalism'.

Clinton Rossiter.
(Photograph from Cornell University Archive)

me. 'You guys from Cambridge are capable of picking up any new skill or subject far faster than our kids. You'll have no trouble.' And I didn't; not at least from the undergraduates I taught. I read assiduously: Rossiter's own books on the American presidency and political parties and countless others he recommended, and gained rapidly in knowledge and authority, at least as far as my students were concerned. Sometimes, Rossiter had to be away from campus and, on those occasions, he would often ask one of his postgraduate assistants to deliver the 'big' lecture in his place. My turn came round. I prepared something on the US presidency and, when the time arrived, marched up to the lectern and, for the first time in my life, addressed an audience of several hundred, summoning up as much energy and enthusiasm as I could muster for the occasion. Too much, possibly. One of my postgrad colleagues, the charming Usha Mehta (sister of the Indian writer Ved Mehta), came up to congratulate me afterwards and asked, only semi-jokingly, if I was thinking of going on to be an actor.

* * *

The Government Department at Cornell had more than its fair share of prima donnas on its faculty, each vying with the others for fame and glory. These personal rivalries were compounded by a more fundamental split that represented a deep and genuine fissure which existed throughout the profession. There were the political scientists proper, people like the brilliant and fast-talking Ted Lowi, a man with a head for statistical and behavioural interpretations of politics at both the 'leadership and grass-roots level', as he would have said. George Fischer liked to think of himself as representing this school of thought. Directly opposed to them were the theory men such as Mario Einaudi, the wily old European aristocrat who chaired the Department, plus the moralistic disciples of Leo Strauss of Chicago such as the constitutional lawyer Walter Burns and the highly strung political theorist Allan Bloom, a man given to dismissing logical positivism with a jovial remark like 'Hot Ayer' (and later famous for his bestselling book, *The Closing of the American Mind*). To these theory men, particularly the Straussians, the very words 'political science' were anathema. Straddled between these two groups was the gadfly, cynic and professional devil's advocate Andrew Hacker, a man who liked to think he could turn his deft and combative intelligence to whatever approach was currently the most provocative – usually to demolish it. The Department also contained others with area specialities (such as John Lewis in Chinese studies and the Southeast Asia expert George Kahin) as well as some, like Stephen Muller, whose intellectual and personal predisposition seemed to lead towards the containment rather than the exacerbation of disputes. But the split between the political scientists and the theory merchants was profound and acrimonious, and it became a passionate and obsessive topic of conversation not only between the principal protagonists but also amongst all of us in the Government Department at the time.

A pivotal but uncomfortable position in this debate was occupied by Clinton Rossiter. Rossiter was the best-known figure on the Cornell campus, a classicist from the Midwest who had (like me, as he often reminded me) switched subjects at graduate level and moved over into American Studies. He became expert on the early period of the American Republic and became intrigued by the careers of the men who exercised political power. To Rossiter, the important figures of American history were the big power brokers, Alexander Hamilton (the greatest man never to have become President), Lincoln, 'Teddy' Roosevelt, FDR and his current hero, Jack Kennedy. He loved these men, savoured the use of their nicknames and scorned the failures. Polk was a bigger figure than you might have thought because he enormously increased the size of the country, whereas Woodrow Wilson, although 'one of us who made it', was incapable of decision when it really counted. Rossiter was really a 'great man' manqué who, instead of being one, wrote and taught about them. Once in a seminar on the presidency I asked Rossiter whether he didn't think that certain historical periods might require a leader who could exercise a calming influence upon the times, someone who might deliberately allow contentious issues to remain a little blurred and permit government activity to lapse a little. His answer was couched, typically, in the language of thrusting and competitive masculinity. 'What do you want, Dan,' he asked with a twinkle in his eye, 'a eunuch in the White House?'

Rossiter was the one person in the Cornell Government Department who was by temperament and intellectual inclination more of an historian than either a political scientist or a theory man. Like Hacker, he tried to straddle these two tendencies among his colleagues but he did so with great unease. This was the man to whom, for better or for worse, my own fortunes were to be closely linked.

Cornell Arts Quad.
(Photograph from Cornell University Archive)

Chapter 17

Testing Times

I was registered to do a PhD degree, not because I particularly wanted a doctorate but because otherwise I would have had to leave Cornell after a year, and there was nowhere else I particularly wanted to be and no job I particularly wanted to do. The PhD programme was a way of remaining in the USA for a few years and of deferring the decision about what I was to go on and do afterwards. Before leaving the UK, I had been encouraged to stay on in Cambridge and do a doctorate there; this would have entailed three more cushy years in residence and a thesis on some suitable episode in English constitutional history. But life at Cornell, on a teaching assistantship worth a mere $1,700 per annum as I struggled with the graduate-level study of subjects I'd never touched before, seemed less cocooned from the real world than Cambridge, more of an adventure, more stimulating. It was the lack of safety nets that attracted. So a Cornell PhD it was to be, if only to postpone other decisions.

In order to do a Cornell doctorate you had to cross a number of bridges: an oral qualifying exam in your second semester, then some two years of seminar credits followed by a rigorous series of take home 'comprehensive' exams followed by another oral, and a thesis and yet another oral. The whole process could take five years. None of your three-year Cambridge stuff. An American PhD might have carried less international prestige than one from Cambridge. But Cornell – its Government Department at any rate – would make you sweat blood before it would bestow those coveted letters upon you.

During my second semester, Clinton Rossiter suggested that I undertake the ritual of the qualifying exam. He and two of his colleagues would take me out to lunch at the Faculty Club, after which we'd simply chat over coffee. No need to be stiff and starchy about it, the way they do things at Cambridge, eh Dan? That seemed fine, though I wasn't sure quite what was expected of me or what I was capable of offering. I remained profoundly ignorant of the Russian system of government despite having attended George Fischer's seminar (supposedly) on the subject. Rossiter was now my mentor and I was hectically busy making my first acquaintance with the

US Constitution, De Tocqueville and all the basic textbooks on American history and politics. What could I say in my oral exam other than that I would be happy to try and work my way slowly up from my humble nursery slopes towards the peaks of genuine scholarship?

Came the day of the oral in February 1962. That morning, I met Messrs Rossiter, Hacker and Bloom and we walked over towards the Faculty Club. Somewhat self-consciously, I watched this improbable trio as they began to show off to each other and to me. Rossiter told Hacker about an incident at the American Constitutional Convention where one of the Founding Fathers had unceremoniously slapped the huge, gaunt figure of George Washington on the back one morning in greeting and the Great Man's false teeth had fallen out. Later that day, as I recalled this story through my tears, it occurred to me that little men who are fascinated by big men always love banana-skin stories.

We reached the Club and my companions and I sat down to our all-American lunch, our soup and crackers, our garnished hamburgers with potato chips and relish, our French fries and our coleslaw, our ice water, our pie à la mode. We adjourned for coffee. From which point the professional rivalries between these three men floated fully to the surface.

They each asked me a few questions, little bagatelles such as, oh, for instance: what might be the advantages and disadvantages if the United States were to be governed by a system like that of Britain. Simple little questions to which I imagined myself expected to give simple little answers. I stumbled about, made an obvious comment here, pleaded ignorance there, made the odd nervous joke and tried constantly to be amiable and respectful. Since it soon became clear to my interrogators (as I could have told them from the start) that I had little knowledge and few thoughts of consequence regarding my newly adopted subject of American Government, Hacker asked me what, in the whole field of the study of politics, I *did* know anything about. I had never studied politics at all until I came to Cornell, but I told him that I had developed an interest in the recently emerging European Common Market. I talked a little about the cataclysm of the Second World War and the subsequent vision of Jean Monnet and others that the recurrence of such a conflict might be avoided if the formerly warring nations were to integrate their economies and, in time, their political and social institutions. My earliest memories were of war and my earliest fears and hatreds directed towards the Germans and the unspeakable atrocities they had committed. As I had grown older, however, I had travelled a lot in Western Europe and had made many friends in many countries and my own strongest instincts, therefore, were to build up interdependent institutions that would force people of different nationalities to sink the age-old animosities that divided them and to concentrate upon their shared needs for prosperity and security.

I finished as honest an exposition as I could muster of the personal motivation that had led me to want to study government in the first place and, more particularly, my special interest in the system of federal government that seemed to work so impressively in the United States. Perhaps a United States of Europe might one day emerge, I allowed myself to hope.

Hacker was unimpressed. 'That self-revelation is all very interesting, Mr Snowman,' (that dread, cold surname at a time like this!), 'but what are your intellectual interests?' If I didn't know about American Government, did I at least know something about federalism? Rossiter and Bloom got their oar in, too. Had I read Schumpeter? What did I think of Robert Michels on oligarchy? What credence would I attach to a Marxist critique of current moves towards the integration of European political institutions? Or to a Weberian critique? Was I a behavioural man or a theory man? Or merely a vestigial historian? I was absolutely crushed.

We parted and I wandered desolately over to the University Library, went up in the elevator to the seventh floor where my little carrel was situated and sat with my head in my hands. It wasn't just that I had obviously failed an exam or that I had let down those who had put faith in me. Worse, I had just experienced a major setback in my entire image of myself. I had done quite well in school as a mid-teenager, very well in my final years and exceptionally well at Cambridge. The higher the level of challenge, the better I had done. Thinking, as the Sundance Kid said to Butch Cassidy, was what I was good at. I obviously had to make a career of it. I would read and think and talk and write and teach for the rest of my days, and it was only a question of time before I found the right institutional niche for these activities. And then, quite unexpectedly and after being led into a false sense of security, I was brutally told that neither my thoughts nor my expression of them was up to par. Suddenly, everything was in doubt. Perhaps I was really rather stupid. Or facile. Perhaps I had conned all those people at Cambridge into imagining that I was bright simply because they fell for my fluency of style. At last I had been found out, seen through, exposed for the intellectual charlatan that I was. But what could I do?

Where else could I go? I buried my head in my arms on the desk of the carrel and stayed there all afternoon, shaking occasionally.

I later learned that it was almost standard practice for the oral to take the form of a stress interview. I had been tested not only for my knowledge and thoughts but also on my capacity to stand up to pressure, and had failed. If only I had known the rules of the game. But why should the game be played that way? Had I been involved in some sort of initiation ceremony, a formal blooding in the mysteries of higher learning without even knowing it? And revealed as an elk without horns, a cowboy without a gun (or worse)? Sympathetic friends later explained that many Cornell professors, particularly the brighter and more competitive among them, had a need to prove to each other and to their poor students that their intellectual standards were every bit as rigorous as those upheld at more famous institutions like Harvard and Yale. They suffered from the 'Avis rent-a-car complex': we are only second (or third) in the Ivy League, so we try harder. Furthermore, each of my combative profs needed to prove to the other two the greater rigour of his particular approach to the study of politics. These men had their own professional and personal insecurities, their 'publish-or-perish' anxieties, their conflicting needs to arouse both the liking and the awe of their students. Rossiter in particular was forever displaying an exaggerated folksiness in an attempt to be liked, to appear 'one of the boys', while at the same time asserting his grandeur and authority over lesser fry, particularly over those who showed any signs of trying to get too close.

At the time, I was incapable of appreciating any of this. I simply took my professors at face value, assumed they shared the same more or less un-neurotic middle-class civility in which I had been raised and was correspondingly shattered by their rejection – or, worse, their exposure – of me.

* * *

The last time I saw Clinton Rossiter was five years after I had left Cornell, in 1968. I took him out to lunch when he was passing through London after a world-wide lecture tour. He was visibly shaken by the international student assertiveness of that year and disturbed by the accusatory tone of many of the students he had encountered. For a man of such *amour-propre*, proud of his connections with the high and mighty and jealous of his reputation and the respect he thought it ought to bring him, he found the aggressiveness of the New Left almost literally unbearable. As ever, he was walking the awkward tightrope of trying to maintain the dignity he felt to be his due while bending every nerve in an effort to be liked. He swung, as he always did, between self-conscious aloofness and boyish accessibility as though never quite sure which role to adopt and for how long.

He was always like this. I had seen both sides in a rather extreme way during the unforgettable day of the oral exam. During our last meeting, in summer 1968, the alternation between the name-dropping and the rank-pulling on the one hand and the folksy boy-scoutery on the other seemed an ever-harder equilibrium for him to maintain; students were no longer much impressed by either aspect of Rossiter's precarious high-wire act. Two years later, after a period when intimate personal tensions compounded these public ones, this brilliant and much-acclaimed man took his own life.

* * *

After the ordeal of the oral, my parents wrote touchingly to suggest I return to England. But my presence at Cornell was my ticket to the great adventure that was America. I may have been crushed by what I felt to be the imbecility of a little group of professors whose methods seemed to have more to do with the production of battery hens than of contemplative scholars. But this was, after all, the land of Lincoln, of the Metropolitan Opera, of the Wild and Far West and it was for these, and not primarily for a Cornell PhD, that I had made this trip in the first place.

So I stayed. With Rossiter's help and encouragement, I withdrew from the PhD program(me) for the time being and enrolled instead for a humbler MA degree. This would require me to stay on for at least one more year rather than an obligatory three or four, and would guarantee an easier ride with my temperamental teachers and give me just enough time to get to know the wider America beyond the confines of my Ithaca hothouse. Thus, at my moment of deepest despair, the instant at which I had been given the greatest incentive to doubt the value of my brief flirtation with America, what sustained me was the thing itself, the American Dream, that new found land, an almost infinite expanse of both mind and geography which provided infinite opportunities to escape from a bad adventure and to seek out new and more exhilarating ones. It was this that had motivated my visit in the first place. I would press on with my studies but, at the earliest opportunity, would place that whole squalid little episode of the oral exam behind me and pioneer my way to new frontiers.

Chapter 18

Campus Life and Times

American higher education in the early 1960s was still in its bobby-sox-'n-sneakers stage, as yet untroubled by even the first hints of the convulsions that were so violently to disrupt it a few years later. The girls wore skirts, often short tartans or wraparounds, and the boys had crew cuts. Cornell was a big fraternity campus, whole sections of off-campus housing dominated by grand wooden-frame buildings – in effect, club houses-cum-dormitories – that were identified not by their street number but by the Greek letters prominently displayed at the entry point. The first week of each academic year was, for many fresh arrivals, taken up by 'rushing', a system of lavish and often eccentric entertainments by which the fraternities would try to sell themselves to potential new applicants. Members of fraternities (and sororities) would sport their special pin, their key, their ring or whatever, and it was to some a matter of major social significance, particularly in the infinite subtlety of the pairing game, if a 'man' or a 'girl' was a 'D Phi' or whatever. Individual fraternities had great snobberies attached to them; this one was full of rich boys, that one was for the sports brigade while a third was renowned for good academic grades. You couldn't normally be from a poor home (or a black or Jewish one) and be a member of a fashionable fraternity, though some would admit the occasional token outsider. Although the fraternities were blatantly inegalitarian, nobody outside seemed to be clamouring for their abolition. The university authorities, indeed, were probably quietly delighted that the 'frat' houses existed; they helped solve a severe accommodation problem on a small and overcrowded campus, and they encouraged the sons and daughters of rich parents to attend a university which was largely privately financed.

Most of the undergraduates did not live in fraternities or sororities but in halls of residence. Several of these were huge, forbidding structures. To a randy (Americans read 'raunchy') young man, the girls' dorms acquired an air of forbidding yet titillating inaccessibility: impregnable fortresses not unlike those medieval castles in which, according to legend, every attractive maiden had to be locked for her own safety and security. Just as,

Cornell University campus.

Cornell: gorge outside Ithaca.

in the middle ages, there were strict codes that had to be followed by any knight who wished to pursue a lady, so there were all sorts of regulations here at Cornell for any young man hoping to gain access to the denizens of these modern castles of delight. In courtship, as in so much else in America, rules had to be followed if one were to have any hope of success.

Undergraduates at Cornell were constantly being assessed, tested, labelled, categorised and re-assessed so that anyone who wanted to pass through the system successfully had to stick closely and precisely to the prescribed work pace. Most people worked far harder than the people I'd known at Cambridge. Professor Andrew Hacker told me one time (amiably enough) that here in America I had to work '25 hours a day!' This was the Puritan Ethic. This was what had made America great. And Cornell was great. Did Cornell have a Harvard/Yale complex? Maybe. The fact was that the University Library spewed out a mass of humanity when it closed every evening at 11.30 pm – rather as the pubs did in England. Except that the kids at Cornell were drunk with work. The entire undergraduate body had to work at roughly the same rhythm, one imposed by the objective and external standards of the university and its teachers. In practice, this came to mean that most students would work long and hard throughout the week but would knock off with total abandon at the weekend. On Friday and Saturday nights, all hell would break loose. Friday night was party night, a night for eating and drinking, socialising and sexualising, for singing and swilling and vomiting. During the working week, the Puritan Ethic reigned supreme. On Friday night, the Pursuit of Happiness took over.

If you can't beat 'em, join 'em. In time, I found myself slowly fitting in with the Cornell way of doing things and watched as I became something of a 'square' during the week and a 'swinger' at weekends. I was never thrilled by this routine and always did my level best to subvert it. But without much success. If you wanted to survive, you obeyed the rules. Flexibility was a mug's game. So I, too, began to work long and hard during the week, longer and harder than ever before. And at weekends I tried to pack in all the many other activities that went to make up the whole man: the socialising, the shopping, the concerts and films and plays, the political and literary magazines, the decent food and drink, the little trips out of town. And the women. The correct time to pursue the maidens in their fortresses was at weekends and no other time would do.

* * *

Romance at Cornell was different from romance at Cambridge. There was something more public about it, more formalised, ritualised. At Cambridge, where almost every student had a room of his or her own, it was not necessary for anyone to know who (in the words of the venerable limerick) did what and with which and to whom. At Cornell, almost everything took place in a social context. When I first came to Cornell, I was given a booklet full of helpful advice to the foreign student. You may have heard, it said, that American girls are more free and independent-minded than girls in other countries. However, while this may be true, it went on, you should not assume that a social invitation to tea, for instance, is meant to suggest any romantic intent. We had been warned! But how then did you pursue these free and independent-minded creatures if occasions that seemed to you to be at least potentially romantic were merely social? Most undergraduates at Cornell lived in communal accommodation of one kind or another, shared not only bathrooms and kitchens but often bedrooms as well. In these big dormitories, one telephone would usually service an entire corridor, so everybody was forever taking messages for (and overhearing) everybody else, and no new assignations could long remain secret. The men were not normally allowed in the women's rooms except on two precisely prescribed Sunday afternoons per term when the door had to remain open and, as the Dean put it, 'all four feet had to remain on the ground at all times' (though whether bottoms could touch the floor at the same time was never specified). Inevitably, therefore, undergraduate necking and petting occurred in full public view in the large downstairs lounges of the girls' dorms as each Friday and Saturday evening ground inexorably towards its close. 'PDA', this lounge-room activity was dubbed, or Public Display of Affection – although it often looked rather more like a public display of acquisition by eager young men anxious to demonstrate the effectiveness of their courtship procedures. For the more adventurous couples, particularly those whose passions were likely to be aroused before the evening was through and whose geographical explorations had extended beyond the confines of mouth and waist, the dormitory lounge was kids' stuff. Their favourite spot, particularly if one of them had access to a car, was the drive-in cinema, known variously (depending on the stage of intimacy reached) as the 'passion pit' or the 'finger bowl'.

Cornell is situated in a glorious stretch of country overlooking Lake Cayuga, one of the so-called Finger Lakes. The area is laced with gorges, ravines, waterfalls and spectacular hilltop vistas. For five or six months of the year, Upstate New York was at best cold and at worst frozen. It was never just 'raining' or 'snowing' in Ithaca, we would joke, but 'Ithacating'. But when spring suddenly sprang, when the snows magically melted, the torrents gushed forth and the leaves miraculously reappeared on all those stately but denuded trees, it was impossible not to feel a sense of exhilaration. This transformation was duly marked in the University Calendar with an official holiday, Spring Weekend. One friend told me the Ithaca spring always made him feel like a grub crawling out from under a stone, though I was put in mind of the prisoners in Beethoven's *Fidelio* blinking in the light of freedom after release from their subterranean imprisonment. The glorious physicality of the Ithaca spring cried out for romance. But the rules of knightly chivalry were hedged about with steps and signs and tokens and taboos. Reputations rose and fell in the capricious breeze of rumour. This or that girl 'did' (the men would whisper knowingly) but most girls 'didn't'.

It was in the spring of my second year at Cornell that I developed a relationship with a lovely young art student at the university, Alice Ann Harris. My assault on the medieval fortress of desire was finally crowned with success.

Book 4

'Go West (and South), Young Man!'

Chapter 19

Getting Out of Ithaca

One of the reasons I had come to Ithaca was to be able to get out of it. For all its physical beauty, its hills, woodlands and adjacent lake, Ithaca had many of the limitations of a small community in an isolated spot. So almost the entire student body of Cornell would stage a mass exodus whenever there was even a brief vacation period. A number of East Coast cities were between about five and eight hours' drive away and, while few Londoners at the time would normally have considered driving to Edinburgh for a weekend holiday, students at Cornell were quite inured to the idea of a brief trip to Montreal, Boston, New York, Philadelphia or Washington. Most did not own a car but there was a well-oiled mechanism, of which I took frequent advantage, for getting in touch with those who did and sharing the gasoline costs of a long ride. My tripping began on a modest scale: Thanksgiving in November 1961 with relatives who lived in Utica, a small industrial city in Upstate New York. But Christmas and New Year were spent in New York City and Easter 1962 in the capital, Washington DC.

In New York, the skies were blue, the streets grey and icy and the downtown sidewalks dotted with jovial bell-ringing Santas trying to make a fast buck for this or that good cause and with scurrying bodies struggling with vast gaudy packages and parcels. I went up the Empire State Building (twice – I left a book up there the first time), visited the Frick and Guggenheim art exhibitions as well as the Metropolitan Museum and Museum of Modern Art, walked up and down Fifth Avenue and across Central Park, enjoyed the noise, the bustle, the racial mix and the ubiquitous merchandising of the Upper West Side, and looked up chance acquaintances who had told me to do so if I ever happened to be in New York. And I managed to get a number of times to the Metropolitan Opera, in its original home just south of Times Square, where I revelled in the superhuman voice of Birgit Nilsson cannonading across that gaudy old house, the Italianate grace of Richard Tucker, the brazen appeal of Jon Vickers breaking every rule of voice production and a series of wildly uneven productions.

Washington had to be seen in the spring. Although I just missed the 1962 cherry blossoms, the city, with its long straight boulevards, its great parks and its white marble buildings glistening in the early summer sunlight, looked ravishing. It still maintained something of the character of an elegant Colonial town and I was pleasantly taken aback by the family-sized proportions of the White House which I had somehow expected to be on a scale with Buckingham Palace. My host, AE 'Dick' Howard – later to become a distinguished constitutional expert and, at the time, law clerk to Justice Hugo Black of the US Supreme Court – lived just across the Potomac River in Alexandria, Virginia. He showed me around the District and its environs (the white areas, at least; I had virtually no knowledge at that time of Washington's huge and growing black hinterland), and he would tell me that such-and-such a Cabinet minister lived here, or that he regularly played tennis with the son of Senator so-and-so who lived there. There was an inbred cliquiness to Washington society, an atmosphere present in any one-industry town, particularly if that industry is politics, but which to an outsider seemed to render almost absurdly personal and parochial the massive issues of US domestic and foreign policy.

This was the height of the Kennedy mania and every news stand displayed an inexhaustible range of papers and magazines featuring the President, Jackie, their children and the wider family and friends and yachts and Hyannis homes. During a visit to the White House, through all the rooms that Jackie had had overhauled and redecorated, the snake of tourists passed by a door behind which, the guide informed us, the President was meeting a group of people. Could we all keep as quiet as possible as we wouldn't want to disturb the President, would we? These were innocent days. There had been scarcely more than the most perfunctory security check on any of us as we entered the building. Rather, an air of almost naïve optimism, of trust, hope and pride in all that Washington had to show. The President looked well set for another six years in the White House and his brother Bobby was coming up fast as an eventual possible successor. The Kennedys were attractive, intelligent and stylish, and people talked of the White House as Camelot. All the bright young American political scientists whom I knew at Cornell and elsewhere were entranced and had visions of being granted access, one day, to the Round Table. Spring was an appropriate time to visit the Washington of Jack Kennedy.

Not everyone was bitten by the Jack-'n-Jackie bug, however. I met a lady who worked in the office of the newly elected Republican Senator from Texas, John Tower, a diminutive figure of great intelligence, one of the most right-wing figures in the Congress and thought to be one of the front-runners in a possible renaissance of the Republican party in the South. Tower's outer office was full of political literature of an extremely conservative stance which lambasted such Kennedy policies as federal medical care to the elderly or federal aid to education. I was introduced to the Senator who told me that he, like President Kennedy, had once been a student at the London School of Economics when it was under the left-wing influence of figures such as Harold Laski. Tower had enjoyed his stay in England, he assured me politely, but added pointedly that, unlike JFK, he had not been much impressed by the 'socialistic' atmosphere that pervaded the LSE. I met members of Tower's staff and was even shown the signature machine with which many of the more routine letters from his office were signed (and remember wondering ruefully whether some of the autographs I had collected and valued as a youngster had been signed by machines!).

One of the Senator's aides, a tall girl from Amarillo in the Texas Panhandle named Wendy O'Brien, told me that her daddy was Dean of the Cornell Law School and that I was to be sure to introduce myself to him when I got back to Ithaca. Perhaps I could visit with them in Texas during the summer.

Chapter 20
Panhandling

When the summer arrived, a few weeks later, I was weakened by an attack of chicken pox (which everybody should have long before the age of 23) and, although determined to get far away from Ithaca and see something of the big, wide United States, I had no firm plans. I had written, as a result of a suggestion from Dean O'Brien, to *The Amarillo Globe-Times* offering my services as a sort of temporary Englishman-in-residence but had received no reply. The academic year was drawing to a close when one of my students offered me a lift down to East Texas (a mere 300 miles from Amarillo – the sort of distance I had begun to take in my stride by then). So, in late June 1962, skinny and spotty and with 50 dollars in my pocket, I took off on the 2000-mile drive to the Lone Star State.

A few days later, having taken a bus across Texas to Amarillo and rented a room for an initial week, I went nervously across town to the offices of the *Globe-Times* and asked if I could see the editor. It was 3 July 1962. When the editor appeared, I told him I was the English student who had written a couple of months before to tell him I would be on my way. What, I asked as boldly as I dared, would he like me to do? There was, of course, nothing he would have liked me to do more than to have gone straight back to Cornell. But he was embarrassed at not having replied to my letter promptly and rejected my offer. It was the eve of Independence Day and the Rodeo was in town. Why didn't I go along with the rodeo reporter that evening and write an Englishman's view of the proceedings? If he liked it, he'd print it.

I had only the vaguest idea of what a rodeo was and did not even know until that day that the locals stressed the word's second syllable over the first. That evening, I duly went along, ate my first snow-cone, saw my first Shriners, enjoyed the temerity of the rodeo clown and learned to appreciate some of the finer points of authentic cowboy athleticism. Afterwards I returned to the old wood-frame boarding house where I was staying, climbed heavily onto the veranda, through the mosquito-net door, up the stairs and into my hot and clammy den where I tossed and turned all night worrying desperately about how to concoct an attractive

'Dan "Tex" Snowman.'
(Photograph and caption from *The Amarillo Globe-Times*, 4 July 1962)

and light-hearted piece about the rodeo. The article *had* to be a success. I simply couldn't contemplate what I would do if it wasn't. I certainly couldn't presume on the friendship of the O'Briens and was determined not to contact them unless and until I had landed (as they said at the rodeo) on my feet. I laboured mightily with that damned rodeo until, in the early hours of Independence Day, I hit upon an approach that I thought might do the trick. I wrote as if I were a seasoned Texan rodeo-goer but had had the misfortune of sitting next to an ignorant visitor from England whose incessant comments I was able to incorporate into the eventual piece. This formula enabled me to poke gentle fun both at the Texan aficionados and at myself, and the double caricature worked. The editor and his colleagues liked it. More than that, they put it on the front page of the July 4th edition alongside a lead story of a big speech by JFK, and featured a photo of me wearing a Stetson with the caption 'Dan "Tex" Snowman'.

For forty days I stayed in Amarillo, wrote an Englishman's view of whatever was going on in and around town, was invited everywhere, went on the road with all and any of the paper's reporters and got lost with the Entertainments Page editor one day in the middle of a king-sized ranch when our car broke down on the way to a cattle round-up ('"Abominable" says Snowman' read the headline over my story the following day). I met the O'Briens who made me welcome and went horseback riding on their estates, was taken to see some of the spectacular canyons on the outskirts

Horseback riding in Texas, 1962.

Daniel in Texas Canyon, 1962.

of town and attended millionaire barbecue parties and poor-boy Mexican cookouts.

This was the land of Paul Newman's *Hud* (which was being shot when I was there) and of *The Last Picture Show*. I also wondered at times whether Amarillo wasn't perhaps one of the most reactionary communities in America. Certainly, it was one of the few places in the country whose Congressman and Mayor were members of the extreme right-wing John Birch Society (whose founder, the paranoid little candy-manufacturer Robert Welch, told me one day that he thought the British National Health Service communist-inspired). Amarillo's school and college libraries had banned John Steinbeck's novel *The Grapes of Wrath* as dangerously socialistic.

The old frontier spirit of rugged individualism was vigorously alive in the Texas Panhandle back in 1962, and it was to this that many liked to attribute the great prosperity that had come their way. But woe betide anyone who thought to question this central tenet. The benefits Amarillo had to offer from helium, oil or cattle may have been enormous, and the city's population had shot up since the turn of the century from 2,000 to over 140,000. But you had to subscribe to the local ethic or you could be virtually run out of town for suspected socialism. People talked big, earned big, ate and drank big and loved and hated big. The local murder rate was prodigious by the standards of any British town of comparable size (everybody I knew had a gun), and so was the number of separate Protestant denominations and churches. President Kennedy was almost universally excoriated and people were not slow to crack the most blatant anti-Catholic jokes. Everybody seemed anxious to get rich quick and personal generosity was unstinting; as a visitor from Britain, a country once great and for whose sins of socialism I could scarcely be held personally responsible, I was accorded princely treatment from all I met. But for the black and the brown and the poor and the indigent and the politically heterodox, there was scant sympathy or help. Ibsen's enemy of the people would have felt himself in familiar territory, and so would many of those who, a decade or less before, had lost jobs in more liberal environments like New York or Los Angeles because of supposed links, generally imaginary, with communism. As I watched spurs and Stetsons flash in and out of muddy but air-conditioned Cadillacs, I could not but reflect upon the extraordinary coexistence between spectacular material advance and equally unadulterated ideological conservatism.

For nearly six weeks I worked and played in Amarillo and the Texas Panhandle and enjoyed my status as an exotic fish in a small pool. The elusive wider world, I was discovering, was made up of a vast chain of pretty small ones and my temporary celebrity in this particular spot on the map helped blinker me for a few weeks from the more oppressive aspects of Panhandle parochialism. I knew, however, that my novelty value would soon erode and people would start demanding to know my personal opinions about such prominent and polarising issues as 'socialized medicine', the 'Negro problem' or the ways President Kennedy or Chief Justice Earl Warren were helping the communist cause. As limey-in-residence, I could make jokes, plead ignorance, bounce awkward questions back at other people or hide my views beneath a complex analysis. Since I was acutely aware that my own views on almost any major political issue were likely to be diametrically opposed to those of most Amarilloans, I frequently resorted to evasions such as these during the course of my stay. But it would only be a matter of time before such ruses would wear thin. People would stop giving me the benefit of the doubt and I would be unmasked and revealed as an effete, pinko snob.

Chapter 21
In Dixie Land

In the best Western tradition, I knew one should always quit while winning, so it was in high spirits and with a good reputation that I took my bags to the Trailways bus station a few days into August and took off for the Old South. For a further six weeks, I travelled through the heart of the Old Confederacy, staying with a succession of wealthy and welcoming white Southerners, courtesy of the English-Speaking Union, and all were duly impressed by my Cambridge degree and what they took to be my educated English accent. I listened to jazz in New Orleans from Preservation Hall's Eureka Band and ate seafood in the Vieux Carré, toured a paper mill alongside Mobile Bay, travelled by bus along Sherman's route of devastation 'from Atlanta to the sea' and watched the nuclear ship *Savannah* arrive for the first time into its home port, a superb 18th-century city whose New World rectilinear street plan was beautifully interwoven with Old World squares. I went on to Charleston and sailed out from the harbour and saw Fort Sumter where the Civil War began, and eventually made my way back slowly up the eastern seaboard to New York and thence Upstate to Ithaca in time for the new academic year.

My trip through the South took place during the 'centennial' of what most people called the American Civil War and some Southerners – whites at any rate – the War Between the States (and a select few the War of Yankee Aggression). Throughout the former Confederacy states were memorials, statues, special commemorative books and films and exhibitions, and re-enactments of the great battles in which more men donned Confederate uniform than had ever done so a hundred years before. The South may have lost the war militarily but I was told repeatedly that Northern power had never been able to vanquish the spirit of the South. Indeed, the centenary of the war helped stimulate a renaissance of Southern pride. In almost every city below the Mason-Dixon line the Stars and Bars, that symbol of Southern defiance against the North, was flying alongside, or even in place of, the Stars and Stripes, while 'Dixie' was often treated with the deference of a national anthem. The South was 'genteel' and 'cultured', people would tell me insistently, and point to the beauty of the magnolia or azalea displays or the old-world courtesies with which Southern men supposedly treated their womenfolk. The North, by contrast, was brash and noisy and dirty. The South believed in the right of the individual to determine his own destiny and of the locality to run its own affairs whereas in the North they permitted big government to ride roughshod over local interests and preferences. White Northerners, I was frequently told with bitter emphasis, were forever claiming to have no prejudice against the 'Negroes' as a race and it was true that white Southerners did; but whites in the South would often have a deep and sentimental affection for individual blacks with whom they had contact whereas the hypocritical Northerners would often make life hell for the blacks in their midst.

This question of race was paramount. Although people would tell me about the dangers of communism (domestic and/or international), the threat of socialised medicine, the overweening power of the brothers Kennedy and of the federal government or about the virtues of States' Rights or the elegance of the Southern way of life, there generally lay behind all these subjects, only thinly disguised, one all-important topic. Race.

By 1962, largely as a result of massive waves of post-war black migration to the cities of the North and West, Negroes (as they were still called) no longer constituted an overall majority in any of the Southern states, although there were still great areas of black concentration, particularly in Mississippi, Alabama, Georgia and South Carolina. For those who had gone North, there were problems a-plenty, as the recurrent urban riots of the later 1960s were soon to highlight. But the blacks who remained in the South had to live under a rigid ('Jim Crow') system of segregation, imposed in the aftermath of the Civil War and still formally upheld by the highest political and legal authorities in the region, which thrust its way into every detail of daily life. There were clearly marked Negro and white drinking fountains and toilet facilities in bus depots and in State office buildings, and separate black and white hotels, swimming pools, churches, restaurants and cafés. The job ads in local papers would specify whether a post was intended for white or black applicants and many of the more menial jobs were reserved for Negroes only. Housing patterns were rigidly segregated as were health facilities. Overt sexual relationships between black men and white women were, if known, likely to arouse the most brutal hostility from white men, though they themselves would not infrequently take insouciant advantage of black women.

Segregated facilities in the Old South

The system of segregation, still profoundly and widely entrenched, was nevertheless coming to be questioned. In 1954, the US Supreme Court, in a unanimous decision written by Chief Justice Earl Warren, had declared that separate facilities were inherently unequal and were not to be tolerated. A few organisations in the South – a bus company here, a school there – had changed their ways accordingly. But many leading figures, such as Senator Herman Talmadge of Georgia, had publicly expressed their contempt for the Court's ruling, and all over the South in 1962 were placards bearing the slogan: IMPEACH EARL WARREN. In Birmingham, Alabama, I stayed with a crusty old pair of Anglophiles who told me how they regretted that Britain's socialists had given independence to places like Jamaica, and added with pride that the local opera and a number of golf courses in Birmingham had been temporarily closed in order to avoid having to comply with the Court's desegregation order. As they spoke, a young black couple walked quietly along the other side of the street. 'Can you imagine sitting next to something like that at the opera?' my hostess expostulated, and I wondered silently how singers like Leontyne Price or Marian Anderson would have replied.

In Atlanta, I met one of the Justices of the State Supreme Court of

Georgia. He told me that the state legislature had long been gerrymandered in such a way as to give added weight to Georgia's white voters and effectively disfranchise most black citizens. But re-districting had now been ordered by the US Supreme Court so that, gradually, the races would become more equitably represented.

'I suppose that is only fair,' I ventured.

'You might think so,' he answered. 'But if you give a Nigra a real vote, he wouldn't know how to use it.' He reminded me smugly that 'we have ways' (the poll-tax and the literacy test, for example) of preventing the ignorant from even being able to register to vote in the first place, so the US Supreme Court could huff and puff all it wanted.

I agreed that it was arguably inconvenient for democracy to give the vote to people who might not always use it wisely. But could not the ignorant be educated into the responsibilities that accompany political privilege?

'Ever tried educating a Nigra?' laughed my interlocutor and brought our conversation to a skidding halt.

As I walked through the grounds of the State capitol, I reflected on the fate of any black Georgian who might have had the ability and courage to challenge the corrupt white-administered literacy tests and who, if he had pressed his case far enough, might eventually have qualified for an appearance before this bastion of egalitarian justice. 'It took our white civilization 2000 years to reach its present high standards,' many Southern whites told me (conveniently forgetting the indescribable atrocities so recently committed by the supposedly pure Aryan descendants of Dürer, Goethe and Beethoven). 'So how can you expect *them* to achieve our level when they've only been out of the trees for a few generations?'

At first I winced whenever I heard comments such as these, but I soon learned to expect them almost as a matter of course. The racist rhetoric was all of a piece with the grotesque statements about the putative evils of socialised medicine and of communism as well as the repetitive clichés about the culture and civility of Southern life. All were, in essence, expressions of extreme unease by a society that felt itself to be under intense and growing pressure. The civil rights movement was just then beginning to find its stride. Martin Luther King had been a name to reckon with in the South ever since the successful Montgomery bus boycott of 1955–56 and by the time I was first in the South, in 1962, liberal whites were beginning to come down from the North to join the struggle and bring it to nationwide attention. That summer, travelling through the Old Confederacy, I found myself passing through many places in which integrated Freedom Rides and lunch-counter sit-ins had recently caused anger among many local whites, and there was much resentful talk about the disgusting behaviour of Yankee beatniks who had no right to come South and disturb a perfectly contented society. 'Our Nigras are happy with the way things are,' I was told, 'and we don't need left-wing Northern pseudo-intellectuals coming down here to lecture us on how we should live. Why don't they put their own house in order first?' By exaggerating both its virtues and the perils to which it felt itself exposed, Southern white society was implicitly acknowledging the strength of criticisms heaped upon it from outside as well as the capacity of its critics to force it to make fundamental changes.

Staying with one upper-echelon, white family after another in what were often elegant ante-bellum homes, I felt as if I were touring the great aristocratic country houses of Britain in spring 1914 or the homes of the Viennese elite in 1937. A long-established way of life was shortly to be dramatically overthrown. Yet those with a vested interest in the *status quo* were almost wilfully avoiding or misreading the signs. I knew that I had to return, sooner rather than later.

Finally, in September, I got back to (relatively) familiar territory, alighting at last from my bus at New York's Port Authority station. Immediately, I found myself confronted with what my elegant, genteel Southern friends would have lambasted as the typically loud, brusque manners of the North. And I loved it. 'That your baggage?' some guy shouted at me, without even the courtesy of a 'Sir'. He was only trying to be helpful, I figured. Another, in response to my request for directions to the Upstate bus depot, simply pointed a finger and yelled, 'Down there. Left!' I felt at home, at last.

* * *

Back in Ithaca, I settled comfortably into my new agenda: a one-year extension, during which I would teach American Government to small classes of US undergraduates while researching and writing an MA thesis under the supervision of Clinton Rossiter. Rossiter's books on the US presidency and its political parties had made him something of a national celebrity. I attended his regular lectures and was able, through a combination of luck, judgement and hard work, to become an effective teacher of the 'sections' placed in my charge. I read avidly all I could about the theory, history and structure of American politics and, like many another in Kennedy's America, became intrigued by the personality and powers, actual and potential, of the President. Just as Franklin Roosevelt, 30 years before, had promised Americans a 'New Deal', Kennedy offered a 'New Frontier'. Like FDR with his 'Fireside Chats', the handsome young President was determined to address the nation directly, in his case via press conferences which were broadcast live on television. I watched these, mesmerised, and wrote a paper comparing and contrasting them with the British parliamentary practice of 'Prime Minister's Questions' (which was not yet broadcast). This was the height of the Cold War, and in October 1962 my friends and I watched Kennedy on TV as he revealed the presence of Soviet missiles on nearby Cuba. We were within range if these were ever launched against the USA, and it was impressive to see how the President and his advisers negotiated their way successfully out of what had for a while seemed potentially the most dangerous crisis the world had ever confronted.

When, in due course, it became necessary for me to settle on a subject for my thesis, I suggested to Rossiter that something on the powers of the presidency might be just right. Decision-making in the White House, perhaps, peppered with a little historical perspective. I finally settled on a topic: President Truman's decision to drop atomic bombs on Japan. The research and write-up preoccupied me for the rest of my time at Cornell and was to lead to one of the most memorable encounters of my life.

Chapter 22

New Frontiers

My second and final year at Cornell was far more fulfilling than my first. Academically, I had an exciting project to undertake: one of my own choosing and to which I felt I could do proper justice. I moved to a larger apartment where one of my roommates was Martin Schain, a fellow postgrad in the Government Department who was to become a life-long friend. Meanwhile, my relationship with Alice added colour and spice to my life.

So did the fact that I had by now joined the Cornell Glee Club, adding Walton's *Belshazzar's Feast* and Prokofiev's *Alexander Nevsky* to my choral repertoire and singing my first Fauré *Requiem* under the by then legendary Nadia Boulanger. By now in her mid-70s, Boulanger had long ago studied composition with Gabriel Fauré and become his chief assistant at the organ of the Eglise de la Madeleine before going on to become coach to many of the leading American composers of her time such as Elliott Carter, Aaron Copland, Roy Harris and Virgil Thomson. As she rehearsed us at Cornell, Boulanger would tell us every now and then that 'Monsieur Fauré' (who had died in 1924) liked a particular passage to go 'a bit more like this', and we would all try to comply.

The choral highlight of my US years was learning the Beethoven Ninth by heart and singing it in spring 1963 in a pair of concerts with the Philadelphia Orchestra under Eugene Ormandy. While we were in Philadelphia, half a dozen of us, despite warnings not to do so, 'snuck' into the concert hall one morning where we knew the orchestra was to be rehearsed by Otto Klemperer. From a distance, dead still and anxious not to be noticed, we watched as the diminutive Ormandy stood next to the gaunt, giant Klemperer, introduced him to the orchestra with the usual courtesies, then left them to get on with their work. They were rehearsing Beethoven's Sixth Symphony, the *Pastoral*, and I remember being surprised at how slowly Klemperer took the usually jaunty *Scherzo* movement (the 'Ländler') and wondering whether that was because, crippled by a plethora of infirmities, the old man couldn't conduct any faster. Suddenly, we became aware of a figure sidling over to us. It was Ormandy. 'Now we're in for it!' we thought. In fact, what Ormandy said, with his charming Hungarian accent, was: 'As you know, Dr Klemperer does not like people sitting in on his rehearsals.' Pause. 'But I think that if you sit over there,' – and with a smile he pointed further back, into a side area of seating obscured by shadow – 'you'll have a better chance of not being seen!' A generous gesture from a man whose music-making contained similar warmth; I still remember the way he encouraged his oboist to shape the solo in the middle section of the Scherzo movement of the *Ninth* – a passage most conductors just race through in strict time.

* * *

The 1960s were affluent, optimistic times on both sides of the Atlantic. In Britain, seven 'New Universities' were being set up, all of them in attractive locations and committed to the high ideal of revitalising the nation's intellectual and imaginative life. The first and most widely publicised of these was the University of Sussex. An entire campus was being erected near Brighton at Falmer. Designed by Basil Spence, the architect of the new Coventry Cathedral, it was scheduled to open in September 1963. Might I be interested in applying for a job at Sussex, asked my father in a letter which contained a job ad he had cut out from one of the Sunday papers. Why not, I thought, and wrote a letter to the Sussex authorities offering my services. A correspondence ensued with Asa Briggs, one of the University's founders and, in due course, I was offered a lectureship starting that autumn.

By June, I had completed my thesis, achieved my MA and been offered an attractive job on my return to the UK. Before I returned I knew I had to travel. In summer 1962 I had gone South. This year it had to be the Far West.

* * *

For a hectic week in early June 1963 I drove with two other young men across Upstate New York, Pennsylvania, Ohio and Indiana then on to St. Louis, down through the Ozarks to Tulsa and the giant spread of Oklahoma City, and on to Amarillo, where I spent a night with some of my friends of the previous year. Thence, across the long, straight highways of New Mexico and (after a sleepless three hours in a dingy motel room at a remote spot in the Arizona desert) to the stupendous vision of dawn breaking over the Grand Canyon. For all too brief a while we watched, awestruck, as there unfolded before us a display quite magisterial in its grandeur: purple in the shadows, scarlet and vermilion and even yellow in the sun, a constantly shifting kaleidoscope of shapes and colours and textures created by the elemental forces of earth, water and sunlight.

This was the summer of Dean Martin's 'Hazy, Lazy, Crazy Days' and the 'Hang Me, Dang me' song. For hour after hour, day after long day, the three of us sat uncomfortably cooped up together and passed from one local radio catchment area to the next, listening to the same popular songs and perhaps a handful of others pouring repeatedly from the car radio. Our own silence was sullen and watchful, broken irregularly as one of us would come out with a new example of the adverb joke or 'swifty' that was all the rage at the time: 'I'm not afraid of crocodiles, said Captain Hook off-handedly' (or 'disarmingly'), one of us would contribute. To which another would respond with something said by Jayne Mansfield 'flatly' or Maria Callas 'sharply'.

When the going got rough, the jokes became sicker ('I have cardiac trouble, murmured Eisenhower half-heartedly') or just plain dejected ('I'm a disinherited peer, said Sir Alec Douglas-Home, crestfallenly'). And my personal favourite: 'Oh, well, I suppose I'll just have to assume corporeal shape again, sighed Jesus, dispiritedly'.

And on it went, roundly and squarely, gratingly and pregnantly, sternly and conventionally, as the three of us, tense and tired, pushed crazily and hazily on through some of the most glorious scenery in the world.

The owner of the car had a girlfriend in Las Vegas whom he told us grimly he just couldn't wait to see. When we got to Vegas, the other guy left to go on by bus while the girl-and-car-owner became appreciably more relaxed. He, she, it and I spent a lazy day at Lake Mead, the desert lagoon created by the vast Hoover dam that controlled the waters of the Colorado River, and then, after a brief foray to the Vegas 'strip', pressed on through the cool of the night towards Los Angeles and the West Coast. We crossed the Nevada–California border (and the state's no-fruit-or-vegetables check) in the early hours, and drove on, with the dawn breaking in our rear mirror, towards the city of the angels. By about 6 am, I had taken over the wheel from my exhausted companions and, although I did not have a valid US driving licence, successfully negotiated our way through a dense early morning fog around San Bernardino, onto the unfamiliar freeway system, right through the Los Angeles rush hour and out into Studio City where, at about 9.30 am, we finally stopped. I paid my respects and my share of the gas, crawled into a sleazy motel, slept for an hour or two and then, not knowing any better, went out for a walk around town.

I made many discoveries that summer and one of them was that Los Angeles was far too big and spread out for one to exist without a car. There was, to be sure, a public bus system (known, ironically I could only presume, as the 'rapid transit' system) but the buses were infrequent, slow and never went to or from the locations I wanted. You could die waiting for a bus in Los Angeles – and, indeed, most of the people waiting for one did look pathetically old. Everything in town was bespattered with garish advertisements and it seemed only appropriate that almost all the seats at the bus stops carried commercials for 'funeral homes'.

The problem of carlessness was severe in a city whose entire social and physical fabric seemed to have been built around the existence of the privately owned internal combustion engine. But, like Voltaire's Candide, I generally found solutions lying alongside my problems. I wandered along Hollywood Boulevard just in time to see the darlings of the movie industry arrive at Pantages for the LA premiere of *Cleopatra* and then, through contacts with a remote cousin whom I contacted, found myself staying with a generous-minded family of anglophiles for a few nights. With their help and guidance, I was able to enjoy the grand tour: Disneyland, Griffith Park, Farmers Market, the Paramount studios and the glorious beaches and, when it was time to move up the coast to San Francisco, they drove me to the Greyhound Bus station.

I had arrived on the West Coast from Ithaca in seven days. But I took seven weeks to return. I rode the cable cars in San Francisco, visited the old silver-boom cities in northern Nevada, spent Independence Day at Salt Lake City (where I became the only person I knew to have sat on both the Great Salt Lake and the Dead Sea), took a 400-mile detour up through Wyoming to Yellowstone National Park and the glorious Grand Tetons, helped make hand-churned ice cream on a farm in the heart of Willa Cather territory* and got bitten by the Frank Lloyd Wright bug and visited every building of his I could find in Wisconsin and Illinois. As I travelled across the US, the local press everywhere was busily reporting the latest news and gossip concerning the Profumo scandal just then unfolding in Britain, and this enabled me to obtain an unusually widescreen perspective

* Cather's 1915 novel *The Song of the Lark*, for example, features a young girl raised in a tiny and remote township in the Mid-West whose only form of self-expression is when she is allowed to play the organ of the local church or sing in the choir.

on American attitudes towards matters of sexual morality. In Minnesota, a Swedish Lutheran family mentioned the case with some embarrassment and attributed Profumo's 'escapades' to his 'Italian blood', whereas friends in New York, eagerly expressing what in those days passed for sexual liberation, congratulated me on the fact that Profumo was 'the first English official in years to have been found with a *woman*!'

At last, in September, I returned to Ithaca with a thousand little stories and one big one: how Harry Truman told me why he had dropped the atomic bomb.

Chapter 23

Harry (Truman) Sends Regards

I had worked assiduously on my MA thesis throughout much of the 1962–63 academic year, examining the history of the Manhattan Project and the extraordinary confluence of scientific, military and political considerations that led to Hiroshima. Then, while planning the outlines of my summer trip across the USA to the West Coast and back, I realised I would – or could – pass through Missouri. I wrote to ex-President Truman telling him of my work and asking if I might meet him. A letter came back, addressed to me at the Department of Government, Cornell University. The envelope included no stamp; just the printed signature of the ex-President:

> Dear Mr Snowman:
> Mr Truman will be glad to see you when you are in this part of the country. If you will telephone C Lifton 2-1061, when you arrive in the area, a time will be set up for you to come in.
> Sincerely yours,
> (signed) Rose A. Conway
> Secretary to Mr. Truman

I called his office from St Louis, Missouri, on 14 July 1963, and was told to present myself at the Truman Library in the President's home town of Independence, just outside Kansas City, at 9 am two days later (the 18th anniversary of the first atomic bomb test in Alamogordo, New Mexico).

I was shown into an open-plan office. Rose Conway was working at a desk in the corner and told me that Mr Truman came in every day; he was currently working on a new book: *History for Teenagers*. A few minutes later, Truman appeared. He was dressed in a lightweight, loose-fitting, blue-and-white striped cotton suit that gave his 79-year-old tummy plenty of room to expand. He looked at me with an open-mouthed, jaw-protruding grin as though slightly amused by my temerity. We shook hands and he beckoned to me to sit down.

I told him, with what I took to be appropriate respect, that I had been studying American politics at Cornell and his immediate riposte was that

I 'should've come and learned it out here ringing doorbells. They know more about politics out here than in those big East Coast schools,' he grinned.

My particular project, I said, had been a study of presidential decision-making and, in particular, his decision to drop the atomic bomb. He broke through my deferential manner with a guffaw.

'That was no decision!' he said, demolishing with a single pre-emptive strike the entire basis of my thesis.

Truman, who had become President barely four months before Hiroshima upon the sudden death of Franklin D Roosevelt, had been convinced by FDR's advisers, notably the venerable Secretary of War, Henry L Stimson, that dropping the atomic bomb on people was the one initiative that might bring the war in the Pacific to a rapid end without the need for a protracted and bloody invasion of the Japanese islands, which might have cost a million lives. In other words, Truman had had little option other than to order the bomb project to proceed. Indeed, if he had been the kind of person to have said 'No' to such a proposal, he would hardly have been elected Senator from Missouri in the first place or been chosen to run with FDR as Vice-President.

'That wasn't a decision!' Truman repeated, with added emphasis. 'Do you know about those bombs the Germans were developing in World War I? The big ones that were designed to fall on Paris?'

I nodded.

'That's all the atomic bomb was. A big bomb to end the war. And it did end it too! I had given the Japanese a warning of what we were going to do and received a sassy reply. Well, they knew what was coming, and it came.'

As I understood it, the USA at the time had manufactured only two atomic bombs: the Uranium-235 'Little Boy' bomb, dropped on Hiroshima on 6 August 1945, and the plutonium 'Fat Man' bomb dropped on Nagasaki three days later.

'We had lots of 'em,' Truman told me with another wicked grin.

'Did you? I know you said they'd rain upon the Japanese if they didn't surrender, but I thought that was just to frighten them.'

'Well, once the first one was made, others could be easily constructed.'

I asked him about the great secrecy that surrounded the Manhattan Project. During the War, before his nomination as FDR's Vice-Presidential running mate in 1944, Missouri Senator Truman had been Chairman of the Senate's Special Committee to Investigate the National Defense

President Harry S Truman.
(Photograph from Audiovisual Archives, Harry S Truman Library)

Program. Later, in his *Memoirs*, he had mentioned that he nearly found out about the Manhattan Project but was persuaded by Stimson not to send investigators into certain war plants. Was this true?

'Yes, Stimson asked me if I would be good enough to call off the investigations. But I knew about the project.'

'Through the Committee?'

'Sure. That's what it was for – to investigate large wartime expenditure. This thing cost two billion dollars, you know.'

Did Truman really know about the Manhattan Project before becoming President? Or was I hearing a combination of bravado, hindsight and the right of the elderly to embroider the facts? If Truman's Senate Committee had found out about the Manhattan Project, who else was in the know? What about all those Congressmen who had had to vote for the appropriations? Did they know what all that money was for? It seems not. Truman told me that Stimson and others (he mentioned General George C Marshall) had persuaded the Congressional leaders of the importance of this funding.

'You mean they voted for all that money and didn't know where it was going?' I asked.

'Yup. But you must remember – this was wartime.' He reminded me of the importance of secrecy during times of war, and how this was a concept perfectly familiar in the UK. A cue, I felt, to ask about British participation in the Manhattan Project. How much did Churchill know?

'As much as he wanted to know.'

I tried to press the former President. 'You mean he preferred to leave all the responsibility with you, the Americans?'

'No. But he wanted to be able to report fully to Parliament.'

Churchill, at least according to Truman, didn't want to know what he didn't want to know.

Truman made a few complimentary remarks about Churchill and various other European contributions to the atomic bomb project – especially those of émigré physicists. Then it was time for another Truman squib.

'Of course, the dropping of the bomb wasn't the biggest decision I had to make as President.'

'But surely it had the biggest effect.'

'No. It wasn't the biggest or the most important. The biggest decision was to go into Korea.'

I reflected that I had obviously chosen the wrong topic for my thesis and should have picked on the 1950 intervention in Korea. How, I wondered aloud, does a President reach a decision of such importance?

'You simply look at the facts,' Truman told me. 'Nobody had access to all the facts except the President.'

'True. But on many issues, you must have had doubts. You'd come to a decision, change your mind, wonder whether all the information before you was accurately reported and so on?'

'Yes, of course. But I'd check up on the facts, and then come to a decision – and then go on to the next one. I've never lost any sleep over any decision I've had to make.'

And that clearly included the bombing of Hiroshima and Nagasaki. By now emboldened, I told Truman I had always had visions of the President of the United States pacing the corridors of the White House, like Lincoln during the Civil War, weighed down by the pressure of the job.

'I was never under any pressure in the White House.'

My scepticism must have shown, for Truman leaned forward and added, confidentially: 'Your Winston Churchill was the same, you know.'

Clearly, this was a man keen to appear decisive, even unreflective, the man who famously told people that 'if you can't stand the heat you should keep out of the kitchen'. It was almost as though he thought that weighing the pros and cons was a sign of indecisiveness, of weakness – something of which President Kennedy was at the time being frequently criticised. A great many decisions, Truman told me, have to be made by the President and by him alone. I mentioned the famous motto on his desk: 'THE BUCK STOPS HERE'. Did he acquire that attitude in the White House?

'Nope. Why, I ran this county (Jackson County, Missouri) the same way years ago'. Truman looked out of the window and mused about his early days in politics as part of the legendary Prendergast machine. And he emphasised once more how he ('and your Winston Churchill') always got on with whatever was the next job in hand.

Eventually it was time to go. 'Well,' he laughed, as I made to stand up, 'it's nice that you youngsters are able to think about these things long after the event and decide what should or shouldn't have been done at the time!'

After this parting shot – warm, but provocative to the end – President Truman pulled his portly frame out of his seat, shook my hand and waved me goodbye.

By this stage in his life, Truman was a benign, grandfatherly figure. He was getting a good press in his old age and was frequently held up as a shining contrast to his 'bumbling' successor in the White House, Dwight D Eisenhower and to *his* successor, the 'inexperienced' John F Kennedy. Our meeting took place at the height of the Cold War, two years after the erection of the Berlin Wall and just a few months after the Cuban missile crisis. Widely credited with the vision and decisiveness that led to the Marshall Plan, the creation of NATO and the 'Truman Plan' that helped keep Greece and Turkey from Communism, Truman was something of a national icon by now. And he clearly enjoyed telling incredulous 'youngsters' about the old days when giants stalked the land and he, Harry Truman, had stood up to them and made the world safer (as he saw it) for the rest of us.

There was no hint of doubt or regret in anything he said to me about any of his actions as President, and he undoubtedly went to his grave a few years later confident that his 'decision' to drop the atomic bomb was the right and inevitable one. All debate about the dangers of nuclear radiation, for example, or whether the bomb was really used to impress or scare the Soviets, was dismissed out of hand as the dreamings of people who had nothing better to do than speculate about matters which they weren't competent to judge. As far as Truman was concerned, the bomb was intended to end the war with minimum loss of life (that is, no *American* loss of life) – and it did so.

* * *

I returned to my hotel in nearby Kansas City, invigorated by the spirit of that feisty old man in the striped cotton suit, and straightway wrote down, as accurately as I could recall, precisely what had been said. I didn't tell Clinton Rossiter that my MA thesis on presidential decision-making was based on a 'decision' that wasn't. He might have made me write an entirely new one on the decision to enter Korea. But I did send a telegram to London a couple of days later to congratulate my cricket-loving father on his 50th birthday:

WELL BATTED FOR HALF CENTURY.
STOP. HARRY SENDS REGARDS.

My parents later told me they were thrilled with the telegram but found 'Harry' a mystery. In some ways, so did I.

Book 5

University of Sussex

1963–67

‘A New Map of Learning’

Chapter 24

Balliol-by-the-Sea

'Drawing a new map of learning' was how Asa Briggs liked to express the ambitious aim of the new University of Sussex. Sussex was the first of the seven New Universities in Britain, products of a brief period of optimism sandwiched between Harold Macmillan's 'Never Had It So Good' election of 1959 and the approach to young adulthood in the mid-1960s of the post-war baby boom. That optimism was to some extent whistling in the dark by those in charge of the nation's affairs, as successive Chancellors of the Exchequer resorted to a series of increasingly ineffective 'stops' and 'goes' in order to try and regulate what was acknowledged to be an overheated national economy. Nevertheless, there was throughout these years a cheerful sense that Britain's undoubted problems were all susceptible to solution if only the right policies were adopted and applied, the 'right' policies being generally construed as those that advocated expansion of one kind or another. By the 1960s, the pump-priming ideas of Keynes seemed almost everywhere in the ascendant, optimistic New Frontier liberalism reigned in Washington and was much admired throughout the rest of the Western world, and in Britain a succession of Tory governments and

Asa Briggs.

their Labour opponents vied with each other as to whose policies could bring people more refrigerators and washing-machines and television sets. 'More', most people seemed agreed, generally meant 'better'. It was in this climate of opinion that work began in England on the new universities, all to be custom-designed and sited in some of the loveliest spots in the land – the first new universities (other than one at Keele) since the depressing urban agglomerations of the 1920s.

'Balliol-by-the-Sea' was how Sussex came to be dubbed by some commentators quick to notice the Oxbridge background of most of its founding fathers. John Fulton, the Vice-Chancellor, was once a Balliol philosophy don, as was the Senior Tutor, Patrick Corbett, while the historian Asa Briggs, Dean of the School of Social Studies and later Fulton's successor, had commenced his brilliant career at Oxford's Worcester College (to which he later returned, with a peerage, as Master). In its teaching methods, too, Sussex followed Oxford in some ways, notably in its emphasis on the value of the tutorial system and its exam structure of prelims after two terms and then nothing until a series of finals at the end of the third year. In other ways, however, the University of Sussex was determined to break new ground as it attempted to graft on to British higher education some of the intellectual breadth and rigour offered in the best universities in America. Thus, students at Sussex, while specialising in, say, Physics, French or Economics, had to cross intellectual boundaries, to study their 'major' field within a carefully structured context of various 'minor' subjects. The new map of learning eschewed traditional academic departments; rather, Sussex was structured around series of interdisciplinary 'Schools of Study'. I was a Lecturer in Politics in both the School of Social Studies (Dean: Asa Briggs) and the School of Anglo-American Studies (Dean: David Daiches). One of the topics that interested me was 'Urbanisation in America', a good topic for an inter-disciplinary seminar. For students in Social Studies I might collaborate with a colleague whose special expertise lay in the statistics of demographic change, while a similar seminar for the School of Anglo-American Studies would be undertaken alongside a literary expert who would introduce recent work by the likes of James Baldwin or Saul Bellow.

Employed at Sussex as an 'Americanist' I soon discovered that a number of my academic colleagues had also spent time at US universities. Interest in matters American – both popular and academic – was probably at its height around this time. People sought the latest books by the current crop

Arthur at University of Sussex, 1963.

of celebrity American authors, flocked to catch the latest American 'movie', learned to talk about 'grass roots' and 'touching base' and, in the wake of the Kennedy assassination, strove to learn more about the American political system, the US approach to everything from food to firearms and the sheer size and variety of the country itself. With the advent of jet travel, more and more people were able to visit the USA: the nation under whose economic, political and military protection post-imperial Britain was in many ways content to nestle. Meanwhile, Departments (or 'Schools') of US Studies were sprouting up at many of the more go-ahead universities in Britain and attracting substantial student applications and some highly talented and creative teachers. At the new University of East Anglia, for example, the faculty included the novelist Malcolm Bradbury and the writer and broadcaster (and biographer of Arthur Miller) Chris Bigsby. At Sussex, a year after my arrival, we were joined by Marcus Cunliffe. Marcus was made Professor of American Studies and, in true Sussex style, was expert on both the political and the literary history of the USA. The influence of American ideas at Sussex was almost tangible: in the introduction of language labs, for example, and the study of statistics and computer skills

Daniel and student, University of Sussex, 1963.

for social scientists. The very terminology we used was often borrowed from that used in the States: not only the 'major' and 'minor' subjects, but the university itself was a 'campus' (the Oxbridge word 'quad' was never used) and the teaching staff the 'faculty' (elsewhere almost a synonym for a 'department' – another of the taboo words at Sussex).

There were other, non-American influences at Sussex. Basil Spence, the architect, used to tell us how the original designs – a series of low brick constructions lying in a wooded valley with each building forming a social nucleus on its own courtyard or fountain, the various nuclei connected by long open walkways – had been inspired by Mediterranean architecture. The recurrent low arches in particular, he said, were copied from the Coliseum in Rome. Other European influences, too, were evident at Sussex. Britain's application to join the Common Market was on the table just when the university was being set up and one of its four initial 'Schools of Study' was in European Studies. A special centre was established at the university a few years later for advanced European scholarship.

* * *

Schloss Leopoldskron, Salzburg.

As an 'Americanist' with pan-European interests, I had the privilege of attending a month-long event in early 1965 at the Salzburg Global Seminar devoted to aspects of American foreign policy. Based at Salzburg's stately and venerable Schloss Leopoldskron (former home of the theatre producer Max Reinhardt) and founded after the war in the late 1940s, the institution was dedicated to the enhancement of intellectual and cultural links between the USA and post-War Europe, and it was here, on 10 January, that I joined an array of bright young men and women from across western Europe and the USA. Together, we attended (and participated in) a succession of lectures and seminars led by some of the western world's leading intellectuals designed to cover, inter alia, some of the political, military and ideological aspects of US foreign policy, America's relationships with the USSR and China, with developing countries and, in particular, its ever-closer links with Europe. I liked, and admired, the global thinking implied by much of what I learned, though I was also deeply aware of the aspirant American dominance that lay behind it.

While in Salzburg we heard of the death of Winston Churchill (24 January, 1965). Everyone present was shocked, duly respectful and especially generous-minded towards the British who were present. One of our colleagues, Raymond Barker, a quiet, thoughtful senior BBC tv producer, made a brief dignified speech and, on the day of the Churchill funeral, some of us went off to Munich where, on tv sets facing outwards in shop windows, we were able to watch some of it live. Raymond later became a good friend while another of the Salzburg attendees, Norman Longmate, was later a colleague of mine in BBC radio.

I greatly enjoyed my month in Salzburg, including the opportunity to explore for the first time this most beautiful of cities and, especially, its Mozart connections. On 28 January, I went to my first *Zauberflöte* (at the Landestheater), a work I saw brilliantly recreated by puppets at the nearby Salzburg Marionette Theatre on another visit half a century later.

* * *

In early February I returned to Sussex, reflecting on how much my time in Salzburg had helped reinforce the cross-national, cross-cultural commitments I had long been harbouring. Sussex, I felt, somehow combined the intimacy of an Oxbridge college, the intellectual versatility and modern-mindedness characteristic of a good American campus and the cultural heritage of Europe: three elements the University hoped to meld into a systematic approach to learning that would revolutionise British higher education. The combination was irresistible to someone like myself, already familiar with each of the constituent elements but impatiently anxious to explore how they might be creatively interrelated. Sussex held out the promise of being the least parochial world I had yet encountered. Its aims were ambitious but the place was attractive, the people who ran it highly competent and the times as propitious as they were ever likely to be. Sussex received massive publicity, had one of the highest application rates in the country, lured many of the brightest and most innovative teachers and researchers in the country and, in general, had every opportunity of turning itself into the outstanding institution of higher education that it was already being labelled by the press.

Chapter 25

Down to Work again

I was 24 when I started teaching at Sussex and it took me some time to get used to my sudden and radical elevation of status. Instead of being at the beck and call of a superior, I received circulars from famous professors who addressed me as 'Dear Colleague'. If I wanted to order new books for the library or initiate a new undergraduate or even graduate course, I had but to give the word. In my own particular field, Politics and American Studies, I knew I was pathetically unprepared, having come to both for the first time a mere two years before. But the authority with which I was vested by the much-heralded institution to which I was now attached gave my limited expertise a ring of authenticity from which my students no doubt benefited.

When I first saw the university, in September 1963, the student union and social activities building, Falmer House, was up and open and some classes had been held there during the previous year. But much of the campus was still a sea of mud supporting a flotilla of cranes and terrapin huts. The first teaching building proper, the Arts Building, was more or less finished and I tramped across to it on the day it was formally opened, sat in my cement-smelling office, pulled the plastic covering off my new desk, checked the phone and the heating and lighting, and pronounced myself inwardly pleased. Before long, I was initiating new 'prelim' courses, instituting a special subject on the history of the US presidency, teaching interdisciplinary seminars with clever colleagues, attending interminable meetings and sitting on committees that discussed everything from the pay and conditions of lab attendants to the size and colour of the Senior Common Room cushions.

The glamour and excitement of this new career brought its fair share of problems and insecurities. What was I to say when people asked me, by way of casual chat, what I was 'working on'? Or whether I agreed with their estimate of some book I'd never heard of? Almost everyone on the 'faculty' was older than me and more experienced; but I knew I'd soon be expected to give as good as I received, to talk about *my* field, *my* research, *my* negotiations with publishers, *my* innovatory approach towards my students, *my* offers from other universities. I had left Cornell with all my degree requirements completed so that, unlike a number of other young lecturers who still had MA or PhD theses to write, I was genuinely bereft of any legitimate 'research area'. There is only so much one can say about President Truman's decision to drop the atomic bomb. I tried to have my thesis published, but my material was of less interest to publishers than the new 'revisionist' interpretations just then being produced by Gar Alperovitz and David Horowitz. And in any case, the subject had become in my mind a vestige of my intellectual past rather than a starting point for further research. I was good at juxtaposing the original ideas of others, packaging them attractively and communicating them with wit and lucidity to people less familiar with them than I was. However, I had doubts about my own ability to develop those original ideas in the first place. Did I really have the intellectual tenacity and imagination to push back the frontiers of my 'field' and make the sort of mark that alone would constitute the ultimate justification of a career in the academy? I wondered, I doubted, and I took refuge in my abilities as a teacher.

Here, too, I was not sure I really had the expertise required. But, as one wiser and older colleague (all of half-a-dozen years older than me) told me one day: the best way to learn anything is having to 'output' it. You won't learn merely by reading endlessly or listening to other people's lectures. You've got to say it out loud yourself or write it and refine what you've written. That way, you'll learn it and remember it. He was right. I recalled that when preparing for exams I would sometimes sit on my bed and explain to my toes the basic causes of (say) the Industrial Revolution or the First World War. I'd list and explain each in turn as clearly as I could and, by so doing, isolate the points on which my memory or analytical skills fell short. And, of course, never forgot those particular points again!

So I lectured, and became good at it. Sussex did not put great store on lectures, so those I chose to give were few in number, carefully prepared and (I hope) delivered with no more energy than they warranted. As for the tutorials that constituted the principal teaching method at Sussex, I discovered that I had a gift for provoking a stimulating and challenging discussion between my students and myself and that, unlike some of my cleverer but less Socratically inclined colleagues, managed to resist the temptation to turn tutorials into monologues.

Outside the university, too, I lectured regularly and extensively, mostly under the aegis of the Workers Educational Authority, and this provided a small but much-needed source of additional income. The WEA, despite its already quaint-sounding name, was in many ways a precursor of such later organisations as 'NADFAS' and the 'University of the Third Age': a go-ahead organisation of mostly retired people keen to remain mentally and socially active. I also wrote articles for a variety of journals, among them not only the university's own paper but also *New Society* – and the *New Statesman* for which I did a piece about the controversial Robbins Report of 1963 which brought about a huge expansion of university education (including a doubling of the student numbers at Sussex from the original limit of 3,000). For the *Jewish Chronicle* I wrote about the similarities and differences between the social and political attitudes of American Jews and blacks, and some of my earliest book reviews were published in *Tribune*. I found myself being invited to do a number of broadcasts, too, and at one point applied on a whim for a production job at the BBC that I saw advertised and for which, rather to my surprise, I was shortlisted.

Overall, I relished being an Americanist at Sussex, especially after the arrival of Marcus Cunliffe, and soon found myself helping to develop new courses, drafting reading lists, setting and marking exams and sitting on further planning committees.

The last time I visited the University of Sussex was on 4 December 2014. The occasion was the launch of a book about Asa Briggs, edited by Miles Taylor (former Director of the Institute of Historical Studies, London). Asa was there, at 93 his usual engaging self, and was happy to sign copies of the book. He died in March 2016 and I wrote his obituary for *The Times*.

At Sussex (outside the Arts Building, 4 December 2014).

Chapter 26

To Swing or not to Swing

Socially, as well as professionally, these were bitter-sweet years. According to all that the mass media were purveying at the time, they should have been unalloyed bliss to an attractively endowed young man in his mid-twenties, securely installed as a lecturer at the most glamorous of Britain's new universities. This was, after all, the era of the Beatles, of Carnaby Street, Biba and Mary Quant, of David Bailey, Jean Shrimpton, Twiggy, Julie Christie and the young David Hockney. Colours and textures were in. So was the pill. Britain may (as Dean Acheson put it in 1962) have lost an Empire and not yet found a role. But for younger people what was supposedly important was the here and now, and their heroes and models were the 'beautiful people' who set the styles of a generation brought up after the War was safely won and reaching adulthood when the Empire was safely lost.

The heart of the action was supposedly in 'Swinging London', but the University of Sussex was not far behind. Sussex was one of the few universities in the country to maintain close to a one-to-one sex ratio in its student body, and it was said to have the most attractive and sophisticated girls: the rich and confident sisters of the brilliant young men who still made a beeline for Oxbridge. Macmillan's Home Secretary, Henry Brooke, sent his daughter to Sussex. The young tennis player Virginia Wade was at Sussex, too, though it was the beautiful Jay twins (daughters of the MP and occasional Cabinet minister Douglas Jay and sisters of the broadcaster and diplomat Peter) who garnered the most publicity. Many of the Sussex girls gravitated towards literature and European Studies but there were plenty, too, who showed an interest in the history and politics of America. Back they would come, week after week, with their long sleek hair, short skirts, fishnet-textured tights and Courrèges boots and sit back in deep chairs, cross their legs and recite to me their latest essays. I gazed down from my desk and tried to concentrate on the matter officially in hand. It was all positively awe-inspiring: Fiona or Felicity on the political function of the mass media in modern technological society, Sarah or Suzanne on the social correlates of voting behaviour, Angela or Annabelle on the role of the Cabinet in parliamentary and presidential systems compared. A splendid effort, Vicky, though I wonder whether your argument might have been a little modified if you had made more use of the Lincoln letters; oh, and Gwyneth, do you think you could let me have that copy of the Brogan book back next week? See you, Katharine, 'bye. There they were in the refectory, a magnificent hall built around a superb view of the Downs, and there they were in the film club, looking even more enticing in the flickering light as they pushed past to get to their seats. They stood confidently by the roadside hitch-hiking back into Brighton, leaving the trains and buses to those with weaker gifts of persuasion. And there they were in the summer months, lounging enticingly on the grassy hills above the university, caressing a sheaf of notes here or a pimply young man there.

To the casual visitor, the 'scene' could look tantalising. Yet in many ways it was more apparent than real. Most of the young men and women at Sussex were primarily hard-working students with a serious interest in their studies. Indeed, the University as a whole was something of a bastion of heavy cerebration, a bulwark against the onrush at the time of the cheap and the cosmetic. At Sussex, the heroes were not so much the Beatles, the Stones or Bob Dylan but such composite cultural luminaries as Proust–Joyce–Mann, Freud–Jung or Schoenberg–Webern–Berg. Modern, modernist, mould-breaking, avant-garde, yes. But avowedly highbrow.

For myself, in my mid-20s, I wanted to appear 'with it' while also remaining above it; part of 'the scene' yet comfortably distanced from it. On the one hand, I was anxious to appear to my students as being open-minded, direct, robust and accessible. Vicky and Fiona – and Bill and Ed, too – had to know that I was their sort of bloke and that they could come to me whenever they liked with their problems. Yet I also wanted to remain soberly responsible for the maintenance of standards in a rapidly shifting world, the more so as I wished to be taken seriously by my colleagues and superiors. Thus, I would wear a Harris Tweed jacket, a white shirt and sober tie and grey flannel trousers with turn-ups, my hair conventionally parted and my black lace-up shoes shined – and wonder why lunchtime conversation did not flow easily when I went and sat at a table with a group of students. I didn't enjoy dancing or smoking or the social atmosphere at the student parties to which I was occasionally invited. But I was equally discomfited by the bourgeois cosiness I felt I saw among some of my faculty colleagues.

Chapter 27
Alice

In some ways, my relationship with Alice helped me to avoid having to confront these disconcerting issues. Alice was 3000 miles away but when we had parted back in August 1963 we had agreed that she would in due course leave the USA and come and live with me in England. This presented me with a dream of potential bliss – plus underlying anxieties. Was I sure that Alice was the right person to become my life partner? If so, how would I be able to break to my loving parents the news that this non-Jewish girl was planning to cross the Atlantic in order to be with me? Alice was an irregular correspondent and between moments of happy anticipation I went through periods of sustained doubt about the seriousness of her commitment and, indeed, of my own. Was I maintaining my determination precisely because the odds against the relationship working were so high?

The landmarks during those sometimes painful months stand out like monuments in a desert. The day after I had returned from the USA, Saturday 28 August 1963, pictures of the great civil rights march in Washington DC were beamed onto our television screens in England. Alice was at the rally, as were Marty Schain and several other of my Cornell friends, and I would have been there with them had I not been booked to sail back to the UK on the *Queen Mary* a few days earlier. As my parents and I watched Martin Luther King's great 'I have a dream!' speech together, I did not mention Alice. Indeed, I did not do so until my 25th birthday, 4 November. That evening I contrived to take my father to Covent Garden to see what he said was his favourite opera, Verdi's *Don Carlos*, and I thought a man-to-man chat during the course of an expensive and happy evening might make things easier for both of us. It didn't.

Two and a half weeks later came the hammer blow of President Kennedy's assassination and I crumbled for a few days, numbed at the enforced realisation of how closely and insecurely I had attached my identity to that of the President, and of my profound emotional attachment to those in his country. There followed a desolate Christmas with my parents,

Alice.

the television news full of jailbreaks and Cyprus – followed, finally, by a chilly day in February 1964 when Alice's storm-tossed ship berthed at Southampton and I took her 'home' to a grim bed-sit in Brighton's unfashionable end, Kemp Town.

* * *

We had met in March 1963 at Cornell and we split up in September 1966 in London. During those years we had our adventures: marriage in her father's back garden in suburban New Jersey followed by a drive down, and then back up, the entire Eastern seaboard of the USA, with civil rights work and the Democratic Convention thrown in; the visit to Salzburg when I was a Fellow at the American Seminar; hitchhiking trips to the Aldeburgh and Edinburgh Festivals in 1965 and to Venice the following spring where I had a series of lectures to deliver. We went to Peter Brook's *Marat/Sade* and *US* at London's Aldwych theatre and sat high up at the side of the Covent Garden stage and orchestra to watch Solti and Peter Hall bring the orgy scene to life in Schoenberg's *Moses und Aron.* Meanwhile, Alice worked away assiduously at her art studies, first in Brighton and then as a daily commuter to a college in London. She developed into a first-rate painter.

Portrait of Daniel by Alice, 1963.

As a non-citizen, Alice could only look on as I cast one of the seven votes in the 1964 general election that enabled Denis Hobden to become the first Labour Member of Parliament ever to have been returned from the county of Sussex. And as an American of decidedly cynical views, Alice did not discourage my leadership of a campus movement to protest against Harold Wilson's support of Lyndon Johnson's Vietnam policies. But in all these activities, and many less memorable, there remained an emotional distance between us. Could I honestly be confident, I would sometimes ask myself in the dead of night, that this was the woman with whom I wanted to share the rest of my life? And the answer invariably came hurtling back. No. I never had that confidence. And nor, I suspect, did she. My parents and others had told me that no marriage between a Jew and a non-Jew could work successfully and, for reasons entirely different from those they may have had in mind, this sadly proved to be the case. It was not so much a question of believing or not believing in the same things. Rather, it was a question of culture, of shared values, similar attitudes, similar kinds of upbringing perhaps.

Ten years later, when I was happily married to a woman who happened to be Jewish but was as non-observant as I was, I felt no such pressure. Nor, I think, did she. Moral: if you are Jew-ish but you don't choose to conform to traditional practice, it's much easier if you are married to a Jew!

Chapter 28
Civil Rights

In 1963, the civil rights movement developed momentum, engineered a dramatic confrontation with the segregationist authorities in Birmingham, Alabama, and went on to stage the giant rally in Washington DC at which Martin Luther King addressed a crowd of 250,000 black and white listeners and spoke eloquently of his dream of a society free of racial discrimination. President Kennedy eventually acknowledged the moral justice of the civil rights cause and shortly before his death put his authority behind a bill to outlaw racial discrimination in places of public accommodation. This became law a few months later in 1964, a year that saw the Southern-based integrationist civil rights movement reach the acme of its influence with a series of voter-registration campaigns. Hundreds of white students from the North went to Mississippi and other Southern states to work with local black leaders in an attempt to bring about change by enfranchising millions of citizens who had hitherto been denied the vote. The volunteers set up 'Freedom Schools' at which blacks would be taught their constitutional rights, and how to insist upon them, and persuaded sympathetic lawyers to come to the area to take up civil rights cases free of charge. And they monitored the actual processes of voter registration and also trained black poll-watchers to supervise subsequent elections. The response of local whites was sadly predictable. Every civil rights worker was constantly liable to harassment: traffic tickets when no violation had been committed, telephones that rang at odd hours or were tapped or disconnected, mail that disappeared or was opened, absurdly high bail for petty offences. In addition, there were a number of more serious incidents: cars mysteriously burned, homes bombed, civil rights workers abducted and even murdered. It was rumoured that, at various strategic points in Mississippi, certain factories were being used as arms depots by whites fearful of a massive 'Negro revolution', and in McComb in the Southwest of the state an electronic buzzer system was said to have been installed to warn the good white folks to get into their specially constructed shelters in time. Rumour and counter-rumour spread throughout the South and many whites regarded the civil rights movement and its black and white workers with something close to panic.

Although I had returned to England a year earlier, I was back in the USA throughout the summer of 1964. On 20 July Alice and I had our US civil marriage ceremony in her father's back garden and the following day we drove South to Mississippi where, in the 'Freedom Book Store' in Jackson, the state capital, we picked up some of the most grotesque hate literature I have ever seen. We then drove up to Fayette County, Tennessee, a rural area lying just above the northern border of Mississippi, where we stayed for a while with a black family and gave a helping hand to a Cornell-sponsored voter-registration campaign. Many of Fayette County's population of around 25,000 were impoverished black sharecroppers living eight or ten to a room in corrugated iron shacks. Although blacks outnumbered whites by more than two to one, the ratio of black to white citizens who were registered to vote was more or less the reverse. The object of the Cornell project, therefore, was to help local Negroes to register and, in general, to know and make best use of their constitutional rights. The immediate incentive was to help them elect a liberal-minded (white) candidate for sheriff during a forthcoming county election but the broader aim was rightly depicted by our diehard segregationist opponents as the ultimate destruction of a way of life.

What duty was it of mine to help black people in Tennessee to register to vote? Answers were easy enough to find. I believed in egalitarian democracy, abhorred racism and felt that, although a foreigner, I had every right to involve myself in a campaign that promised to be a practical application, on a tiny scale, of principles which to me were sacrosanct and universal. Indeed, I experienced during that brief period a closer affinity between the general theories to which I subscribed and my capacity to put them into practice than at any other time in my life.

But if the Fayette County project produced a sense of genuine moral fulfilment, it also posed a number of dilemmas. There was, for instance, the basic question of the language and the environment in which to clothe our message. It would have been useless to speak to people from a simple rural background in the language of sophisticated political philosophy. To the black population of Fayette County, the sort of appeal that made the greatest impact was that of fundamentalist Christianity and the institution that carried the greatest authority was the church. We clearly had to capitalise on this, and yet it was with some unease that I heard myself, English suburban Jewish boy that I was, standing up in church and making passionate speeches, with a touch of fabricated American accent, about how the Good Lord would be real pleased if all you good folks would get right down there and register to vote.

'But our boss man has told us not to go reg'ster to vote,' many genuinely bewildered people would tell us, adding that they didn't dare go against his word unless they could be absolutely sure that they had something tangible to gain by doing so. Could they be certain that the election of a liberal-minded sheriff would radically alter their lives in the ways we had told them it would? And how sure could we all be that the liberal candidate would win? Suppose he didn't; then what? Questions such as these would surface again and again after the church meetings, in people's homes and in chance encounters in the fields or in local stores. The local people looked to us, looked up to us, and our response was often evasive and patronising. 'Sure everything's gonna be just fine,' we would say, 'just you go register to vote.' Yet, like all reformers, we sometimes promised more than we could be sure of delivering and our moral fervour occasionally took over from our intellectual integrity. On election day itself, for instance, I ferried great numbers of black voters to the polling stations and reminded them on the way exactly where to put their 'X' and told them how this would help put an end to racial discrimination in the county. I knew that I had been participating in a propaganda campaign that involved telling lots of little lies for the sake of one blazing truth. There are moments in life when the end must justify the means, and this was one of them. Or so I told myself.

On election day there was a big Negro turnout but the segregationist candidate was returned as sheriff with a comfortable majority. Some blacks had probably spoiled their ballots and others had no doubt lost their nerve at the last moment. But it was also clear that many ballot boxes had been stuffed and the results in several parts of the county rigged. Our shock and disappointment was nothing compared with that of the local blacks, who were outraged by the result, fearful of its implications and understandably upset with us for failing to deliver the promised goods. 'It's alright for you,' they would say with some bitterness, 'you don't have to stay here and face the music.' On the day Alice and I left Fayette County, someone was doing a brisk trade selling the Black Muslim newspaper *Muhammed Speaks*. The Muslims had always rejected any offer of white help in the struggle for black rights and now, even in the South, black Americans were beginning to give notice that they would henceforth solve their own problems in their own way. We had tried to help, had been found wanting and were now dismissed. Throughout the South the message was the same; the civil rights movement had done its work and started a revolution in which its own concepts and methods were fast becoming obsolete.

* * *

There were other indications, too, in that summer of 1964 of the changes that were to come. In July there was a riot in New York's Harlem district in which people were killed; this was to become the prototype for a succession of inner-city combustions across the nation over the next few years. The Harlem riot began as a result of an initially commonplace police incident which rapidly acquired the stature of tragedy. Sparked off by this incident, the resentment of Northern urban blacks against all who wielded authority over them burst forth in an angry explosion of indiscriminate destructiveness. I was in Mississippi when the Harlem riots occurred, and local whites could hardly contain their frenzied derision. To them it was a 'race riot', although most of the victims of the orgy of shooting and looting and burning, like the perpetrators, were black. 'Those Yankees had it coming to them,' they whooped. 'Coming down here and telling us how to treat our Nigras right. When did our Nigras ever riot against us like that?'

A further indication of what America would be like during the later 1960s occurred in the arena of party politics. 1964 was a presidential election year. In the spring and early summer of that year, the final touches were being put to the composition of the Mississippi delegation to the National Convention of the Democratic Party which was due to convene in August in Atlantic City, New Jersey. Mississippi was essentially a one-party state and the local white Democratic power brokers ran it almost as a medieval fiefdom. This year, however, civil rights activists had worked to get local Negroes enfranchised for the first time and, despite the acute dangers to all involved, had managed to build up by this means a parallel delegation whose members were mostly black.

I was in Atlantic City with Alice when the two rival delegations presented their credentials. All along the boardwalk there was a buzz of excitement and anticipation as the Convention gathered. In the middle of one conclave, a rising star of Texas politics was giving an animated interview to a TV crew while, a few yards along, a bunch of Bobby Kennedy groupies were giggling about how they had caught a glimpse of their idol (who, one had constantly to be reminded, was not actually running for any office). Out at sea, a little boat was blaring the tasteless 'Hello, Lyndon' song (to the tune of 'Hello, Dolly') at everyone on land and, in the further distance, at the far end of the beach smiling down at the gambolling Democrats, was a huge poster of the despised Republican front-runner, Barry Goldwater, bearing the much-parodied slogan 'In Your Heart You Know He's Right!'. Meanwhile, right up against the Convention Hall itself, were the black and white members of the Mississippi Freedom Democratic Party (MFDP) holding banners and placards, singing songs and shouting slogans and insisting that their delegation rather than their lilywhite rivals should be given official accreditation.

Behind closed doors the party's top figures worked out a compromise by which they hoped everyone would abide. The official Mississippi delegation would be seated but so would two of the MFDP delegation as representatives 'at large'. And next time round, in 1968, no effort would be spared to ensure that delegations from every state would be genuinely representative.

The old-style liberals in the MFDP urged acceptance. 'Step by step' was their philosophy and they argued that any offer of a move in the right direction, however small, was to be eagerly grasped. The young black militants, however, took the opposite view. Under no circumstances, they argued vehemently, should the MFDP accept a situation in which an all-white delegation from their state would be seated and granted full voting rights. The immediate situation was won by the old-style liberals. But by their acceptance of compromise, they were deemed to have signalled their preparedness to abide by the rules of the white establishment and were derided for doing so by their erstwhile allies, the new black radicals. Henceforth, the radicals would move ahead on their own, brook no compromise and neither seek nor accept further help from well-meaning white liberals.

The dilemma at Atlantic City brought to a head the tensions that had been building up among the ranks of the civil rights volunteers. It seemed the days of the Southern, rural, integrationist movement were now essentially over. Soon, the multiracial dream of civil right leaders such as Martin Luther King would be discarded as the whole impetus became more militant and shifted away from the South to the great urban centres of the American North and West. As new black leaders like Malcolm X came to be featured in the headlines, King became somewhat marginalised, his attention shifting towards new topics such as America's military involvement in Vietnam. As for the idealistic old civil rights slogan, 'We Shall Overcome', this began to be outmoded as a new more strident cry took its place: 'Black Power!'

Chapter 29

Vietnam and Beyond

Throughout my time at Sussex, the USA was prosecuting what seemed an ever more violent war in Vietnam. The Vietnamese war was a kind of localised proxy for the wider Cold War of the time. Like Korea earlier, Vietnam was divided into a Communist-inspired north (led by their National Liberation Front) and a pro-Western south. Many in the US and elsewhere were disturbed by the aggressive presence of Western forces in Southeast Asia, and some were worried in Britain about what looked like official UK support for dubious US policies. At Sussex, I came to be centrally involved in a university-wide protest against the support offered by Prime Minister Harold Wilson of America's Vietnam policies, and this activity brought together many of the cross-currents that ran through all aspects my life during the Sussex years.

The focal occasion was a visit to the University in July 1966 by the Prime Minister (along with the recently retired Australian Prime Minister Robert Menzies, the American human rights activist Ralph Bunche, the violinist Yehudi Menuhin and the physicist PMS Blackett) to receive an honorary degree. Wilson had uttered not a word against President Johnson's drastic escalation of the Vietnam war – the huge increase in American troop numbers and fire power, the bombing of North Vietnam and the mining of its principal harbour, Haiphong – and had, indeed, appeared to many to be grovelling to the American president with more enthusiasm than even Britain's parlous economic position could possibly have necessitated. A number of students and teachers at the University, most of them feeling that the people had elected a Labour government and been let down by it, set up an organisation to consider how best to bring their concern to the Prime Minister's attention. The object was not to prevent Wilson from coming to Sussex or to disrupt the proceedings while he was there. On the contrary, it was felt that his presence might provide an opportunity to persuade him to speak his mind on a major subject about which many felt he had been disingenuous and lily-livered.

A number of preliminary steps were taken, notably a survey of the Brighton electorate that revealed (with detailed figures to prove each point) that a majority were 'opposed to American action in Vietnam, opposed to British support of that action, and opposed to the bombing of North Vietnam'. Then, on 16 June, the following letter, signed by more than 100 members of the Sussex faculty – over a third of the entire teaching staff – was dispatched from the University to the Prime Minister at 10 Downing Street:

> Dear Prime Minister,
> There is at the University of Sussex, as in all parts of the country, a considerable body of opinion that deeply regrets the British Government's unqualified support for American actions in Vietnam. The undersigned, who are all members of the University staff, realise that America's problem in Vietnam is a complex and delicate one and that the British Government's decision to support the USA is based on a consideration of many factors and, no doubt, pressures. We nevertheless feel that Britain has a duty to demand, at the very least, that the USA should:
>
> stop bombing North Vietnam
> state publicly that she is prepared to recognise and negotiate with the National Liberation Front
>
> We would be grateful if you would take advantage of your visit to the University at the forthcoming Degree Ceremony (13th July) to explain why you continue to give unequivocal support to the USA on the question of Vietnam. We would like to know, in particular, how you think that successful negotiations are likely to occur if the above two demands are not met by the American Government.
>
> If you feel that it would be inappropriate for you to make a policy speech at a Degree Ceremony, we would remind you that many important American officials, among them the President and Secretary of Defence, have recently made policy speeches at similar occasions.
>
> We look forward to your visit to the University and hope that you will address yourself to the issues that we have outlined.
>
> Yours sincerely…

My signature was the first to appear and I had been the person principally responsible for the collection of the rest, and it was I who, somewhat self-consciously, had posted the letter, by registered mail, from a Brighton Post Office. By way of reply, we eventually received a formal letter from an aide acknowledging ours and referring to various statements on Vietnam made by the Prime Minister in the House of Commons. But our own letter was meant for a wider audience. We released the text to the Brighton *Evening Argus* a week before the degree ceremony and also announced that many

Hand Tailoring Bernard Luper

Evening Argus

NIGHT EXTRA

Monday July 11, 1966 — Incorporating the SUSSEX DAILY NEWS — Fourpence

Angry Brighton councillors want . . .

£18,000 'FINE' FOR REBEL UNIVERSITY

BRIGHTON councillors, angered by the suggested Vietnam protest at Wednesday's University of Sussex graduation ceremony, may ask the council to "fine" the university £18,000 a year.

Target of the protest is the Prime Minister, Mr. Harold Wilson, who will receive an honorary degree at the Dome. Councillors regard the planned demonstration as yet another example of extremism at the university.

The £18,000 represents Brighton's share of the £58,000 which five Sussex education authorities contribute each year from rates to the university. The grant was raised a few years ago, from

BURGLARS FACE LIFE SENTENCES

Crime-busting recorder starts city's clean-up

MINI-HEARINGS WILL SPEED JUSTICE

Brighton Evening Argus, *11 July 1966.*

students and faculty members intended to wear white arm bands as a silent sign of protest against the war in Vietnam and those who were helping Lyndon Johnson to aggravate it.

The *Argus* scented a good story and milked it for all it was worth. One headline declared that 'Angry Brighton councillors' wanted to fine the 'rebel university'. Another, headlined 'Reds are Blamed for Varsity Protests', quoted one local councillor as saying that the proposed demonstration was the work of Communists and another that 'students should…not get involved in international affairs which they know nothing about'. Money, he and others apparently averred, should be withheld from the University until it changed its 'constant Left-wing and protest-about-everything' image. These and similar stories always went on to quote a response from me, generally to the effect that we were not Communists and had no intention of disrupting the degree ceremony but had merely asked the Prime Minister to explain to us an important aspect of his Government's policies, and that we had a lot of support from students and faculty alike – both of whom were, in fact, rather well-informed about Vietnam.

Among the distinguished visitors who came to attend the degree ceremony were a number of US university presidents including Grayson Kirk of Columbia (himself to receive an honorary degree on their collective behalf), Kingman Brewster of Yale and Milton Eisenhower of Johns Hopkins. They needed someone to chaperone them, put them on and off buses, take them to and from all their VIP appointments, and who better to do such a job than a junior lecturer in American Studies! Thus, on the day of the graduation ceremony around which so much tension had been building, I was given privileged access to the inner sanctum of official activity. Unlike anyone else on the Vietnam Committee, I was at the VIP dinner thrown the night before the ceremony by Lord Fulton (as the Vice-Chancellor had by then become) and was in the Brighton Dome for the ceremony itself the next morning. Here, Wilson did talk briefly about Vietnam, making what I thought the vacuous suggestion that the protesters ought instead to address themselves to the Chinese Embassy. And I went on to the Top People's buffet lunch where I chatted to Blackett and to Dame Patty Menzies, and spent the afternoon taking the American visitors to the Fultons for tea. And all the while the local press was full of what a dangerous and radical agitator I was!

I enjoyed my absurd double role. Grayson Kirk and company were polite to the point of condescension, only Brewster of Yale engaging me in substantive conversation about the background to the Wilson letter. What had led to the protest? What did faculty and students in other parts of the country feel about Vietnam and Britain's attitude towards it? Had other politicians distanced themselves from American policy more effectively than Wilson? How did I see the war developing? What other issues were engaging the political concerns of people on British university campuses? Nobody else among the VIPs showed any active or serious interest in what was happening, though Fulton called me aside from time to time for reassurances about the peaceful nature of the protest. Within two or three years almost all the US university presidents on my bus – most spectacularly Grayson Kirk – had been ousted from their jobs. The only one to go from strength to strength as the era of student protest gathered steam was Kingman Brewster. He was later to become America's Ambassador to the United Kingdom.

* * *

One day, Marcus Cunliffe popped into my office. He had been asked by the publishers BT Batsford if he would write a book outlining American history from the end of the First World War to the present. He couldn't undertake this himself, he told me; he was too immersed in some new research he was undertaking about George Washington. But would I like him to put forward my name instead? The book would be part of a series aimed at the 'general reader', Marcus explained, and would in due course include similar outlines of the post-WWI history of Britain, Germany, Russia, China and perhaps others.

I leaped at this unforeseen opportunity: a chance for me to 'output' material about which, while supposedly expert, I frankly did not at the time know anything like enough. I was given a contract, got down to work and started on a book that, true to the latest historiographical turn, would eschew old-fashioned political history and, instead, give emphasis to the broader social, cultural and economic trends of the previous half century. The 1920s, the so-called 'Jazz Age', would become in my hands the 'Age of Rose-coloured Nightmares', and I went on to write of not only Roosevelt's 'New Deal' but also the widespread poverty of the Depression years, the themes and counter-themes of US foreign policy, the struggles of wartime, post-war suburbanisation, racism in North and South and the civil rights movement, and the (then current) war in Vietnam. Work on the book took me to a number of libraries, though the memory I most relish was working in the great round Reading Room at the British Museum where every major scholar of the past century or two had sat before me (most famously Karl Marx). I relished this commission, worked on the assignment assiduously, and even obtained from Sussex a sabbatical term during which to finish it.

By the time I completed the book, published in 1968 as *USA: The Twenties to Vietnam*, I had been offered an irresistible initial attachment to the BBC as a radio producer. Lord Archie Gordon,* head of talks and documentaries, phoned me one afternoon in 1967, told me how they needed someone with a knowledge of American politics during the run-up to the following year's US elections and asked if I might be interested. Apparently, I had done a good interview at the BBC earlier in the year and this time they had a job for which they thought I might be ideal. I had a word with Asa Briggs about the offer and he, already at work on what was to become a 5-volume history of broadcasting in the UK, was kindness itself. 'Go ahead, Daniel,' he said. 'I think you'll enjoy it. See how things work out and, if you want to come back to Sussex, just give me a ring.' I called Lord Archie and said yes, I'd be delighted to accept his kind offer. It was initially for six months, over the course of winter 1967–68. After that I'd know for sure which was the world for me: the academic world or that of broadcasting and the media.

Not long afterwards, I proudly took the completed manuscript of my

* In 1974, Archie succeeded his elder brother to become Marquess of Aberdeen and Temair.

book in to Batsford, in London's Fitzhardinge Street just off Manchester Square, to present to my editor Peter Kemmis Betty. I had finished it ahead of my official deadline; one wouldn't want to break a contract after all. Peter was delighted. He smiled and said: 'That proves you're not at heart an academic'. 'Why?' I asked innocently. 'Because they all deliver late! At the BBC, programmes have to be done on time.'

Book 6

BBC Years (1)

'Educate, Instruct and Entertain'

Chapter 30

Old World, New World

While I was finding my way into BBC production, I wrote to a distinguished American historian asking if I might record an interview with him. He wrote back to say 'Yes' but added that, since everything he had to say on the relevant subject was in his book, he wondered why I wanted him to say the same old things all over again. He ended: 'I shall never understand the electronic media!'

His letter was friendly, but tongue-in-cheek. I wrote back in the same vein: 'I happen to have in my office the only copy of a dialogue recorded in Ancient Greece between Socrates and Plato, which I plan to wipe soon so as to be able to re-use the tape. It contains nothing that Plato did not write in his philosophy books, so I take it that you would not be interested in hearing it…'

* * *

I joined the BBC in autumn 1967 after four years at Sussex, along with a young man called Russell Harty who became a colleague in Talks before going on to become a celebrity TV interviewer. Another new recruit was Lord Hill, former 'Radio Doctor' and Tory Cabinet Minister, provocatively plucked by Harold Wilson from the (commercial) Independent Television Authority as Chairman of the BBC's Board of Governors. Hill's remit was to 'sort out' the liberal-minded Director-General Sir Hugh Greene (brother of novelist Graham) and the merry cohorts he liked to promote. And if that were not enough, September 1967 also saw the introduction of the new, streamlined radio networks: Radio 1 (to beat the pop pirates like Radio Caroline), Radio 2 (to replace the Light Programme), Radio 3 (in tandem for a while with the Music Programme and Third Programme), and Radio 4 (in place of the old Home Service). In a speech I made to mark my retirement from the BBC at the end of 1995, I said – only semi-jokingly – that I dated the decline of the BBC from the month I joined!

Nobody in the BBC gave me anything so vulgar as a brief, remit or job description when I arrived, but Archie Gordon and his senior colleagues made it clear that they would like me to help enrich the airwaves over the course of my six-month attachment by calling upon my contacts and supposed expertise not only in matters American but in history, politics and culture more generally. I was initially encouraged to turn my hand to production of scripted talks, particularly though not exclusively for the Third Programme (or Radio 3) which, when I joined, included in its schedules something like fourteen hours of speech programming per week. The Controller of Radio 3 at the time was PH Newby, a quiet, thoughtful man whose offers meetings, held every Thursday morning, were the most civilised I ever attended at the BBC. Howard Newby spent his weekends writing engaging novels and was recipient of the first Booker Prize while, around the table, were highly cultured fellow producers such as the poet George MacBeth, the film critic Philip French and (by now close to retirement) such legendary feature producers of an earlier era as Douglas Cleverdon and Geoffrey Bridson.

I quickly learned that a 20-minute talk would involve commissioning someone, probably an academic historian or critic, to write and read some 2,700 words ('no abstract nouns or passive verbs') on a topic of broad general interest. The result would conveniently fill a concert interval. Before my contract came to an end I also produced my first radio documentary; it was about Martin Luther King.

I loved my new work at the BBC and relished the sheer cultural breadth to which I was encouraged to aspire. At Sussex, for all its much-vaunted cross-disciplinarity, I had nonetheless felt it incumbent upon me to try and keep abreast of the latest academic research in my field: to read learned articles in the *American Political Science Review* about (say) trends in Republican affiliation in rural Wisconsin or the applicability of Weberian theory to post-industrial work patterns. I felt faintly guilty if I went to see the latest French film or tried to catch up with Camus or Primo Levi: I wasn't keeping up properly with my core subject. At the BBC, by contrast, aspirations to intellectual versatility were often rewarded (however superficial they may have been by academic standards). When my six-month BBC contract approached its end in March 1968, the powers that be told me they would like to place me on their permanent, pensionable staff but that no post would be available for the next two years. However, if I was interested, they could help bridge the gap by giving me an interim extension from June until the new job became available in 1970. I jumped at the chance. But what to do during the next three months without a job to sustain me? I would go to America, armed with a BBC tape recorder. I had not been to the USA since 1964; but this year, 1968, looked set to be every bit as dramatic.

* * *

In April, shortly before I left for the States, Martin Luther King was assassinated in Tennessee, the state in which I had undertaken civil rights work four years earlier. King's influence among America's black community was considerably diminished by this time, as more overtly militant individuals, notably the leaders of the Black Panthers, stoked up the rhetoric. But in the wake of King's murder, a series of riots occurred in many parts of the country with black citizens angrily venting their wrath against white racism. On university campuses, meanwhile, across the USA and much of western Europe, successive waves of student protest immobilised hitherto supposedly respectable homes of learning. In New York that spring, I visited the campus of Columbia University and found it to all intents and purposes closed. A witty student placard declared: 'If You Are Lost, You Have Come To The Right Place!' Later, I watched as a huge anti-Vietnam demo marched through mid-town Manhattan, led by a banner proclaiming: 'LBJ: Pull Out – Like Your Father Should Have Done!' Soon afterwards, Lyndon Johnson pulled out of the presidential race. Who would replace him as the Democratic front runner?

From New York, I went on to Washington DC. Here I received a message that Chaim Raphael, a distinguished Anglo-Jewish scholar and civil servant, had had to withdraw from a (paid) US-wide lecture tour he

Columbia University, NY: Summer 1968.

was about to undertake under the aegis of the Jewish organisation B'nai B'rith. Was there any chance I could take his place? Absolutely, I replied – and immersed myself, in some desperation, in all and any material I could find that might link my growing knowledge of US politics and society to the interests of Jewish audiences. I eventually alighted upon the idea of suggesting similarities and differences between America's black and Jewish populations. They were similar, I would suggest, in that both groups tended to be politically on the liberal-minded left, but different in that American Jews were mostly from wealthier, better educated backgrounds. Jews, indeed, were the only upper-middle-class socioeconomic group in America whose political instincts were on the left. Or that, at least, was my hypothesis. It saw me through, and the tour took me across via Minneapolis to Winnipeg in Canada, thence to Seattle, down the West Coast to Los Angeles and San Diego. In LA, I watched Robert Kennedy as he campaigned for the Democratic presidential nomination. Six days later, he too was murdered.

Everywhere I went across America that spring and early summer, I recorded interviews, impressions and the bustle and noise of a great but troubled nation. Back in London, I recorded a few more; James Baldwin came in for an interview, as did (Ambassador) Kingman Brewster. In August I followed the news closely as the Democratic Convention in Chicago finally nominated Vice-President Hubert Humphrey as their presidential candidate. But Humphrey's triumph was greatly overshadowed by reports of the angry protests near the convention hall (that led to the trial of the 'Chicago Seven'). That autumn, I edited all the material I had recorded, and produced and presented a substantial radio portrait of America as it limped its way towards November's presidential election. I called the programme 'Grave New World'.

Chapter 31
Back in (and out of) BH

After all my American adventures, it was good to return to Broadcasting House, attend civilised meetings and propose and produce serious programmes presented by thoughtful contributors. 'Dons talking to dons,' the critics might scoff. But at Howard Newby's meetings we felt that there was value in inviting an intelligent and communicative speaker to share with a non-expert audience the deeper background to (say) the 1968 Soviet invasion of Czechoslovakia or, a few years later, the Allende regime in Chile. Often, Radio 3 might commission a talk with no hook other than the fact that the speaker was believed to be capable of talking well and to have something of interest to say: David McLelland on Karl Marx, Jean Seznec on Michelet or Idris Parry on Goethe. Geoffrey Webb gave a pair of talks around this time on theology and iconography in the Middle Ages while the poet and critic (and my former Sussex colleague) Laurence Lerner presented two meditations on the fiction of the Enlightenment. These were the years when EH Carr was commissioned to present seven talks on the early history of the Soviet Union and Isaiah Berlin broadcast his celebrated lectures on Romanticism. The function of (what we still thought of as) Reith's BBC was, famously, to 'educate, instruct and entertain'. I liked to think that our programmes did all three.

The standard fee for a straight talk was not princely (I always felt obliged to explain to the speakers I produced), but if the broadcast was well received it might be repeated at a later date, and stood a good chance of being printed in the BBC's weekly magazine *The Listener*. In addition, I was able to point out that a Radio 3 talk might reach thirty or forty thousand people. How many lectures would a university don have to give before getting his or her message to that many? Actually, what the BBC's audience research statistics showed was that such a programme might occasionally reach 0.1 per cent of the population (i.e. 50,000) – give or take a margin of error of 50,000! Perhaps I should have told my speakers that, like a Cup Final team at Wembley, they would have an audience out there of 'up to' 100,000...

There were scripted talks on Radio 4 as well, though here the emphasis tended to be more on personality, memoir and anecdote ('René Cutforth recalls His Life and Times') and less on argument, explanation or analysis. On both networks there were also several other kinds of history programmes: interviews (Samuel Eliot Morison on the European discoveries of America), imaginary conversations (Hume meets Voltaire), lots of historical drama and those archetypal radio creations, the documentary and the dramatised feature. Radio 4 presented a three-part series on the voyages of Captain Cook ('The Continent that Never Was') and a number of features about events and people within the memory of many still living: Passchendaele, Thomas Masaryk and (as part of a series of radio portraits of non-conformers) Annie Besant.

But the most frequent purveyor of historical features, dramatisations and reconstructions, especially about the great events of the 20th century, was probably 'Study Session', the educational ghetto slotted in between 6.30 and 7.30 pm every weekday evening on Radio 3. In early 1970, while still on a short, non-staff contract with the BBC, I was invited to present a 10-part Study Session series entitled *Britain In The Sixties*. These programmes dealt with Britain's place in the wider world and went on to cover some of the recent trends in the nation's form of government, its economy, race relations and youth culture, all of which gave me a good opportunity to interview some 35 or more of the major public personalities of the time, from Cabinet Ministers and trades union leaders to various leading figures in Britain's pop culture.

* * *

One of those I interviewed for the series was the current Minister for Health and Social Security in the government of Harold Wilson, the formidable and famously combative Richard H Crossman. We met in Crossman's office alongside London's Elephant and Castle. I set up my Uher tape recorder and microphone, checked speech levels, and set things in motion. After about 18 minutes, the interview concluded, I thanked Crossman. He looked at me, amiably enough, offered me a cup of tea and said: 'I suppose you're going to cut this tape into snippets!' I pleaded guilty, and we fell to talking about the problems involved in making documentary programmes. He said the best way, of course, would be for the interviewer and interviewee to spend six hours together and then, when they were really ready, they could record an ideal, brief, uncuttable interview. But Mr C accepted that this was not possible. I later used portions of the interview in three of the programmes in *Britain In The Sixties* and, in a fourth, I referred in my script to Crossman's comments about snippets. All this was done with the greatest editorial integrity, I thought. Indeed, so pleased was Graham Tayar, my producer, with the value of Crossman's contributions to the series that he wrote to thank him for agreeing to the interview and, as a courtesy, sent him copies of the relevant scripts.

Some months later, I found myself producing a substantial documentary feature about the broadcasting of news and current affairs. From the outset, I was keen to try and persuade Crossman to contribute to this programme. Accordingly, I spoke to the people at the Department of Health and Social Security and was told, a few days later, that Mr C had agreed to be interviewed. An appointment was made: at 7 pm, after what, I was told, would be a very packed and demanding day for the Minister. Crossman, delayed by a vote in the House of Commons, arrived at the DHSS at about 7.20 pm. I was shown into his room. He asked me to remind him what the interview was all about and, before I had got very far, launched into a tirade about the pernicious, degrading way in which I had used the previous interview I had recorded with him. As he spoke, he was pacing up and down, and the angry words flowed in torrents. I tried to remind him of our conversation over tea: hadn't I made it clear then that the interview would be used, after editing, in a series of radio documentaries? The anger was unabated. 'What a way to treat a Cabinet Minister!' he railed. I replied that I considered I had used the interview with integrity and asked him in what ways he felt I had misrepresented him. He sidestepped this. I was not sure whether the core of his resentment was that the interview had been edited at all (which he knew it would be) or that I had misused the passages that had gone into the programmes (a charge which I would have been prepared to rebut). But Crossman was in no mood for rational discussion, so I assumed his irritability arose, in part perhaps, from other matters currently on his mind. It was not impossible, I thought, that my programmes might have offended his pride: there was Richard Crossman, tucked in amongst a great many lesser fry. But I did not think he had realistic grounds for complaint.

When we got back to the purpose of my visit, Crossman said that he would only do the new interview with me about the broadcasting of news and current affairs if I promised, in writing, that it would be transmitted *in toto*, unedited. And he added things about the tape being destroyed after transmission and not kept in the archives. In reply, I said that I would undertake not to edit anything he had to say, but that I would therefore need him to speak for no more than a maximum of about 10–12 minutes. In that case, he said, he would have to have time to sort out his thoughts more clearly and I'd have to come back to do the interview some other time.

I had obviously caught Crossman on a bad day (something his civil service underlings discreetly underlined to me as I left the Department at around 7.35 pm). Crossman was notoriously temperamental and it was precisely this passionate disposition that helped make him an irresistible broadcaster. But even allowing for the exaggerations of a man in a bad mood, his comments raised a major question of principle: what rights does a person who has agreed to record an interview have to stipulate the form or circumstances of the eventual broadcast? And, in particular, does a member of the government have any particular rights in this respect? The following day, I told Archie Gordon about what had happened. He was his usual sympathetic, understanding self. But clearly it would not have been in the interests of the BBC to lose the goodwill of a senior member of the current government. It was decided that Lord Archie would write to Crossman, say how sorry he was if any offence had been given by the BBC, but outlining the importance of the Corporation's editorial independence. And there, so far as I know, the matter rested. I never did that follow-up interview with Crossman, but I can't say my eventual programme was any the poorer for his absence! Ditto, the BBC Sound Archives.

* * *

The archives provided a huge boon to any radio coverage of the 20th century. No BBC programme about the British monarchy was complete without Edward VIII's Abdication speech, complete with Reith's introduction; any documentary on the history of World War II was likely to include Neville Chamberlain intoning the famous words: 'I have to tell you now that … this country is at war with Germany.' Occasionally, it was possible to explore archives from further afield. In the later 1970s, I produced a 26-part educational series on *World Powers in the Twentieth Century*, a project covering the domestic and international history of China, the USA and the Soviet Union during the 50 years or so following the end of the

First World War. This was an ambitious project, two years in the making and, in addition to using standard BBC recordings of Mao, Stalin, FDR and so on, I visited various archive sources in the USA and brought back little-known recordings of people like Al Smith, Huey Long and Father Coughlin. Some years later, when producing programmes about the polar regions, I was able to obtain excellent recordings of Shackleton (from the ABC in Australia), Peary (from the US National Archives in Washington DC) and Nansen (from Norwegian Radio).

* * *

By summer 1970, I had become a fully-fledged, 'permanent' member of BBC staff with my own office, secretary, salary (and guaranteed pension) and direct access, whenever I wished, to all the BBC's resources: not just its studios and editing suites but the archives and library, a 'book room' containing a wide range of recent publications, the BBC's collections of sound effects and gramophone records, and a huge range of human expertise on which I could call at any time. My job was to come up with interesting ideas for programmes, argue the case at regular meetings chaired by the Controllers of Radio 3 and Radio 4 and, assuming the idea was accepted (and most were), go away and produce them. In order to do the job well, it was understood that I would need to cultivate a wide 'intelligence network' and keep up with what was going on in the news, in the academic and publishing worlds, in the arts and in the wider cultural world more generally. If I felt I should see some much-talked-about theatrical production, buy a particular book or take a famous visiting novelist, philosopher or historian out for lunch, I was free to do so and in due course, armed with the receipt, simply claim the money back, regardless of whether or not a particular programme materialised as a result. Sometimes, my programme proposals required me to travel abroad: to Paris or Rome, perhaps, or the USA or further afield. If the proposal had been accepted, the travel was duly paid for. Did the BBC waste money? Did producers fritter away their afternoons with long bibulous lunches at nearby pubs? Perhaps in some instances. But to me, the freedom of the prevailing regime throughout much of the 1970s and '80s brought out the happy workaholic in me. I could do anything, read anything, go anywhere, meet anyone – and all I had to do was to edit and disseminate the highlights of these variegated experiences in the form of good radio programmes. I threw myself into my work, producing talks, interviews, discussions and documentaries on a wide variety of cultural and historical subjects.

I particularly enjoyed helping to develop the broadcasting careers of such younger talents as Susan Hill, Aled Jones, Norman Lebrecht, Roy Porter, Edward Seckerson and Lucie Skeaping, all of whom were to become good friends. But much of my work was with well-established broadcasters like Bernard Crick, Robin Day, Bill Grundy, William Hardcastle, John Vaizey and Lord Hailsham. Hailsham, with his gammy leg, preferred to cycle than to walk anywhere and, in addition to presenting a number of serious, quasi-philosophical programmes, did a delicious short talk for me in which this formidable ex-Lord Chancellor regaled listeners with how much he relished edging his illegal way across a red light or up a one-way street the wrong way. As a fellow cyclist, I had to acknowledge that I knew the feeling!

One of the people with whom I made a number of programmes in the early 1970s was the recent American émigré to Britain, Harvey Matusow. Notorious in his homeland, he was a one-time Communist who had spied on his comrades for the FBI, before going on to a career as a professional

Lord Hailsham and Friend cycling into the BBC.

witness, telling 'all' to such as the House Un-American Activities Committee (HUAC) and Senator Joseph McCarthy's Government Operations Sub-Committee. Eventually undergoing a crisis of conscience, Harvey recanted almost all of his testimony, and in a subsequent book, *False Witness*, disclosed that McCarthy's aide Roy Cohn had encouraged him to lie on oath. Harvey was taken to court, found guilty of perjury (ironically not for the many actual lies he'd confessed to, but for allegedly slandering Cohn), and jailed for nearly three years; post-jail, he threw himself into the artistic avant-garde but, finding neither forgiveness nor acceptance in the leftist circles where he desired it, he left the USA to live in England.

The Harvey I befriended soon afterwards, anxious to put that painful past behind him, had now become the personification of the ageing, amiable, artsy hippy, living in Ingatestone in Essex (where, under his watchful eye, I once spent the night having taken the currently trendy drug known as 'LSD' – an experience that, characteristically, I wrote up in some detail once I had arrived safely home a day or so later).

Harvey was a jovial character and a good broadcaster, and our programmes included a feature about the history of American protest songs, a portrait of the humour, warmth and tension which simmered under the surface of

Harvey Matusow (left) with John Cage, 1972.
(Courtesy of Robert Cohen and Dave Thompson)

New York (which we toured together), another in which we followed an American couple who were visiting England for the first time and a pair of documentaries about the work, lives and practical difficulties facing young artists in Britain at the time. While in England, Harvey, provocative as ever, founded what he called his 'Jews Harp Band (explaining that what he was playing was in fact a 'jaws' harp), a highly prescient movement aimed at limiting the use of computers in matters concerning business or government, and in 1972 he was the principal inspiration and co-founder of a high-profile postmodern arts festival primarily held at Camden Town's Roundhouse and named 'ICES' (International Carnival of Experimental Sound). The Festival featured avant-garde musicians such as John Cage and Cornelius Cardew – and Harvey's partner at the time, the electronic musician Anna (aka 'Annea') Lockwood whose 'aleatoric' compositions, more concerned with process than product, included recording the sounds of flowing rivers or the tapping of glasses containing various amounts of water – and the burning or burying of a piano.

Harvey eventually returned to the USA, found another partner (he married some half-a-dozen times or more), allied himself to new causes, renamed himself 'Job' and moved hither and yon, finally settling in Arizona where, working with his 'Magic Mouse Theater' (under the personal *nom de plume* Cockyboo) he became a popular and well-known presenter of children's radio and tv programmes. Intellectually, psychologically and geographically he was forever on the move, and he died in 2002 from injuries incurred by a traffic accident. I'm really glad I knew him. Some of my American friends would rather I hadn't.

Chapter 32

Music and Musicians on Air

What does a conductor bring to an orchestra that can lead highly experienced musicians to play differently (over and above practicalities about tempo, sound balance, etc.)? Where, in effect, does conductorial authority lie? What was it about a great maestro that enabled an orchestra to play better? How did he (they were virtually all men in those days) assert his authority? Did it help if the players feared him? Or loved him? Back in spring 1969, soon after my return to the BBC and renewal of my contract, I produced a 60-minute documentary examining the personal and psychological relationships that developed between orchestral players and their conductors. The topic was originally suggested to me by David Gerver, who went on to present the programme. David was an academic psychologist whose particular expertise was the workings of the brain among people who were simultaneous interpreters.

In order to pursue these ideas, I watched a number of conductors at work in rehearsal and recorded interviews with them, our eventual haul ranging from the already celebrated (Boult, Bliss, Boulez) to younger maestri such as Haitink (then 40) and the 24-year-old David Atherton.

David (Gerver) was also keen that we include an interview with Yehudi Menuhin, the famous violinist who, by then, was conducting more than he was playing. On arrival at Menuhin's house on Highgate's elite The Grove, we were ushered in and told the maestro would be down soon. In due course, a pair of orientally slippered feet became visible descending the stairs, then a pair of ballooning Indian trousers over which hung a loose, multi-coloured cotton shirt-cum-kaftan. David and I rose in respectful anticipation of what we were sure would be a spiritual and perhaps meditative greeting from the great man. Instead, he sat us down briskly, said he didn't have much time and asked us to tell him precisely what we wanted of him. Once the microphone was switched on, Menuhin reverted once more to spiritual mode, telling us how his desire, as a conductor, was to transfer the sense of the music 'from the eye to the ear'. 'Once it's in the ear,' he added with a beatific smile, 'it's in the heart.' After we left, David and I had much fun reflecting on the deliciously mixed occidental and oriental signals we had received that morning!

But our greatest coup was to persuade the management of the BBC Symphony Orchestra to let us accompany the band on a tour of Holland and Belgium in January 1969 led by their young Principal Conductor, Colin Davis. This would enable us to get to know the players (and record interviews with them as we pleased), sit in on rehearsals and, of course, interview the maestro. 'Be careful about how you treat Colin,' the orchestral manager warned us gently a few days before we departed. 'He's exceptionally talented but doesn't fully realise it and thinks he's just an ordinary person like everyone else.'

The orchestra were duly told that David and I would be accompanying them, and on 14 January we all assembled at the BBC's Maida Vale studios to be taken by bus to Heathrow at the start of a five-day foray that would take us to Rotterdam, Antwerp and Amsterdam. We travelled everywhere with the orchestra, stayed in the same hotels, shared meals with the players and attended all the rehearsals and concerts in each venue. This enabled us to get to know the orchestra extremely well and garner a collection of sometimes remarkably frank interviews from distinguished elders, such as the great harpist Sidonie Goossens (who reminisced about working under Toscanini some 30 years before) and the orchestra's down-to-earth principal viola player Harry Danks, to many younger and more recent recruits.

David was wonderful company throughout the project and proved to be an excellent broadcaster. He was also a talented mimic. He would put on an old-world, quasi-Edwardian mien as he pretended to be addressing 'Sir Adrian', or would adopt the gentle, almost quizzical intonation of Haitink who, having struggled to articulate the various ways a conductor might assert authority, concluded with a sigh, 'There are *so* many ways to do it…'

* * *

I had many other music-related encounters around that time. Two in particular were quite extraordinary. Both issued in substantial programmes, yet each raised major issues of an almost philosophical nature which, at least on air, remained unresolved. The first was in spring 1969 when I went to Bayreuth with the Wagner expert Geoffrey Skelton to record extensive

Winifred Wagner at home in Wahnfried.

interview material with the venerable (English-born) Winifred Wagner, widow of Wagner's son Siegfried and daughter-in-law of his formidable wife Cosima. By now in her early 70s, Winifred had run the Bayreuth Festival throughout the 1930s and had notoriously been a close friend of Hitler. After the war, her sympathies with Hitler and the Nazi party led to her exclusion from the Festival, which was henceforth managed by her sons Wieland and Wolfgang. But when Geoffrey and I visited Winifred she was still living in the composer's old house, 'Wahnfried' (today a museum), and it was there that we recorded a succession of autobiographical interviews with her in her perfect if slightly German-accented English. Winifred was polite, forthright, courteous and honest. She was one of the very few older-generation Germans I ever met (and I visited often) who did not tell me how anti-Nazi she had been. On the contrary, the Nazi party had done all it could to boost the noble flower of German cultural nationalism, she said, and Hitler, who genuinely loved the works of Wagner, had done all he could to support her work at Bayreuth. That was not, Winifred emphasised, to condone all the barbarous and evil things that were carried out in the name of the regime. But whenever there was a problem with, for example, a singer Winifred had wanted to retain at the Festival but who had (say) a Jewish wife or a tendency to homosexuality, she knew she could always solve things via a quick call to her friend the Führer. We asked her about her memories of Wagner's widow Cosima (who died in 1930) and

Winifred gave us a vivid picture of the way the local townspeople had always smiled and bowed to the elderly *grande dame* as she undertook her social rounds.

One morning, after recording continuously for something over an hour and a half, I asked Winifred if she would like to take a break. No, she answered, she was perfectly happy to carry on. At which point Geoffrey reminded me that Frau Wagner was perfectly used to sitting immobile for great lengths of time: through (for example) the opening act of *Götterdämmerung*, which was considerably longer. Laughter all round.

Half a dozen years later, Winifred gave a similar, and similarly controversial, interview to the film-maker Hans-Jürgen Syberberg, which was shown worldwide.

* * *

The final music-related programme of 1969 (which happened to have a starring role for Cosima Wagner's father, the composer and pianist Franz Liszt) came from a suggestion by Howard Newby. Howard phoned me one day and asked if I knew anything about Rosemary Brown. She was a musical 'medium' who claimed to be in direct touch with long-dead composers such as Beethoven, Chopin, Liszt and Brahms. The spirits of these and other such figures, apparently, would contact Mrs Brown, speak to her directly and dictate new compositions which she would dutifully write down. Various experts had examined these pieces and concluded that they were, indeed, very much the kind of music their supposed composers had been creating during and towards the ends of their respective lifetimes. Was Mrs Brown a fraud? A hoaxer? Was she really a thoroughly trained musician trying to conceal her highly sophisticated skills under a cloak of mystery? Or was she genuinely gifted with some kind of extra-sensory perception (ESP) denied to the rest of us? One way or another, Mrs Brown and her work were beginning to create quite a furore in musical circles. I set out to investigate.

I made an appointment with the lady and went to visit her in her home in Balham where I found a gentle, quietly spoken woman, recently widowed and of modest means and mien, who evidently had no great pretentions as a musician. She had always liked music, she said, and could play a bit on the piano, but her chief love as a youngster had been ballet. Whatever else she was, I got the firm impression that Mrs Brown was no clever musical virtuoso trying to trick the rest of us. But, equally, I could not quite credit the idea of the spirits of the dead dictating new compositions to her.

Once again, I turned to Geoffrey Skelton as my presenter and, accompanied by a BBC recording engineer, we made a date to go to Mrs Brown's house and watch her at work. She wrote later that she had been quite apprehensive as the time approached. Could she be sure that any of her composers would choose to communicate with her (let alone dictate a new piece of music) while the gentlemen of the BBC were present? What would happen if none of the composers got in touch that day? Maybe the BBC would pour scorn on the entire enterprise and make her look ridiculous. Mrs Brown turned to Liszt and asked him what he thought. Liszt reassured her. 'You must go ahead,' she later reported him as having said; this is 'one thing we have all been waiting for, and it will be a step forward'.

'I can't guarantee that anything will happen,' Mrs Brown warned us anxiously while we were setting up. But, to her relief (and ours), Liszt appeared to her before long, 'as reliable as ever, looking very calm and composed and telling me in his rather Victorian, slightly pedantic manner he was willing to communicate a new piece of music'. To which Mrs Brown asked him to make sure it was 'something spectacular'.

It was. The piece he dictated had a key signature in six sharps and the

Rosemary Brown takes dictation from Liszt.

music was in 5/4 time in the right hand against 3/2 in the left. All this Mrs Brown found somewhat bewildering as she began to write down the notes that Liszt dictated. I would have expected Mrs Brown (or Liszt) to have progressed through the piece as a whole, writing a first few bars and then moving on to the next section. What was astonishing, to me at least, was that she began to write the individual notes in the left hand only, one by one. 'Was that a 'B', did you say?' she would ask Liszt, correcting it to a 'D' or 'E' on receipt of his clearer instruction. Only after she had written down the left-hand notes of the first few bars did she return to the beginning of the piece and, as though undertaking a totally unrelated task, write down the notes to be played by the right hand. As she did this, Mrs Brown seemed to have no sense of how the piece as a whole was constructed or how it would sound. After writing all the notes of the first 20 bars or so, she tried playing the piece but was soon defeated by the key and time signatures. Geoffrey offered to take over, and gave us what were the opening bars of what was later named *Grübelei* ('Meditation') which, the composer and Liszt expert Humphrey Searle told us, was 'the sort of piece which Liszt could well have written, particularly during the last fifteen years of his life when he was experimenting with new ideas'.

Rosemary Brown became widely known (and celebrated) in sections of the music world, and went on to publish a couple of books describing and

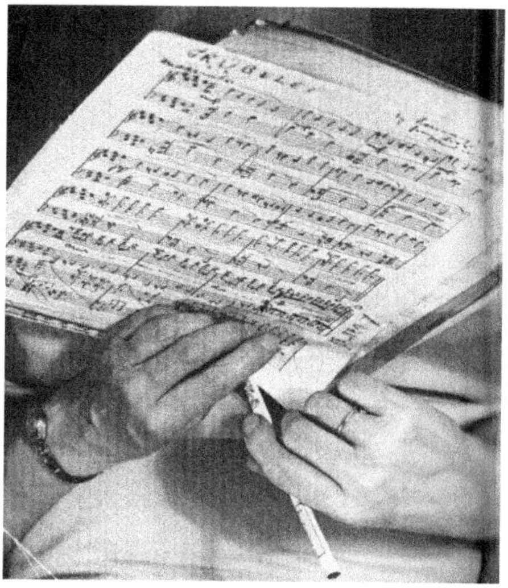

Liszt's Grübelei.

attempting to explain her insights and experiences. In the first, *Unfinished Symphonies: Voices from the Beyond* which appeared in 1971, she described in detail our visit to her in a chapter devoted to Liszt (from which the quotations above and the *Grübelei* photo are taken). A year or so later she gave me the opening of a string quartet dictated to her, she said, by Brahms. I showed this to the Amadeus Quartet and they, too, acknowledged the extraordinary authenticity of its Brahmsian writing.

What was the truth about Mrs Brown and the music she claimed had been dictated to her by long-dead composers? For our Radio 3 programme, I consulted a variety of experts, supporters and sceptics in a quest to understand what was a quite extraordinary phenomenon. Did Mrs Brown have a 'sixth sense'? Was she gifted with 'extra-sensory perception'? She was not unique in claiming to receive direct communication from the dead, and a number of musicians over the years had attributed their ability to improvise in the style of earlier composers to their being in touch with the spirits of the departed. But Mrs Brown claimed to be doing more than this. She saw the dead composers, she told us, spoke to them and heard what they said. But how, I wondered, had Beethoven, Liszt and the rest learned to speak English? Did they have heavy foreign accents? What sort of clothes were they wearing and what age did they appear to be? Before Geoffrey and I visited her, I spoke to the brilliant and ever-provocative BBC musicologist Hans Keller and he suggested we get her to ask Mozart (who lies in an unknown, unmarked grave in Vienna's St Marx cemetery) precisely where he is buried. Alas, Mozart did not appear to Mrs B, nor was she able to give us more than rather general answers to our accompanying questions.

For a long time after the programme had been broadcast, I was asked where I stood on the Rosemary Brown mystery. She herself seemed to have no doubts about the authenticity of what she was telling us: that the spirits of dead composers were communicating through her in order to present us with new pieces of music to enjoy. But surely, many asked, she must have been, deep down, some kind of fraud hoping not to be found out or too rigorously interrogated. I found myself rejecting both these views. I didn't for a moment believe that she was doing what she seemed to believe she was doing. But neither was she a fraudster. On balance, I edged towards the view that Rosemary Brown was a genuinely modest lady who, while liking music and being drawn to it, perhaps underrated her own musical imagination. Like many music lovers, she could recognise the style and personal traits of some of the famous composers of the past but lacked the confidence to believe she herself could write fully fledged compositions in the style of any of them. Any first-year composition student can write a chorale in the style of Bach or perhaps thump out a reasonable imitation of a typical Verdi aria or the tumultuous opening of a Beethoven-style sonata. But only the most adept (and highly trained) could produce a complete work in the authentic musical language of one of the great composers of the past. It seemed to me just possible, therefore, that Rosemary Brown did perhaps have skills of this level but that what she lacked was the confidence to acknowledge this fact to herself. She was therefore having to resort to the psychological subterfuge of imagining herself the handmaid of these great composers, and it was this and only this that allowed her to give public expression to the musical impulses that lay deep within her.

Chapter 33

Anniversaries

There was nothing like an anniversary to persuade the BBC schedulers that a programme was required. Sometime in the middle of 1969, my friend David Gerver pointed out that at the end of that year the conductor Sir John Barbirolli would be celebrating his 70th birthday. A good excuse, I thought (and my Radio 3 bosses kindly concurred), for David and myself to sit in on some wonderful music and meet some interesting people. Soon we found ourselves watching Barbirolli rehearsing (with the New Philharmonia Orchestra) at Cecil Sharp House in Camden Town. The work was Mahler's First Symphony. Barbirolli, diminutive, all eyebags and an affectionately gruff voice, couldn't quite get the effects he wanted, so he borrowed the first cellist's instrument and illustrated there and then. Few conductors could do that! Then, David and I went to visit Daniel Barenboim and his wife Jacqueline du Pré – who, famously, had recorded the Elgar Cello Concerto under Barbirolli. At the time, the couple had a basement flat in Upper Montagu Street in Marylebone. Barenboim was just setting out on his career as a conductor (a few days earlier I had watched him rehearsing the London Mozart Players at the Rudolf Steiner Hall). When we arrived, Jackie was out doing some shopping, so 'Danny' made us some coffee and engaged us in the most interesting, highly articulate conversation about Barbirolli's particular gifts and qualities as a conductor. Then Jackie turned up, pretty, smiling and with an exuberant innocence that was fetching yet (I remember thinking) somewhat naïve alongside the multilingual sophistication of her husband. When we turned on the microphone to interview her, Jackie burst out, like a child at a party: 'Happy Birthday, Sir John!' It was a great shock when Barbirolli died, just a few months afterwards.

Some years after I had left BBC staff, I returned to the subject of John Barbirolli and, to mark the centenary of his birth in December 1999, presented a series of illustrated interviews with his widow, the redoubtable Lady Evelyn (produced by Radio 3's Andrew Lyle). Evelyn lived in Buckland Crescent, just up from London's Swiss Cottage: a warm and lovely lady, by then in her late 80s but with her memory and her wit undiminished with age.

Evelyn Barbirolli.

Evelyn Rothwell had been a well-known oboist whose early engagements had included a stint in the orchestra at Glyndebourne soon after its foundation. She married Barbirolli in 1939 and went to live with him in New York where, three years earlier, he had taken up the somewhat daunting role as Toscanini's successor at the New York Philharmonic. Barbirolli and Toscanini had both started their musical lives as cellists. Indeed, the young Toscanini had played in the orchestra at the world premiere of Verdi's *Otello* back in 1887, as had John's Italian father and grandfather, both of them violinists. But despite these putative links, Evelyn recalled that John found Toscanini quite irritating at times, denigrating colleagues such as Bruno Walter, for example (whom she and John greatly admired). More congenial was Fritz Kreisler. 'He was not only a great violinist but also an excellent pianist,' Evelyn told me. 'He used to come round to our apartment to relax and while away the hours playing our Steinway.'

When the New York season was over, John and Evelyn would travel west for concerts at the Hollywood Bowl. Los Angeles was packed with talent and the Barbirollis would sometimes spend an off-duty evening with Jascha Heifetz, the cellist Gregor Piatigorsky and pianists such as Vladimir Horowitz or José Iturbi. And, as often as not, said Evelyn, her eyes lighting up at the memory, the man turning the pages would be that gentle music lover, art collector and Hollywood actor Edward G Robinson. For all John's cosmopolitan background (Italian father, French mother), he was born a Londoner and at heart a patriotic Englishman. One day at a party out in California, Charlie Chaplin spotted Barbirolli and came over to talk to him. 'Soon the two men were huddled in a corner talking about old London,' laughed Evelyn, 'two nostalgic cockneys in evening dress at a posh Hollywood party, oblivious of their surroundings.'

Barbirolli spent seven seasons with the New York Philharmonic but, especially once war had broken out, felt he ought to return to England. After crossing a U-boat-infested Atlantic in 1942 to conduct a number of concerts up and down the land, he was offered the permanent conductorship of Manchester's Hallé Orchestra. Wartime Manchester was not much of a match for Hollywood and the Hallé was no New York Phil. But, as Evelyn recalled, that made John all the more determined to get down to business. 'He'd frequently get back at two o'clock in the morning having walked home from Didsbury station after a concert in some chilly out-of-town cinema or music hall.' John drove himself hard, often sleeping for only three or four hours a night, and Evelyn sensed he was afraid that inactivity might bring on the bouts of depression to which he was prone. But Barbirolli gradually managed to build a provincial band into one of the best orchestras in the country. When tempted with top posts at Covent Garden and the BBC, he turned them down. It was for Barbirolli and the Hallé that Vaughan Williams wrote his Eighth Symphony. He inscribed it to 'Glorious John'; the nickname stuck.

If the Hallé was home, Barbirolli was always happy to try and fit further engagements into his busy schedule. He loved opera, and Evelyn recounted how much she and John had relished Kathleen Ferrier – a great singer and a wonderfully ebullient friend – and how devastated they had both been at Ferrier's untimely death. The first time I saw Barbirolli was when he was conducting opera: a performance of *La bohème* at Covent Garden to which I had been taken on 4 November 1953, my fifteenth birthday.

Evelyn was wonderful company; we remained friends after our BBC interviews had been recorded and broadcast, and would occasionally dine together. A bright, attractive and engaging personality to the last, Evelyn Barbirolli died in January 2008, a day after her 97th birthday.

* * *

In 1976, to mark the upcoming 200th anniversary of the US Declaration of Independence, I went to New York, Chicago and San Francisco to collect material for what became a pair of celebratory programmes. While in New York, I met the veteran writer and broadcaster Alistair Cooke. He took me back to his apartment on the Upper East Side, asked about the project and gave me plenty of practical advice as I prepared to set out for the next two cities. Every now and then, Alistair would go over to his bookshelves and dig out a volume he wanted me to see. They were arranged like a map of the USA: those on Boston or New England along the top right, with New York and Washington a little lower, while books on California were well down on the far left-hand side. He stretched up and dug out one about Chicago, placed along the top, about a third of a way across towards the left. 'When you are in Chicago,' he said, 'do be sure to record the sound of the L,' the Windy City's (elevated) public transport system. And then there were the contacts he gave me. Do get in touch with Mike Royko at the *Chicago Tribune*, he said with a grin, and tell him I sent you. I duly met Mike, who was famous – or notorious – for having written a dangerously frank book about Chicago's controversial Mayor Daley. Mike told me over a drink how his father had known all the big gangsters back in the days of Al Capone and Prohibition. 'Dad always regretted that he had been born in the Ukraine rather than Italy,' said Mike, adding that the old man always felt that if only he had been an Italian, he could have become a really big gangster!

* * *

Three years later, September 1979, saw what people in Britain (but not in China or Japan, Russia or the USA) thought of as the 40th anniversary of the outbreak of the Second World War. What, by this time, did the war mean to the grandchildren of those who had fought in it? I was invited to take over a project, originally proposed by drama producer Hallam Tennyson, which would feature interviews with youngsters from various European countries, each of which had had a very different war. The series, presented by Richard Mayne, was to be called *Forty Years On* and the idea was that it would include material that I would record not only in the UK but also in Germany, France, Yugoslavia and Sweden. The results of my travels that spring and early summer were startling. To British kids, 'Dunkirk' meant a heroic retreat which saved countless British lives thus enabling our forces to regroup and attack the Germans once more. In Paris, a schoolgirl with just enough English to warrant my recording her said hesitantly: 'Dunkerque? Wasn't that when the British all ran for the boats and left us to the Nazis?' In Belgrade and Zagreb I heard a great deal about how it was the Communists who were the principal opponents of Nazi fascism, while in a school in Stockholm youngsters told me how they knew how horrific the war had been and how wonderful it was that their country had managed to keep out of it. In Gothenburg I asked a young lad whether he felt the war got the right amount of attention in school history books. 'I think it gets too much,' he answered. 'After all, it only lasted six years.'

During my travels, I also met people with personal memories of wartime: parents and grandparents of the children who were my primary focus. A young grandmother I met in Berlin, perhaps in her late 50s, explained how, as an adolescent, she had been thrilled to join the *Deutscher Mädel*, the girls' branch of the Hitler Youth. She had relished the smart uniforms she and the other the girls were given to wear, the romantic summer camps, the sports events and the general training they received as they approached young womanhood in what they all thought of as the exemplary society being forged at the time by their beloved *Führer*.

In Munich, once the spiritual home of Nazism, I set off one morning for the nearby suburb of Dachau, site of one of the earliest Nazi concentration camps and by now a museum and memorial. While I was there a group of young German soldiers arrived for an educational visit and, after an initial briefing, they were invited to ask questions and express their views. 'I understand the importance of retaining the memory of the dreadful things the Nazis did,' said one earnest young man in his late teens. 'But the result is that we, who had nothing to do with the crimes they committed, continue to be labelled by the outside world almost as though we did.' He had a point, everybody agreed. But wasn't it right that places like Dachau (not to mention a mass murder camp such as Auschwitz) should be preserved? Well, yes of course, someone else said. But why are we so selective about what we do and don't choose to memorialise from Germany's Nazi past? 'Here in Munich we have made a museum out of Dachau. But there is no plaque marking the Beer Hall where Hitler staged his notorious 1923 putsch.' Not, he hastened to add, to celebrate it; merely to mark it as a location of historical significance. Fair enough, piped up another young soldier. 'But if there *were* a plaque outside the Beer Hall – or the house in which Hitler lived when in Munich – the danger is that the neo-Nazis might leave flowers at these places and turn them into political shrines.' The

THE LISTENER 30 AUGUST 1979

Daniel Snowman

40 years on: is the war 'just history'?

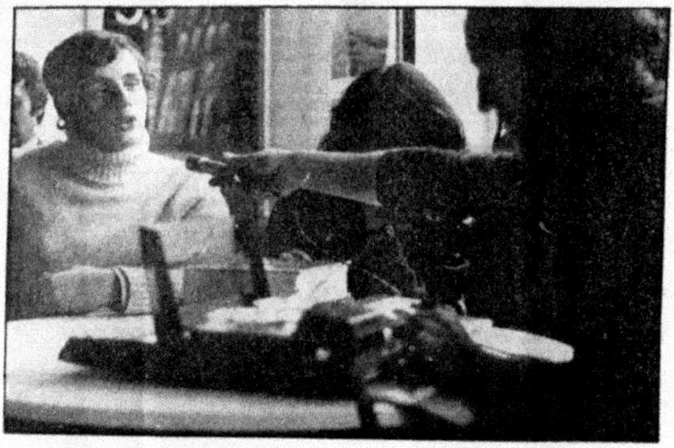

A French schoolboy gives his views on World War Two

Next week is the 40th anniversary of the outbreak of World War Two. Daniel Snowman, author of a number of books on modern history and the producer of 'Forty Years On' (Radio 4, from 4 September), has been asking what the war means to the generation of Europeans who have no personal memories of it.

Hitler inflicted intensive bombing on the USA in World War Two; but the Germans, may, by now, be 'just history'. But everything else I heard from my young friends convinced me that it was history with a difference.

For one thing, most of the youngsters I met (the howler-merchants apart) simply knew so much more about the Second World War than I, at their age, had known about the First. I met British children who could name, and even identify, every British or German warplane, young Yugoslavs

Listener *article, 30 August 1979.*

debate (much of which I recorded) was vigorous, and I found it moving to see and hear the honest integrity with which this younger generation of Germans struggled to come to terms with the barbarous legacy of their recent predecessors. I didn't leave Dachau to return to my hotel in Munich until well into the afternoon. I suddenly realised how hungry and thirsty I was, having had nothing to eat or drink since early morning. Somehow, my minor and temporary discomfort felt deeply appropriate. As I thought back over the day I had just experienced, I decided not to break my fast until dinner time that evening.

At the end of August, just before the 40th anniversary of the outbreak of the War, I wrote an article in *The Listener* to mark the event, and my forthcoming programmes. The article was headed: '40 Years On: is the War "just history"?': a question worth reconsidering as I write these words, over 40 years later.

* * *

In 1983, I was back in the USA just ahead of the 100th anniversary of the opening of the Metropolitan Opera. For this, I went to New York, enjoyed a self-indulgent week going through the sound archives of the Met and recorded interviews with some of the great doyens of earlier times, such as the celebrated mezzo-soprano Risë Stevens, before returning to produce and present a BBC documentary to mark the event. Music and musicians featured in many of my programmes: a pair of long conversations with Plácido Domingo recorded in Spain and broadcast in 1983 (when I was also writing a book about him); a feature about Paco Peña and his work, recorded in Córdoba; a documentary at the Sydney Opera House in 1987 as the company undertook a production of Cherubini's *Medée*, and another three years later as Simon Rattle prepared to make his Covent Garden debut conducting a new production of Janáček's *Cunning Little Vixen*.

Interviewing Simon Rattle, 1990.

Chapter 34

History on Air

In 1970, the year I (officially) joined the staff, BBC Radio came up with a plan entitled 'Broadcasting in the Seventies' the aim of which was to reform its networks with the intention of differentiating them – and therefore their potential audiences – more clearly. Thus, Radio 1 would be the home of the latest ground-breaking pop music while more traditional fare would be on Radio 2. Radio 3 would broadcast classical music, and most speech programmes would henceforth be on Radio 4. Many of my fellow producers (and bosses) were appalled at this new delineation. What had happened, they asked, to Reith's mission to 'educate by stealth', to the idea that someone listening to, say, a Mozart opera or concerto might, by inadvertently leaving the radio on, become unexpectedly absorbed by an interview with a leading economist or philosopher or a documentary about NATO or Plato? The musicologist Hans Keller, by now a leading figure on Radio 3, said that if most of the speech programmes on this network were replaced by music, listeners would increasingly treat the world's finest music as mere background noise ('aural wallpaper') rather than actively choosing to listen to it. Somewhat acrimonious meetings were held between staff and management, and the internal controversy spilled out into the press. On 14 February 1970, *The Times* published a letter signed by 134 members of staff (myself included) protesting at what was seen as 'the abandonment of creative mixed planning in favour of a schematic division into categories'. Twenty-five of the signatories came from Drama and no fewer than 38 from Music. All who signed the letter were breaking their contracts by so doing and in principle open to being sacked. The reforms went ahead, we weren't sacked, the uproar died down and we producers settled down to work within the new, rationalised regime.

During the course of this furore, a new Controller of Radio 4 had been appointed: the youthful Tony Whitby. It was against this turbulent background, and perhaps in part as a sop to the still smouldering ground troops, that Whitby gave the go-ahead for what was to become one of the largest, most ambitious projects in the history of BBC Radio.

* * *

I was always, I suppose, a historian at heart and many of the programmes and series I produced at the BBC examined the historical origins and background of the subjects I chose to explore. Every so often, the cry would go up inside the BBC that we needed to think of new ways of presenting history on the air, especially that of Britain. By 1970, dramatised history often sounded a little dated as yet another intrepid crew cried 'Aye, aye' to the orders of Columbus or Nelson, or the Light Brigade sallied forth once more to what increasingly sophisticated audiences thought of as the accompaniment of coconut shells. Broadcasting, moreover, needed to catch up with important shifts in the intellectual world. No longer was history regarded as essentially the sayings and doings of the great, ostensibly 'value-free' but in fact crudely deferential. Historians such as EP Thompson had been painting a broader picture of the English past, including in their canvas not just the principal actors but also those who were primarily acted upon, the hitherto mute voices of the women and children, the poor labourers, the sick, the indigent, the elderly, the illiterate. What was *their* view of the Napoleonic or Crimean wars, of the press gangs, the bunkers and the battlefield amputations? What was life like for the Lancashire cotton mill worker, the Derbyshire coalminer, the climbing boy, street entertainer or elderly widow a century or two before the advent of the welfare state?

At the same time, some historians were beginning to practise what became known as 'oral history', recording the reminiscences of older people as they looked back over the events of their own lives. What Bartók, Cecil Sharp or Alan Lomax had done for folksong a new band of men and women wielding the latest recording equipment set out to do for history more generally. A controversial departure, oral history was initially dismissed by some as adding little (or perhaps too much) to the sum of human knowledge. I remember visiting the so-called oral history archive at a famous American university (not the one with which I had had the Plato-Socrates correspondence) only to discover that they had proudly transcribed their recordings and destroyed the tapes. 'It's so much faster to work from a text than a recording,' explained the librarian. Apart from which, historical memory can be notoriously inaccurate, with the elderly inclined, deliberately or inadvertently, to embroider what it is they think they are accurately recalling. And the sheer proliferation of recorded oral memories can sometimes be more of a burden than a boon to the historian. Must every oral recording be sanctified as part of the 'historical record'?

Perhaps not. But, as serious oral archives began to be established, parameters fixed and the recorded memories of people who had passed away stored and catalogued, the value of such a resource became increasingly evident.

* * *

Some in the world of broadcasting were sensitive to these shifts in historical method and perspective, and two colleagues in particular tried to reflect them in their programmes: Charles Parker, creator of the *Radio Ballads*, and Michael Mason who masterminded *The Long March of Everyman*. The two men could not have been more different. Charles wore a permanent air of studied resentment, the scars I imagined of endless battles against what he saw as his recalcitrant BBC bosses as he struggled for the right to hymn the working classes on their establishment airwaves. Michael, equally committed to a radical view of society, was a romantic optimist, always inclined to believe that patient explanation would ultimately win

Michael Mason.
(Photograph provided by Michael's son, Andrew Mason)

the heart and mind of even the most sceptical interlocutor. Where Charles would grumble at the darkness, Michael would seek to light a candle. Both would bestow upon their creative work the most infinite care before releasing a programme for transmission, poring over details like a general mesmerised by the minutiae of troop emplacements before a battle. Many of Michael's, indeed, dealt overtly or metaphorically with military history, a legacy perhaps of his own indelible memories of fighting in the last years of World War II. Where Charles's 'Ballads' were radiophonic poems, rhapsodising working-class Britain through the music and voices of the people portrayed, Michael's masterpieces were on an altogether more epic scale. From 'The Bayeux Tapestry' and 'Rus' to 'The British Seafarer' and his final experiments with subaqueous, quadraphonic sound, Michael was Shakespeare, Verdi or Tolstoy where Charles was Flaubert, Baudelaire or Gorki. The two men came together in Michael Mason's hugely ambitious project, and *The Long March of Everyman* resulted in a series of twenty-six 45-minute programmes covering 'themes and variations in the history of the people in Britain'. I was privileged to work alongside Michael throughout the project, and produced half of the programmes.

Chapter 35

The Long March of Everyman

The Long March of Everyman, first broadcast on Radio 4 over the winter of 1971–72, covered British history from the Romans to the present, and called upon the services (as consultants, or programme directors) of many of the country's leading historians, among them Asa Briggs, Theo Barker and Peter Matthias as well as such revisionists as Gwyn Williams, Edward Thompson, Christopher Hill, Rodney Hilton, George Rudé and rising young turks like Raphael Samuel. As perhaps befitted a series with a title of somewhat Maoist resonance, the special feature of *The Long March* was that, as far as possible, the story was told through (as we liked to say) the words and voices of the people themselves: archive recordings for more recent periods of course but, above all, authentic documents – letters, diaries, official pronouncements, gravestone inscriptions, graffiti, popular rhymes, lyrics or jokes – each of which was spoken for us by someone who was today's nearest equivalent. Thus, if one of our historical consultants provided us with, for example, a deposition by a Lancashire wool merchant in a sixteenth century courtroom or a homesick epistle from a West Country mariner in Nelson's navy, we tried to ensure that these were read for us by (say) a minor textile baron from Manchester or a Bristol-based naval rating. This is where Charles Parker came in. Charles, dudgeon held high, could no longer work with his old BBC department in Birmingham and came to us. He scoured the country, Uher in hand, as head of a team that recorded some 800 historical documents in voices and accents that corresponded, as far as possible, to those that would originally have spoken or written them.

The resulting tapes, from all over Britain, were intercut with popular and 'art' music, sound effects, literary excerpts (read by actors) and the edited voices of our historical consultants and programme directors, and the final ingredients were mixed in the BBC's Radiophonic Workshop in Maida Vale. Certain sounds and documents would be repeated, in the spirit of a Wagnerian *leitmotif*, within a programme or even between programmes to make a thematic point: the disciplined, rectilinear beat we created for the Roman legions on the march, for example, found echoes in later programmes as Britain's rigid road network or factory system were established. The intention throughout was to find links, parallels, connections – to concentrate on 'synthesis' rather than 'analysis' – to create what Michael liked to call 'total audio': a series of through-composed sound symphonies that would attempt to evoke the world of ordinary people during earlier periods of British history.

The approach of *The Long March* was innovative in a number of ways: in its attempt to view the past primarily from the point of view of ordinary people rather than the elites who mostly filled the history books (and radio programmes) of the time, in the decision to cross chronology with theme and to emphasise the connections linking historical experience rather than the analysis of its separate elements, and in the free-flowing, unnarrated radiophonic style of production adopted. All this provoked a great deal of critical debate. We had doubtless tempted providence by saying that we hoped the series would 'give back to the British people a sense of their roots', while the cross-cutting of chronology with theme (not to mention the Wagnerian comparison) was bound to cause offence to purists. Some complained that the programmes needed clearer signposting so that listeners could have known who was talking, where a document had come from, and whether we were still in the 16th century or had jumped to the 17th.

Reasonable enough perhaps, and we knew from the outset that we risked losing elements of analytical clarity in the interests of 'total audio'. But we stood by our emphasis on seeking connections and continuities, on presenting history as essentially a seamless web of experience unmediated by extrinsic signposting. Our own contemporary culture, we felt, was in some ways becoming excessively linear, analytical, divisive. Everything, it seemed, was thought to be susceptible of rational explanation by reference to causal relationships between component parts, whether a rainbow, a nuclear bomb or a Beethoven symphony, while no contention could be regarded as 'valid' unless logically demonstrable. But weren't there other kinds of truth, we asked (influenced in part by the prevailing counter-culture of the time), that demanded attention through the totality of what they proclaimed? Whole experiences whose validity lay more in the cyclicity and the interconnectedness than in the causally related subdivisions? Not only the rainbow or the symphony but the great cycles of life, death and seasonality? This, after all, was how we as individuals experienced our own little tranche of history. Later historians looking back at our era might divide domestic affairs from foreign affairs or economic from social factors, the biographies of prime ministers or playwrights from considerations of

Poster for The Long March of Everyman.

housing or transport policy or an analysis of the rise and fall of a killer disease or a particular style of popular music. But to you and me, and undoubtedly to our predecessors as well, topics such as these tended to intermesh as part of the continuous texture of daily life, and it was this that *The Long March of Everyman* set out to try and recreate.

* * *

The Long March of Everyman was conceived in a Britain that had recently found itself plunging deep into a debate about the role of the individual in the national community and, on a wider stage, the role of Britain in the world. Who are the British? Are we, basically, white? And Protestant? Are Kenya Asians (with British passports) British, and should they have the same rights as are normally available to British citizens? What about children or criminals; should they be treated as though they were the same as the rest of us? And homosexuals? How far should individual 'deviants' be permitted to behave as they wish? And (on a global scale) what sort of 'special relationship' should we have with the United States? Should we join the Common Market? What obligations did we have to the former colonies?

These and similar questions, familiar as they may have come to feel a generation or two later, were being fiercely and freshly debated in the late

1960s and early 1970s when options still seemed open and answers not foreclosed. In the aftermath of war and empire, many people in Britain found themselves contemplating their national past with a new sense of urgency and mission. The quest for national self-definition was part of the context that helped create *The Long March*, while the programmes themselves, with their hugely variegated *dramatis personae*, were perhaps our contribution to the debate.

* * *

There was one other respect in which *The Long March of Everyman* embodied the era in which it was produced, and that concerned recent changes in broadcasting technologies. The arrival and enthronement of magnetic tape had enabled radio producers to aim at far higher standards of recording and editing than had ever been possible before. Charles Parker's *Radio Ballads* and Michael Mason's *Long March of Everyman* would have been impossible before tape. In addition, from the mid-1960s, more and more people were switching to colour television sets. This brought a great deal of revenue to the BBC, much to the delight of programme makers like myself, though it also accelerated the already rapid shift in popular attention from radio to TV. More than that, the shift to television and the ubiquity of magnetic recording tape both contributed to a deeper trend that fed back into all modes of communication: a gradual move from an essentially linear culture of speech and print towards a modular one of bullet points, frequent shifts of voice and camera angle and, in general, shorter, sharper forms of expression that, in a later microelectronic age, would lead to what came to be called 'sound bites'. Looking back, it is not hard to see how today's rapidly moving digital culture was in some ways preceded – heralded – by the Goons, Monty Python and the telly commercial with their rapid edits, dissolves, striking juxtapositions and highly economical foreshortenings of sound, speech and meaning. And perhaps by a landmark series of BBC radio programmes that, dispensing with the guiding voice of an authoritative narrator, communicated instead through a constantly shifting succession of richly inter-edited and highly evocative soundscapes. I would be sorry to think that *The Long March* contributed to a reduction in the nation's attention span. But as an exploration of the possibilities of radio montage, it undoubtedly covered new ground. Perhaps that is why, on listening to some of the programmes again, I find they sound a great deal less 'dated' than I had anticipated.

Book 7

BBC Years (2)

1970s and 1980s

Chapter 36
Verbage

What do we mean by 'news'? Under what circumstances might you be tempted to lie, to keep money that you know is not legally yours, possibly even to kill? When you say you are in favour of equality, do you mean of *opportunity* or of *condition*? How might an Argentine intellectual explain and interpret the Falklands War (whoops; I mean that over the Malvinas islands!) of 1982? I enjoyed pushing at the boundaries of popular acceptability, and themes such as these were frequent features of my BBC programmes. Anything a BBC producer thought 'questionable', perhaps for reasons of taste or political sensitivity, had to be referred upwards (we used to call it 'passing the fuck').

In May 1972 I was reprimanded for not having done so. I was producing a BBC Radio 3 series called *Personal View*. The idea of the series was to invite someone with a strong and independent mind to present four 20-minute scripted talks (one per fortnight over the course of two months) in which the speaker would reflect on some topic of current interest. Programmes went out live during the concert interval on a Saturday night. The speaker would turn up around 6pm with a draft script and, with the producer, go over details for an hour or two, punctuated by sandwiches and drinks, and go on air at c. 8.30–9 pm. All very civilised. For this particular run of programmes, my speaker was the brilliant but highly controversial Marxist historian Eric Hobsbawm.

On 13 May, Eric turned up with a script critical of US involvement in Vietnam (this was the time of the 'Easter Offensive', renewed mining of Haiphong harbour etc.). Predictably, he had written an interesting, intelligent, highly provocative but, by his own lights, persuasive job. We discussed details, he agreed to make various alterations and adjustments and the talk went ahead. Back in my office on the Monday I was told that the BBC had received a call from the US Embassy objecting to the programme, and in due course I was summoned to a meeting with the Head of Talks and Current Affairs, Arthur Hutchinson. He was stern but polite, and I remember holding my ground. In his subsequent report about our meeting, Hutchinson pronounced the Hobsbawm script 'seriously unsatisfactory from a policy point of view' adding that it contained observations that were 'manifestly inaccurate, over-generalised or otherwise unacceptable for broadcasting by the BBC'. At the very least, the report said, 'a person of Mr Snowman's intellectual and reasoning capacity' should have pointed out to Hobsbawm 'the demonstrable fallacies in his script' and, if necessary, referred it upwards – and perhaps written an opening and/or closing announcement to the effect that the views broadcast were solely those of the contributor. I agreed to keep a closer watch on future scripts in the series, honour had been upheld on all sides and the US Embassy was no doubt informed that the producer of this nefarious broadcast had duly been hauled over the coals.

* * *

For some years in the 1970s I produced a regular series of short Sunday-lunchtime radio programmes called *Words* in which well-known cultural figures were invited to speculate on aspects of our language and how we used it. Here, too, I had a few close calls. I remember visiting the cultural critic Marghanita Laski in her home adjacent to Hampstead Heath to record one of her contributions. She was in bed recovering from an infection but was nonetheless in delightfully impish mood. How absurd our attitude to language can be, said Marghanita reading her script, as I leaned across the bed with my tape recorder to get close to her. For example, she continued with her cut-glass accent, if she were to say 'F-dot-dot-K' or 'C-dot-dot-T', we would all know the words she had in mind. But if she were to say the full words, the BBC would doubtless consign the script to the waste bin. On another occasion, the young Margaret Drabble drafted a lovely piece about the word 'curse', and how thousands of post-pubic English schoolgirls would giggle over Tennyson's famous lines:

> 'The curse is come upon me,' cried
> The Lady of Shallott.

Daring stuff for a family sitting down to their Sunday lunch. But, after some debate, this too was passed for broadcasting.

Not so a script by Kenneth Tynan, the National Theatre's famously controversial dramaturg. Ken had written a script about the ways we invent words to fit new requirements. For example, he suggested, how about the as yet non-existent word to 'palp' a women's breast? It contained elements of pulp, palpitation and so on; far more evocative than boring old 'fondle'.

This was (if I may put it this way) too hot to handle. My then boss, the Hungarian-born George Fischer, deemed the script unbroadcastable and told me to inform Mr Tynan accordingly. I duly phoned Ken and told him of George's decision. A real nuisance, we both agreed, but what could we do? I then added that, of course, there was nothing to stop Ken, if he wanted to, from contacting a sympathetic newspaper and telling them what had happened... A couple of days later, the entire script was printed, uncut, in *The Guardian*, no doubt to my boss's chagrin!

Towards the end of my period producing *Words*, in November 1976, I wrote a piece for the BBC magazine *The Listener* focusing on the kinds of words that, it seemed to me, could well have existed but happened not to. Why, I wondered, did the French say *descendre* but not *ascendre*? Why did we have 'fratricide' in English but not 'sororicide' or (for Cain and Abel for example) the word 'siblicide'? And how come we could 'visualise' St Paul's Cathedral, but not 'auralise' Beethoven's Fifth or 'olfactorise' a beef curry? I opened my piece in *The Listener* with the mock start of a story:

> There was once a couth young Tasmaniac ballerino who visited London. After some postvarication, he decided to stay. Despite his equanimous mien and the occasional gainly benapropism, he was a shy, even a mortacious lad, a cessant talker, noted for his social sinisterity.
>
> One day, unable to find a job, he ambulated nervously along to a pornutopic day-club that his mother – the social overbitch of her day – had long ago matronised. Wearing one of his mother's blice, and practising a pediflection here and an antitortion there, he plucked up courage and asked for a vidition…

Chapter 37
Hot Places
Southern California

One day, back in the mid-1960s when I was a Lecturer in American Studies at the University of Sussex, there was a knock at my office door. In walked a young man of around my own age who introduced himself as Walter Wells. Walter and I were in many ways mirror images of each other. For a start, everyone said we looked rather alike (particularly in the days when my hair was a bit thicker!). I had spent a couple of years doing post-grad work in the States, and now Walter had made the journey in the opposite direction. We soon became close friends and over the next few years kept in close touch as I moved out of academic life (to the BBC) and Walter moved permanently into it as a professor at California State College, Dominguez Hills in Los Angeles. In June 1968, during my US tour, I met up with Walter in LA and it was with him that I went to watch Robert Kennedy campaigning just a few days before Bobby was assassinated.

I'd always loved southern California, and Walter invited me to take a year off from the BBC and join him for the academic year 1972–73 on the faculty at Dominguez Hills. I had recently been contracted to write a new book comparing and contrasting British and American social values and attitudes, and the opportunity to spend a year researching the topic in the States was irresistible. The BBC generously gave me a year off, with a guaranteed job awaiting me on my return. During my absence, my place was filled by another friend, the Canterbury-based sociologist Krishan Kumar who, in turn, was granted a year's leave of absence by his employer, the University of Kent, another of the prestigious 'new' universities of the time. I was thus able to spend an idyllic year living right by the Pacific (at Hermosa Beach) preparing lectures, doing research for my book and relishing life at the heart of one of the most exquisite and rewarding environments the world had to offer.

People joked that the only problem with Los Angeles was the four elements: the air is polluted, there is no fresh water except what is brought in by pipeline, the earth is subject to quakes and the whole place is so dry that parts of it are frequently ravaged by fire. True. But I loved it. All of it: the coastal routes, the lakes and mountains, the dry flatlands and the deserts. When not working, I sped up and down the freeways, got to know the San Francisco bay area almost as well as greater Los Angeles, nipped south and over the frontier into Mexico, made forays to Las Vegas, Grand Canyon and beyond and made sure to pay my respects to London Bridge which had recently been transplanted to Lake Havasu in Arizona.

During my year teaching in Los Angeles, I was designated Professor of American History and, frankly, felt something of a fraud as I pontificated on the Frontier Thesis or the New Deal to young Americans who, I presumed, had known all about these since childhood. But, as ever, I found that the best way to become expert on a subject was to lecture or write about it. Meanwhile Walter, a gentle sage who wore his learning lightly, would deliver lectures at Dominguez to packed classes of adoring students about the poetry of the early American Puritans, the novels of Nathanael West and Scott Fitzgerald, the imagery in *avant-garde* French cinema, Soviet propaganda posters and much else (he also wrote books about the language of business communication, the work and the wit of Mark Twain, the Hollywood novel and, towards the end of his life, the paintings of Edward Hopper). Walter and his wife Joan and their growing family were living at the time just down the coast from me at Irvine. He was, and long remained, one of my dearest friends.

* * *

Towards the end of the academic year, my father came out to join me in California and we went off on a whirlwind holiday together. He was close to 60 and I was 34. I drove him all over the state and beyond: up the coast to Hearst's Castle, on to San Francisco where we stayed with friends, across to Lake Tahoe and up to historic Virginia City and Carson City, then down through Yosemite National Park and back. Never before had the two of us bonded the way we did during the course of that week-and-a-bit together. It was as though we were brothers, buddies, rather than parent and child. Throughout, he was happy, relaxed, carefree: a delightful and easy companion. I think he tasted a touch of freedom that his normal life did not quite deliver. At one point on our drive he noted that it was a Saturday: not a day on which, as orthodox Jews in Edgware, we or any of our friends would drive a car. But out here, said my dad gleefully, there was no way he was going to encounter anyone who knew him! While we

Daniel in California, 1972–73.

*Arthur Snowman outside the Comstock Assay Museum,
Virginia City (Nevada), Summer 1973.*

were away, his father was ill. How ill, he didn't know but he made one or two long-distance telephone calls and things did not look good. When I finally drove him to LA airport (just up from Hermosa Beach) to return to the UK, he said almost nonchalantly that he didn't know whether his father was alive or dead. He'd find out when he arrived back in England. He did. His father, my grandfather Sam, had just died and the funeral was a couple of days later.

* * *

When I lived in Los Angeles the city had no permanent resident opera company. But the New York City Opera visited the Dorothy Chandler Pavilion in LA for a limited season in late autumn each year, and in November–December 1972 I attended all their offerings. The first was *Carmen* in which the tenor lead, Don José, was played by the 31-year-old Plácido Domingo. Here was a young man with a voice of gold; tall, handsome and – wonder of wonders – capable of acting as well. There was no mistaking the intense commitment of this performer. He was never out of character even when momentarily out of the musical or dramatic spotlight, yet nothing in his singing or acting appeared to be forced. He seemed to ride with the score, swim with the musical-dramatic tide, gain and project strength from his inner understanding of the forces of which he was part. Never before had I heard such lyrical singing allied to such dramatic intensity; hitherto, indeed, I had tended to consider these qualities mutually exclusive. Yet Domingo effected a marriage of the operatic arts with consummate skill and apparent ease.

The Chandler Pavilion was packed for the NYCO performances I attended (another included Beverly Sills performing all three soprano parts in Offenbach's *Tales of Hoffmann*), and I was puzzled why Los Angeles – unlike San Francisco, for example – did not host its own opera company. 'But opera would never take root here,' people told me confidently. 'This is a very fluid, flowing city,' they would add. 'People like to drive the freeways. They like grabbing takeaway food. They love movies. Movies *move*. Like the rides in Disneyland. Also, it's a very visual culture. It's not just films and TV. Look at the billboards, the gas station architecture. It's a culture of show, modernity, movement.'

'But there's lots of music out here,' I would respond cautiously, 'and a great deal of singing talent. Why not opera?'

'Sure there's music, but it tends to be the latest forms of jazz or rock.

Music for the movies, music with lighting effects, music built around stars – or music performed *under* the stars – music that's new, amplified, transient. That's what people enjoy out here.'

I was not entirely convinced. This was a place where, these same people liked to tell me, anything could happen and frequently did. And in any case, the easy catch phrases about the cultural inadequacy of Los Angeles seemed to me to fly in the face of its recent history. For all the razzmatazz, the Hollywood glamour and the sheer prodigality of the Western myth, there was another side to Los Angeles, often ignored by Angelenos and outsiders alike: the presence during the city's great leap forward just before and after World War II of a large colony of outstanding musical and artistic talent. The Los Angeles Philharmonic had boasted Otto Klemperer as its conductor while those two great pivots of 20th-century composition, Arnold Schoenberg and Igor Stravinsky, had both lived here. So had Erich Korngold, Hanns Eisler, George Gershwin and Ernst Krenek, instrumentalists such as the violinists Jascha Heifetz and Joseph Szigeti, the cellist Gregor Piatigorsky and the pianist José Iturbi (and, for a while, Arthur Rubinstein) and a host of distinguished conductors, among them Bruno Walter. Los Angeles had also been home to writers such as Thomas Mann, Aldous Huxley, Nathanael West, Franz Werfel, Bertolt Brecht and others, while the lure of the movie industry had brought novelists of the calibre of F Scott Fitzgerald and William Faulkner to the city. When I was living there, the conductor of the LA Phil was Zubin Mehta. Might not such a city become a home for opera?

Fourteen years later, it did, with Domingo playing a pivotal role in its foundation. The 1984 Olympic Games took place in Los Angeles and were accompanied by an Olympic Arts Festival. This featured a visit by London's Royal Opera Company which included a production of *Turandot* with Domingo and Gwyneth Jones. The Arts Festival proved a huge success, and Domingo – Spanish-born and Mexican-raised – relished spending time in what was becoming an increasingly Hispanic part of the USA. We *have* to do opera here, Domingo told everyone who would listen. Two years later, in 1986, the dream came true and the newly formed LA Opera launched its inaugural season with Domingo starring in a new production of *Otello*. From the outset, Plácido acted as the company's artistic consultant. In 2003 he took over as General Director.

* * *

While I was at Dominguez Hills, I was offered a permanent post. I was very tempted to accept. The college and the colleagues were full of goodwill, the pay was good, the pension guaranteed and the workload manageable. Who could not, after a cold, rainy day in London trying to get onto a packed rush-hour train, dream of a life alongside the Pacific Ocean in the hills and dales of Southern California?

And yet… I reflected that Los Angeles (like Cambridge or Norwich perhaps) was a kind of *ne plus ultra*: perfect in its way, but not on the way to anywhere or anything else. Physically or metaphorically. True, the *LA Times* was a good newspaper, and they might have me do an occasional article or book review. And maybe I could get to know people at some of the better universities in the area: USC or UCLA, perhaps, or up the coast, those bright beacons of learning at Stanford and Berkeley. But I found myself looking back over the Atlantic at London, with not only the BBC but a host of galleries, museums and publishers, some 50 top-class theatres, five world-class orchestras and all that opera. And a short distance away, any time I felt like making a brief foray, all the cultural and intellectual *richesse* of Paris, Berlin, Munich, Vienna, Milan, Venice and beyond. Los Angeles, I felt, was on the edge of nowhere else. London lay at the very core of all I valued. So I returned.

* * *

Over the years, I re-visited Southern California many times. When I was there on a US tour in 1990, I visited Walter and Joan in Irvine, and again in 1996. By then, Joan was already suffering from cancer and she died soon afterwards. In due course, Walter, by now retired from Dominguez, met his new partner Shelley (later his wife) and they came and settled in London, a couple of hundred yards from where I was living at the time. Walter remained a close (in all senses) friend until he died – just a few months after the death of poor Shelley – in October 2015.

Chapter 38
Very Hot Places
India, Nepal, Bangladesh, Thailand

During the mid-1970s I went on a six-month attachment to the BBC's World Service in Bush House after which, rather than return to Fischer's 'Talks and Docs', I was invited to join the BBC's Further Education Department. It was here that I produced *World Powers in the Twentieth Century*: the largescale, multi-sourced, archive-based series mentioned earlier. This project was accompanied by a book by Harriet Ward that tied in with a current school O-Level syllabus (what we'd nowadays call GCSE). Various smaller-scale projects followed and then, in 1982, something truly – and literally – global. A couple of years earlier, the former German Chancellor Willy Brandt had issued a major report on international development issues; it was entitled *North–South: A Programme for Survival.* The Brandt Report brought to worldwide attention not only the relative levels of wealth and poverty in the countries of the North and South but, critically, the longer-term dangers to the planet as a whole of the growing discrepancy between population and resources.

When my grandparents were born, world population was estimated at just a little over 1 billion. By the time of the Brandt Report this had risen to some 4.5 billion and projections suggested that early in the new century this figure would have shot up to over 7 billion. In Britain (particularly in England) people would sometimes talk of their densely populated little island with its increasingly crowded cities, the amount of food imported from abroad and the supposed problems caused by occasional waves of immigration. Discussions of international affairs tended to be dominated by the Cold War, very much a North–North issue, with some consideration to the possible mediatory role of what was coming to be labelled the Third World. But few gave much thought to the serious implications of a planet characterised by a rapidly and alarmingly deteriorating ratio of people to resources. I proposed a major eight-part BBC Radio project entitled *A World in Common* in which each programme would home in on issues of both local and global significance such as population rise and density, food, health, energy, trade, aid, urbanisation, education and much else. And the title of the opening programme? A kind of *leitmotif* for the series as a whole: 'Is Your End of the Boat Sinking?'

In order to undertake such a project, I would have to find a way of obtaining interview material and actuality from all parts of the globe. As overall consultant I enlisted the help of William Clark, formerly Anthony Eden's press secretary and later the director of the Overseas Development Institute and a Vice President of the World Bank. Bill Clark proved an invaluable source of advice and contacts, putting me in touch with friends at the World Bank and the United Nations – in particular, the UN Development Programme (UNDP) whose Director of Information, Erskine Childers, grandson of the famous Irish patriot and author of *The Riddle of the Sands*, was to prove particularly helpful and encouraging. In addition to visiting the UN in New York and the World Health Organisation in Geneva in autumn 1981, where I recorded a number of initial interviews and made further contacts, I contacted my old Sussex friend and erstwhile colleague, Emanuel de Kadt, and invited him to co-present the series with me. Emanuel would visit parts of Latin America gathering interview material, while I would undertake what was to prove the trip of a lifetime. On 18 October 1981, I flew to Rome, home of the UN's Food and Agricultural Agency. From Rome, my schedule took me on to Cairo and Alexandria and thence to Delhi, Kathmandu, Dacca, Bangkok, Penang, Kuala Lumpur, Singapore and finally, in mid-December, to Sydney where I linked up with my family (who joined me there) for Christmas and New Year. We then returned to London in January 1982 after a stopover in Jakarta.

Throughout this global odyssey, I was able to record interviews with leading figures in national and local governments. But I also made a succession of field trips: to cotton works in Egypt, to the crowded street markets in Delhi and the dangerously eroding banks of the Ganges, to a factory in Kanpur and a UN 'Food for Work' project in rural Bangladesh. In sun-drenched Cairo, I was almost run over – just along from an auto dealer called Shady Motors – as cars raced uninhibitedly over a zebra crossing, while in Thamel, on the edges of Kathmandu, I was welcomed at a café called The Snowman's Cave where the kindly boss could scarcely believe the name on my passport.

I had never seen poverty of a kind, or on a scale, such as I encountered during the course of this trip. Walking along the increasingly treeless

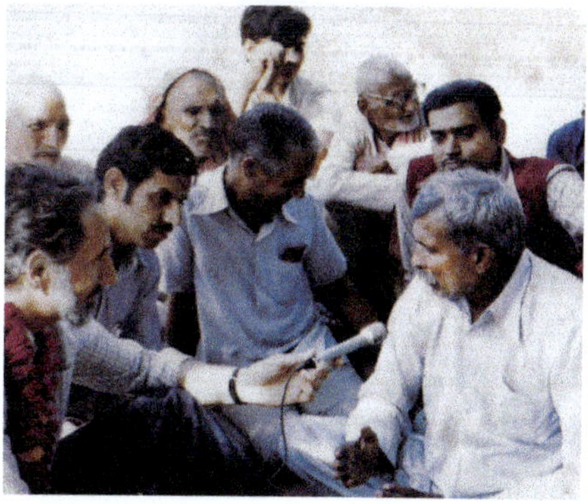

India/Nepal/Bangladesh 1981.

foothills of the Himalayas, I encountered a weary-looking woman, wrinkled and almost toothless, as she struggled to carry a heavy load of water back to her dwelling place. It transpired that she was in her late 30s, had had something like 20 pregnancies, and was simply performing one of her regular daily chores. In Bangladesh, I visited a small, remote village. Here, every family had its own little hut, often overcrowded with a host of rowdy children, and a nearby patch of soil – divided by a grass ridge from that of its neighbours – on which to grow its essential victuals. I remember thinking deeply subversive Leninist thoughts: why not remove the grass ridges between the sparse allotments and communalise the land, thereby doubling the size of its potential output? And didn't people in the Third World know about contraception, I wondered? Some did, it was explained to me, and I later visited a clinic in Dacca where I saw a long line of young women queuing up for confidential advice. But for the vast majority of the population in a desperately poor country like Bangladesh, having a lot of children – especially boys – was widely regarded as a kind of pension plan. Daughters might marry into other families. But the role of grown-up sons was to care for their elderly parents.

In an even more remote agricultural location in Bangladesh, armies of skinny, scrawny, unshaven and bare-chested men dug away at the ground, struggling to fulfil the goals assigned to them by benign but watchful representatives of the UN. I was nearly overcome with heat, thirst and general exhaustion just watching them, hour after hour, and remember the waves of relief and shared goodwill when, at the end of the day, the workers were rewarded with plenty of healthy food to eat and guaranteeably clean water to drink. Never again, I vowed that day, would I allow myself to complain about the way (for example) some opera singer had slurred a note that should have been taken 'clean', or an orchestral conductor had adopted a tempo that was a tad faster than the score indicated. Such luxuries, I felt, were almost obscene in a world plagued by the poverty and desperation I had witnessed in Bangladesh that day.

I returned from this three-month marathon convinced of the importance of what had come to be called development. That is, the economic development of the poorer countries of the world provided by those that were wealthier. This was partly a matter of basic humanity; nobody should be left as desperate and hungry as some of the people I encountered in the South when there was so much surplus wealth in the rich North. But it was also in the shared interest of First and Third Worlds for the former to help build up the resources of the latter. Thus, it had long been known that people with some level of economic and educational achievement tended to have smaller families than those lower down the social scale. It was not contraception *per se* that would slow down the rapidly rising population of the planet, but economic development. Having become a Europeanist earlier in life, I was now a convinced globalist.

When I got back to London in mid-January 1982, I relished telling my parents about my adventures. I'm glad I had the chance to do so because a month later, in February, my father died. He was 68. Two months later, on 21 April, BBC Radio 4 began weekly broadcasts of *A World in Common*.

Chapter 39

Secretive Places

The Vatican and Castro's Cuba

By the early 1980s, the world press was full of the doings (and alleged misdoings) of the Vatican. Partly, this was on account of its controversial and charismatic Pope John Paul II, the Polish Cardinal Karol Wojtyła until his elevation to the Holy See in 1978 and the first non-Italian pontiff since the Dutch Pope Adrian VI, who had died in 1523. An inveterate traveller, John Paul made over 120 foreign trips during his pontificate and created links of goodwill with Jewish and Muslim leaders as well as his nearest Protestant counterpart, the Archbishop of Canterbury. He declared himself unequivocally opposed to the rule of apartheid in South Africa and the ruthless Pinochet regime in Chile and, crucially, became an active spiritual inspiration to his fellow countrymen as they edged towards the eventual overthrow of Communism. In matters moral and theological, however, the Polish Pope was an unbending traditionalist, firmly upholding Catholic opposition to birth control, abortion, homosexuality and the ordination of women, for example, and what was coming to be known as 'liberation theology'. But the Vatican was also in the news spotlight on account of the alleged misdemeanours of its bank: a principal shareholder in the scandal-racked Banco Ambrosiana whose general manager Roberto Calvi ('God's banker') fled the country to avoid prosecution and whose murdered body was found in 1982, hanging beneath London's Blackfriars Bridge.

Bernard Jackson, a frequent broadcaster on matters religious for the BBC, suggested a year or two later that he and I might make a series about the Vatican. I thought it a splendid idea, made appropriate contacts in the British Catholic community and in due course in Rome, and we set off for a fortnight in the Holy City in spring 1985. Once there, we found the Vatican singularly difficult to penetrate. Bernard and I were given the backstage tour, as it were, and taken by junior prelates to see the Vatican treasures and into some of the holier of the holies. Various men of the cloth gave us polite interviews about the history of the Vatican and the papacy, alongside scholarly explanations of the Vatican's theological, political, social, educational, moral and economic situation over the course of previous decades and centuries. And all were full of respectful praise for the current incumbent of the throne of St Peter. But an interview with, for example, someone from the Vatican Bank, or with the Pope's stern enforcer-in-chief, the German born Cardinal Ratzinger, 'God's Rottweiler' (later to assume the Papacy on John Paul's death in 2005)? Not a chance. Bernard became irritated. Angry even. Here am I, he would say, an observant Catholic, I attend mass every week with my wife and children, and pay Peter's Pence, and they won't give even to someone like me the serious interview that the BBC is offering them. Bernard, I would reply, shrugging my shoulders with my hands turned outward, try to understand. Look. I'm a lapsed Jew and, as such, should be far more frustrated than you. But I understand how they feel. Wouldn't you if you were them? And the two of us would collapse with laughter and go off for another wine-soaked pasta dinner.

In the event, Bernard did an excellent job and the programmes were well received. And we came back with a good publicity coup. The British Ambassador to the Vatican had asked us if we would care to attend one of the Pope's regular audiences. We of course were delighted. Bernard hid

'Pope, meet Bernard!'

a microphone on his person and, as the Pope moved along the lines of attendees, surreptitiously turned it on. I didn't think we would or should use it on air, but I did not want to stop Bernard collecting what might be a treasured souvenir of a memorable moment. When it was our turn to receive the papal handshake, Bernard told the Pope that we were from the BBC and would His Holiness like to say something to the people of Britain? His Holiness smiled and said, 'Oh, I am always saying things to the people of Britain!' and moved benignly on. But we were able to retain a photo of the encounter. I like to think it looks as though I am introducing my two Catholic friends to one another.

The Pope was later beatified and canonized: the only Saint, I like to tell friends, with whom I have ever shaken hands!

* * *

The following year, 1986, Bernard and I took off for Cuba. Here, too, there was a risk of being somewhat frozen out by those we wished to interview: the island nation, just 90 miles off the Florida coast, had notoriously housed Russian missiles aimed at the USA back in 1962 and was still very much an outpost of the Soviet empire, massively subsidised from Moscow. It had been the focus of world news when, in 1980, huge numbers of Cubans had managed to make their escape to Florida in what became known as the Mariel Boatlift. When proposing the programmes – to my BBC bosses and the authorities in Havana – I made it clear from the outset that Bernard and I would not be aiming to uncover controversial aspects of the Cuban political or governmental system. Rather, we wanted to learn something about the continuing role of the Catholic church (which the Cubans proudly told us was not in any way suppressed) and, more broadly, to feature the kinds of things the Castro government would be happy to publicise: their productive agricultural sector, high employment rate, advanced medical facilities and the rest. In other words, the much-touted successes of Cuban socialism.

Bernard and I had a good couple of weeks in Havana, with occasional trips further afield, our interviews and contacts facilitated by the fact that Bernard was a fluent Spanish-speaker. We were accompanied by helpful (and politely watchful) government officials and, although we did not meet Fidel Castro, we were granted an interview with one of his closest adherents, Ricardo Alarcón, Cuba's former representative at the UN and later Fidel's Minister of Foreign Affairs.

With Ricardo Alarcón in Havana.

Between times, Bernard and I had our fair share of adventures. One day we encountered a shifty-looking character who, seeing we were foreign journalists, sidled up to us, keen to tell us (anonymously) of the human rights abuses practised by the Castro regime. We also found time to have a drink at *El Floridita* (said to have been Hemingway's favourite bar) and enjoy an evening of Cuban music. Lynn Geldof (sister of Bob) was living in Havana at the time and we spent some time with her.

In many ways, Cuba reminded me of Israel. Geographically, it was incomparably beautiful, a richly variegated geographical enclave full of healthy, well-fed energetic people proud of their nation and all it represented. The green hills and enticing beaches, the benign climate (except, in Cuba's case, during the autumn hurricane season) – everything seemed ideally equipped to welcome visitors from less privileged spots on the earth. And yet, like Israel, Cuba was also a somewhat beleaguered and isolated political entity adjacent to implacable enemy territory, its economic and military security only guaranteed as a result of huge subsidies from a far-off superpower. A few years after Bernard and I were in Cuba, Soviet communism collapsed and, with it, the hitherto somewhat thriving Cuban economy. It was another quarter century before the island, as a result of careful mediation by a Latin-American Pope and the calculated goodwill of Presidents Obama and Raul Castro (Fidel's brother), finally re-entered, at least for the time being, the normal give and take of international affairs.

* * *

Bernard Jackson and I found ourselves in Córdoba one summer. We were making a programme with (and about) the guitar and flamenco virtuoso Paco Peña who was teaching a course there with the help of the guitarist John Williams and the popular American folk singer known as Rattlesnake Annie. One steaming afternoon, as we waited for what Spaniards incomprehensibly think of as lunchtime, Bernard and I were sitting in the central square sipping cold drinks beneath a parasol, and we began to fantasise about going somewhere cooler. 'How about Antarctica?' Bernard volunteered, only half in fun. An interesting idea, I thought: but how would we ever go about it?

Once back in England, I contacted the people at the British Antarctic Survey and the Scott Polar Research Institute, both of them in Cambridge, and in March 1988 Bernard and I flew to Stanley in the Falkland Islands where we joined the BAS ship the *RRS* (Royal Research Ship) *Bransfield* and sailed south towards Signy, the South Orkney islands and the Antarctic peninsula.

Chapter 40
Cold Places
Arctic and Antarctic

One morning, after a turbulent crossing of the Drake Passage, I awoke early and, sensing that we were now in calmer waters, dressed up warmly and went on deck. I was welcomed by brilliant, almost blinding sunshine and, surrounding us, a vast, horizonless, blue ocean dotted with an irregular army of glistening icebergs that had calved off from the great refrigerator that cools the Southern Ocean: silent testimony to centuries – millennia – of polar glaciation. I was dazzled, not just physically but psychologically, by the pure, raw power and beauty by which I was enveloped. I am not often given to spiritual reflection. But at that moment, awestruck by what seemed the massive and eternal power of the universe, I began to think about the scale of the planet that I temporarily inhabited and the minuteness and essential transitoriness of little me. I turned to face northwards. There, over the curvature of the earth, would be the southern tip of Latin America; the various rocky outcrops that provided the islands we had been visiting and the Antarctic peninsula for which we were heading were, I reflected, geological extensions of the Andes further north. A little to my right, there would be Cape Town and the continent of Africa, then, further on and higher up, the Indian subcontinent, then Indonesia, Australia and New Zealand. I turned around further and tried to figure where the Pacific was placed, and the USA and then, halfway around again, my own little Europe. And I thought of all those crowded millions – billions – of people up there, in all directions, struggling with too much wealth or too little. How obscene, it seemed to me at that moment, that people in the rich world agonised over which brand of tea, toilet paper or toothpaste to buy. As we sailed on, over and beyond 60 degrees south (the official northern limit of Antarctica), I began to feel that I was on a mission to learn something far more basic about not only the ends of the earth but the future of the planet as a whole.

* * *

Over the course of the late 1980s and early '90s I was fortunate enough to make two lengthy voyages to Antarctica and three substantial trips to various parts of the Arctic. The first visit to Antarctica, with Bernard Jackson and courtesy of the British Antarctic Survey, resulted in a series of BBC broadcasts we called *South of Sixty* and which featured interviews with some of the oceanographers, climatologists, glaciologists, geologists and geophysicists who were among our co-passengers on board the *Bransfield*. These recordings were integrated with the sounds of the seals and penguins we encountered once on land, the ice-crunching footsteps and katabatic winds, and on-site descriptions (and further interviews) as we visited the science stations that BAS maintained on the Antarctic peninsula or stood alongside the remains of an old whaling station or the grave of Shackleton at Grytviken in South Georgia. Later, I was invited by the Australian Antarctic Division to join them for a similar (two-month) voyage, this time out of Hobart. From here, we sailed in a south-easterly direction, across the Antarctic Convergence where the warm waters of the temperate zones encounter the icy currents of Antarctica, across the great Southern Ocean that girdles the lower latitudes of the planet, and on down to make landfall a full continent away from my earlier voyage with BAS. Over the next few weeks I was able not only to see Australia's various science bases but we also made courtesy visits to both a Russian and a Chinese station, both of which made us warmly (literally!) welcome.

In the course of these epic voyages, I began to understand something of continental drift, stratospheric ozone depletion, climate change and how and why marsupial remains had been found embedded in the Antarctic ice. But I wanted to know more. In particular, how did the Arctic compare with its polar opposite? In between my two visits to Antarctica, Michael Green, the Controller of Radio 4, had generously accepted my proposal for an ambitious, multi-programme *Arctic Festival* of which I would be in overall charge. Among other things, the Festival went on to include a signature six-part series which I presented and produced while Oliver Walston, best known for his farming programmes, sailed the (Russian) Northeast Passage and presented the results on air, and that inveterate traveller Malcolm Billings made his way to Arctic Canada and revived for us the story of the Tudor-era mariner Martin Frobisher and his discovery of what turned out to be Fool's Gold. Meanwhile, *Woman's Hour* was dispatched to report on the soapstone sculptures and other artworks of the Inuit people of the far north. My own extensive journeyings took me to Arctic Canada, Alaska (including its oil-rich North Slope) and the adjacent northernmost points of Norway and the Soviet Union. Radio 4's *Arctic Festival* was launched in January 1992. By that time, I was sailing south with the Australians.

* * *

The ends of the earth are similar in that both are cold and, in their respective winters, each is shrouded in darkness for some 20 hours out of every 24 and correspondingly illuminated during the summertime. But in most ways they are – literally – polar opposites. The High Arctic is an ocean surrounded by land, the Antarctic a vast mountainous continent surrounded by ocean. Think of the world as a giant Christmas pudding with thick dollops of icing on the top and twice as much and twice as thick at the bottom. Antarctica is by almost any criterion far grander than the Arctic. If you were to imagine a globe of the world with the frozen regions of the far north and south exchanged, the new Arctic would reach down to Stockholm or even Glasgow. At Vostok, the Russian Antarctic base, they were recording temperatures of -80°C, far lower than anything reached in the far north. The Arctic sustains a substantial population of Inuit (what we used to call Eskimos), Lapps (nowadays known as Sami) and other indigenous peoples; nobody in Antarctica can survive for long except a few scientists with long supply lines. Politically, the Arctic is largely controlled by the nations whose land it contains; during the Cold War, the Russians and Americans faced each other across the Arctic, each side building a network of 'Distant Early Warning' sites (the 'DEW-line') and nuclear stations. In sharp contrast, Antarctica is neutral, demilitarised territory subject to an international Treaty; during the Falklands War of 1982, British and Argentine scientists based in stations 'south of Sixty' made a point of visiting each other during the height of hostilities further north. In the far north, huge amounts of oil and mineral wealth had long been routinely extracted from right across the Arctic rim. The Antarctic Treaty of 1961 forbade mineral exploitation of any kind south of Sixty.

* * *

'It must be very lonely down there,' people said when asking about my visits to Antarctica, perhaps imagining me struggling intrepidly across the ice like a latter-day Scott or Shackleton. And there was something forbidding about being one of a mere 3,000 or so people (mostly male) on a continent twice the size of Australia. But what struck me while there was, if anything, the problem of privacy. At all the scientific bases I visited, a small number of people were huddled together throughout the winter months, the personnel and essential supplies only relieved and updated each summer. Nobody was allowed to travel far without at least one companion while a central feature of life on base was the intimacy, the camaraderie, the almost clubby atmosphere prevailing. In Signy, a tiny island in the South Orkneys, social life was a cross between a working men's club, motor repair garage (complete with nudie pin-ups) and college common room. During the day, everyone was solidly at work as teams set off on field trips, collecting samples, analysing the food, age, temperature or excreta of local wildlife, or the growth of the microbes and the mosses and lichens on hillsides ravaged by wind, ice and the ubiquitous fur seals. And at night, after a solid beef stew or mutton curry, people would converge around the bar and tell tall tales into the night until, finally, each would drift off to one of the curtained bunks, the only personal patch of privacy available.

Next day, after a substantial breakfast, it was back to work. One team would be extracting cores from the (sometimes nearly 4 km) of ice covering much of the Antarctic continent. Like tree rings that tell you the age of a tree, ice cores can be analysed to reveal temperature changes over the course of previous decades and centuries and it seemed there was no doubt that, here in the frozen South, average annual temperatures were beginning to rise.

Another team was off to investigate the local penguin colony. Or perhaps the friendly flip-flop fur seals. The fur seals, once hunted almost to extinction, had apparently ceded that dubious honour to the whale. But one result of the decimation of Antarctic whale stocks had been the superabundance of that basic component of the Antarctic food chain, the shrimp-like creature called krill. Fewer whales, more krill. And this in turn led to a proliferation of other Antarctic fauna leading in the case of the fur seals to a stupendous compensatory growth of a once-threatened species. In parts of Antarctica when I was there, fur seals frolicked on every available rock or ice floe. Indeed, they were reproducing at what one scientist ruefully described to me as almost plague proportions, thereby ruining thousands of years of accumulated Antarctic flora. Today fur seals, tomorrow perhaps the whale. And if whales were to reproduce at anything remotely approaching plague proportions, who could know for sure what would happen to world fish stocks and, indeed, the whole balance of nature? Were we setting a trap for our descendants for whom, if global warming didn't get them first, there lay in wait the great sub-oceanic Leviathan?

* * *

My journeys to Antarctica were by ship, but my first trip to the frozen north meant a mere three-hour flight from Toronto. As I looked casually out of the adjacent window, the thick woodlands beneath me gradually became thinner, the vegetation drier and more brittle, the foliage clearly struggling for survival in a harsh climate, their roots tough but shallow in a thin topsoil above intermittent rock and permafrost. Trees, stunted grey-green conifers, often stood at a rakish angle to the ground, their roots struggling to embed themselves in the frozen bedrock. Gradually, as we left the boreal forest of the sub-Arctic, the trembling aspen and balsam poplar gave way to the thickets and heathers of the tundra, while the brave willows and dwarf birches were by now bending almost drunkenly horizontal in their desperate efforts to retain a roothold. I watched as the forestlands of the North Canadian Shield grew ever more sparse, giving way to mosses and lichens that clung to outcrops of rock where they could. At first, the wooded landscape had merely seemed to be interrupted by occasional lakes, still frozen perhaps, winking back at the welcoming sunlight. But as we flew ever further north, the whole vast topography beneath me moved from being lake-spattered land to what looked increasingly like an island-filled ocean. Lakes grew in size, multiplied and became linked one to another like amoebae, the visible manifestations of a continental drainage system that – as in northern Russia – takes dramatic form in a series of north-flowing rivers, most notably in Canada, the great Mackenzie. At the mouth of the Mackenzie (as with the Ob, the Yenisei and the Lena) you encounter a silver sea of gleaming ice. And across this? The great archipelago of the Canadian High Arctic.

* * *

My three Arctic visits, each lasting around three weeks, took place in 1991: to various locations in the far north of Canada in May, then in June to Alaska and in July and August, accompanied by Birger Amundsen from Norwegian Radio, to northern Norway and on into Arctic Russia. All this was just around the time the Soviet system and the Cold War were edging towards their end, and I thus found myself able to move around the Circumpolar North with an ease that, a mere year or two earlier, would have been unthinkable. On the third of these trips, after a brief sojourn in the Norwegian port city of Kirkenes, Birger and I sailed across the Barents Sea to the Russian port of Murmansk, home of the Soviet nuclear fleet, and from there delved deep into the Kola peninsula to spend a day in the tiny town of Lovosero, heart of Russia's Sami community. In Stalin's time, especially during the War, Sami culture was all but obliterated. Many families were removed from the land and the language was virtually proscribed. By the time I visited, a cultural thaw was already becoming visible as children were being educated in the traditional forms of reindeer herding, wearing native costumes and reviving the language of their indigenous forebears.

Similar trends were observable right around the circumpolar north: in Arctic Canada, for example, where I went out with dog teams to meet Inuit elders who told me with pride of the revival of traditional drum-dancing and throat-singing (both of which I recorded for my BBC series), and of the native language, hunting skills and survival techniques they were teaching to their children and grandchildren. As with native people elsewhere (among Australian Aborigines, for example), I heard much excoriation of the abuses imposed earlier by cruel and/or selfish white merchants and missionaries who, uninvited, had tried to 'civilise' them. The result – in the Samilands of northern Norway or the heart of the Kola peninsula, as in the Arctic villages of Alaska or the mouth of the Mackenzie – was a revived native culture that essentially straddled the ancient and the new. One day in Arctic Canada I was welcomed to an Inuit home in the far north: the father showed me the fresh (and still bloody) skin of a caribou that he and his sons had recently hunted and, as we sat down to a hearty meal of caribou meat, they switched on the television to watch tennis live from Wimbledon!

In Iqaluit, on Baffin Island, I met a spirited young Inuk woman who worked for a Canadian radio station. Suzanne was completely fluent in both English and Inuktitut and told me that one of her jobs was to broadcast news stories in both languages. I asked how she managed this during, for example, the recent Gulf War. Were there words in Inuktitut for 'Desert Storm', for example, or 'Scud missile'? Or even 'sand'? She laughed, acknowledging that on matters such as these she had to think fast and offer approximations. 'But everyone says that you people have

ABOVE *Antarctic penguin colony.*
RIGHT *Approaching Antarctica.*
BELOW *In Arctic Canada.*
BELOW RIGHT *The book that arose from my five visits to the polar regions, the weather kitchens of the world where long-term climatic trends are cooked.*

lots of different words for snow', I said, warming to my cold theme. 'Yes, of course,' replied Suzanne, pointing out that in the far north they had lots of different kinds of snow: soft snow, crystal snow, flaky snow, the hard icy stuff that you can carve into blocks if you want to construct an igloo. And they all need a word to describe them. 'Yes, I suppose so,' I conceded – at which Suzanne shot back in her turn that we Brits had lots of words for rain – and for the same reason. We might say it was pouring or showering or drizzling. Indeed! Not only superbly bilingual, Suzanne was also perceptively cross-cultural. We Inuk people, she said, love our children. Our young mothers harness their babies to them, face to face. Yes, I'd seen that, I said with a smile, thinking about the elegant prams used by young parents back home in London and wondering what I was going to hear next. 'But you people put them in what look like shopping trolleys and push them around with their backs towards you!' Game, set and match to Suzanne.

Suzanne interviewed me for her radio station and, inevitably, much fun was made of my absurdly appropriate (or inappropriate) surname. But, as I no doubt repeated *ad nauseam* to people back home, the name 'Snowman' helped open many an igloo door during the course of my Arctic travels.

* * *

Elsewhere around the Arctic rim, economic development had produced environmental destruction, sometimes on a massive scale. From Murmansk, Birger and I returned to Norway by train. As we chugged northwest along a single-track line up and across the Kola peninsula, I watched as the landscape changed. We were some 70 degrees or more north, on the very treeline where boreal forest (or taiga) meets tundra, the soil too thin and sandy and the winter cold too intense to permit any but the hardiest trees and shrubs to grow.

Every now and then the train would halt for half an hour alongside some tiny village with a double track to enable a train to pass from the other direction. At one, we were able to disembark and I mingled with my fellow-passengers: students from Moscow doing a summer job, an old peasant couple who looked as though they had walked out of a Chagall painting and a consignment of pimply young soldiers who, evidently somewhat bewildered, were told that this was where they had to get off. Why? They weren't sure. I soon found out. As the train eventually continued its lazy journey, through dusty grasslands dotted with the occasional struggling birch tree, there came into view a fleet of 40 or 50 military vans parked a mere hundred metres or so from our track. Just beyond them were piles of scrap metal, abandoned trucks and other vehicles and a compact of derelict huts surrounded, like the wagon circles of old, by artillery. The entire site was littered with rusty oil drums and pieces of discarded machinery: a torn rubber tyre here, a gnarled railway sleeper there. What I was witnessing was the last gasp, or yawn, of the Cold War, a demoralised military camp occupied by people whose political and professional *raison d'être* had been eroded by the forces of history. For 40 years, this region had been closed to all but authorised personnel, one of the most militarised areas in the world. Now (mid-1991), a trainful of ordinary civilians, not to mention foreign observers such as myself, could steam past free to observe, comment upon, photograph or film.

Our train journey continued into the mouth of a living hell, the dying forestlands giving way to huge, steaming, slag heaps. My nose began to block and my throat go dry as, through a thick chemical haze, I began to make out the silhouette of tall factory chimneys belching poisonous effluent into this dead, lunar landscape. This was Nikel, a Communist-era town built, as its name implies, to support an important nickel mining and smelting works. Long a source of income, Nikel attracted workers from Moscow, Kiev, Tashkent and further afield, keen to benefit from the high Arctic wages on offer, the decent homes and schools and the relative absence of street crime and other big city scourges further south. In Soviet times, you did not complain (out loud at least) about the asthma, headaches, bronchitis and lung diseases so prevalent in the area. But by the time I was there, people were beginning to talk, even – perhaps especially – to foreign visitors, about the self-evident environmental dangers: the streams of sulphuric smoke pouring perpetually across the town and surrounding hillsides, the crumbling buildings, the hopelessly inadequate healthcare facilities. Salvation, I was told, would not come from Moscow. Russia needed the nickel and was in any case in a state of political and economic turmoil. But perhaps the nearby Scandinavians could help. Or the kind, generous Canadians. Maybe, someone suggested cheerily, global warming might lead to Russian cargo ships being able to sail across the Northeast Passage to Vladivostok and, thereby, hugely increase trading opportunities with the countries of Asia.

What I was hearing was the early stirrings of something unthinkable until then: a nascent sense of circumpolarity. Once safely (and healthily) back in Kirkenes, I encountered Alexei, a young man from Murmansk who was visiting Norway as a tourist. Someone asked him to sign a local petition organised by the local 'STOP DEADLY RUSSIAN CLOUDS' campaign, and he willingly did so. He and the Norwegians were talking vigorously in fractured English. Could such a conversation have taken place five years before? 'Of course not,' laughed Alexei. Russia, it seemed, was coming out of the cold.

While in Arctic Norway, I had the chance to fly up to the Svalbard islands. I spent some time in the capital Longyearbyen and a couple of nights with the scientists in that ultimate Arctic outpost, Ny-Ålesund. One of my happiest memories was how, on a visit to the mining town of Barentsburg, I fell in with a genial and generous group of Russians. We shared food and drink and one of them picked up his balalaika and sang some wonderful sentimental Russian songs. I was entranced. On my return to London, one of them sent me a book of traditional Russian folk tales. I couldn't read a word of it but was thrilled to hear from him.

* * *

After my return from my Arctic and Antarctic travels, I wrote a book entitled *Pole Positions: The Polar regions and the future of the planet*. Was that final phrase a little pretentious? Perhaps. But my polar trips confirmed and reinforced a profound sense of the interconnectedness of everybody and everything on this little earth of ours. Thus, the proliferation of fur seals or the increase of stratospheric ozone, both of them the subject of scientific study, could each contain long-term lessons about the changing ratio of people to resources. We humans are all merely animals and, as such, one element in the global food chain: what we consume, eject, destroy (including our bodies after our death) – everything is cycled and recycled. As for the potential shifts in global climate, the Arctic and the Antarctic are the weather kitchens of the world; it is here that the long-term climatic trends are cooked. One day, as the *Bransfield* sailed gently along the edge of the Antarctic continent through the thin ice and scattered bergy bits of the Southern Ocean, I stood alongside a distinguished glaciologist. Half a century earlier, he told me, these waters would have been frozen. Our ship was, in fact, sailing where, in Scott's day, there was a sheet of impenetrable ice and the ocean level was lower. At the other end of the world, in the far north, I saw icebergs calving off from what until not long ago had been thought of as permanent ice sheets, and greenery sprouting on land which had until recently been covered with almost impenetrable permafrost.

One way and another, it was here at the ends of the earth that future global trends, on land, sea and in the air, could first be identified and most clearly measured. Just as after my extended visits to parts of Asia a decade earlier, I returned from the polar regions to the more temperate zone of England convinced that humanity would be foolish to disregard or underrate the messages clearly demonstrated in the far extremes of the earth. Even if we were to survive nuclear weaponry, terrorism and possible pandemics, I wondered, who knows what levels of Malthusian destructiveness might be visited upon us and our successors from the increasingly warm heavens above or, perhaps, from the deep and rising oceans below?

One result of my book was the emergence of the concept of 'Nominative Determinism': a hypothesis (first proposed in 1994 in the magazine *New Scientist*) that some people seemed to gravitate, perhaps subconsciously, towards areas of work that reflected their names. 'Snowman' on the Arctic and Antarctic seemed to prove the point (as did, for example, the urologists Splatt and Weedon). Fun. But utterly wrong in my case certainly – and no doubt, too, in that of Britain's former Lord Chief Justice, Igor (Lord) Judge!

Book 8

Meanwhile . . .

Chapter 41

Kissing Cousins *and the 'Ifs' of History*

Whatever was preoccupying me professionally or wherever I found myself travelling, I always tried to keep up my reading and writing. Almost to the point of obsession, some might have thought at times! Whether at Cambridge, Cornell or California, at Sussex, the BBC or over the years since, I was forever grabbing a copy of this or that book or article, drafting a new feature or review for publication and, throughout much of my adult life, working (or planning to work) on a new book I was writing or editing. You had to pass the time somehow, I used to joke!

My first book, which the publishers, Batsford, entitled *USA: The Twenties to Vietnam*, appeared in 1968; it was then issued in the USA by Harper & Row as *America Since 1920* followed by a succession of updated editions by Heinemann Educational Books in the later 1970s and early '80s. I followed this up in 1970 with a contribution to an international series focusing on 'Women Who Made History' published by the Geneva-based company Edito-Service. I had first considered undertaking a biography of the hugely talented yet deaf and blind American writer Helen Keller but, in the end, decided to pick another of my heroes (or heroines), Eleanor Roosevelt, the wife and widow of Franklin Delano Roosevelt, the longest-ever serving US President (who died in April 1945). Throughout her time as First Lady and subsequent widowhood, Eleanor was an avowed internationalist and a prominent advocate of women's rights and civil rights more generally. She pressed the USA to join the United Nations in 1945, was appointed a delegate to the General Assembly and went on to become the first chair of the UN Commission on Human Rights.

With Eleanor Roosevelt, as in almost everything else I went on to write, my aim was to understand the people, events, institutions and ideas I was highlighting by placing them within their widest historical context, to cross traditional intellectual boundaries and incorporate social, political and cultural insights and much else. The next book was originally suggested by my former Sussex friend and colleague Peter Burke, one of the most brilliantly cross-cultural intellectuals I have ever known. The publisher Maurice Temple Smith had commissioned Peter to write a book about the elites who governed early modern Venice and Amsterdam, the first of a series of comparative studies Temple Smith was planning to undertake. Peter kindly suggested that I might contribute to the project. The idea was that I would compare and contrast the historical attitudes and values of those two great nations so dear to me, the United Kingdom and the United States. The ever-enterprising publisher liked the idea and the book was duly commissioned.

* * *

I began working on this during my year in Los Angeles, 1972–73. Indeed, as mentioned above (Chapter 37), the new commission was one of the principal reasons I was keen to spend further time in the States, and the academic appointment gave me just the opportunity I needed. Whether I was lecturing, travelling, socialising or simply relaxing, everything seemed to integrate in one way or another with the research I was undertaking for the forthcoming book. Already, when at Cornell a decade earlier, I had noticed what I took to be a more disciplined and perhaps routinised

Daniel at work on typewriter (photo from 1968).

American attitude towards work, and a greater literalism regarding (for example) the wording of law and legislation, or the symbols of rising or falling social status, than anything comparable in Britain. Now, as I became accustomed to life on the West Coast, I revisited, rethought and, when appropriate, adapted some of these earlier impressions.

Americans, I sensed, tended to be more future-oriented than their British cousins. More achievement-oriented, too, perhaps – with achievement likely to be assessed (in a society that had deliberately eschewed official titles of honour) primarily in terms of wealth or status. The US was a society, too, that valued what, for want of a better term, I labelled 'transitoriness'. In Britain, several generations often remained in the same area or dwelt in the same home. In America, a nation whose very history was imprinted with the move across a continent in search of a new frontier, most people I knew seemed recently to have moved their home or job or were contemplating doing so or were changing their car or TV set for a newer and better model. Everyone and everything seemed to be on the move in a quest for improvement. Behind this lay an almost unshakeable optimism, the old American Dream that, if you retained an open mind and were prepared to take calculated risks, problems could usually be solved, things made better. At BBC meetings, the boss would sit at the head of the table, deputies on either side, and programme proposals were sometimes turned down on the reasoned grounds that they might not work. At Dominguez, novel ideas were mostly met with 'Great. Let's try it!'

The book, *Kissing Cousins: An Interpretation of British and American Culture 1945 to 1975*, was initially published in the UK (and in the USA as a Harper & Row paperback) in 1977. Much of the text dealt with historical and current contrasts between the two. But it had become increasingly evident to me, particularly when I returned to study British sources, that the cultural norms and values of post-War America were coming increasingly to infiltrate those of the UK. British people were beginning to talk of 'grass roots' and 'touching first base', placing the accent on the first syllable of 'television' and 'research', becoming ever more litigious and learning to demand their rights and enjoy the pleasures of acquisitiveness. My final chapter was entitled 'The Americanization of British Culture?'

* * *

In one of my BBC projects, I invited several historians to imagine themselves as some all-important figure in the past at what proved to be an important turning point. Suppose, for example, you were Benjamin Franklin in the 1770s; might you have been able to find a way to keep the peace between England and the American colonies and thus avoid the American Revolution? Or could you, as Kerensky, have adopted a different policy towards the Russian Bolsheviks in summer 1917 and thereby pre-empted what in fact became the Revolution of October that year? Later, I expanded the series into a book, with a number of further contributions, and wrote an introduction reflecting on the quasi-philosophical question of whether and to what extent events in the past could have worked out differently. The more we know about the events of the past, I argued, and the further back in time the relevant events occurred, the more they seem to us to have been inevitable. As we turn towards the present and recent past, by contrast, we tend to posit a degree of freewill, of being able to choose between alternative possible futures. The book appeared in 1979. It was published by Robson Books, the company founded by my cousin (and poet) Jeremy Robson. We called the book *If I Had Been… Ten Historical Fantasies.*

A decade or two later, the whole topic of what came to be dubbed 'counterfactual' history had become one of the more controversial and widely discussed amongst leading historians (among them Niall Ferguson and Richard J Evans). It is good to think that we had been able to make an important early contribution to the debate.

Chapter 42

The Amadeus Quartet

It was Jeremy who suggested in early 1979 that I might like to write a book about the Amadeus Quartet. Or, rather, it was an idea suggested to him by his friend (and mine) the poet Dannie Abse who also knew Siegmund Nissel, who played second violin in the ensemble. I approached the quartet, went to have an initial meeting with the cellist, Martin Lovett, and we agreed I should meet his colleagues and perhaps sit in on a rehearsal. Over the next couple of years, I got to know all four members and their families as well as their agents, publicists and record producers, and in autumn 1979 joined them in Munich for a few days where they were recording the Verdi quartet for Deutsche Grammophon.

The Amadeus Quartet were, for almost forty years, the leading ensemble of their kind, certainly in the UK and arguably the world. Three of the members – the leader, Norbert Brainin, Sigi Nissel and the viola player Peter Schidlof – had all come to Britain in the late 1930s as refugees from Vienna and, in the early years of the war, all three had been temporarily interned (when asked where they met, they used to reply 'in prison!'). After release, all went on to do whatever they could to help the war effort and, in due course, found themselves mixing among the musico-cultural circles of northwest London where they met the young cellist Martin Lovett through his Hungarian-born wife (and violinist) Susi Rosza. The foursome launched themselves as the Amadeus Quartet at a hugely successful concert at the Wigmore Hall in January 1948 (where one of the works they played was the Verdi). From that moment until the death of Schidlof in 1987, their path was a triumphant and unparalleled progress, give or take one or two minor problems along the way: a temporary illness, a poor hotel, a cancelled plane, inadequate rehearsal time. For decades, reviews talked about the uniquely 'Viennese' style with which the Amadeus, more than any other quartet, continued to play the great works of Mozart, Beethoven, Schubert and the rest.

I gradually got to know the Amadeus as both colleagues and friends and tried to penetrate both their music and the music-making: the art and the personalities. I sat in on countless rehearsals at the homes of all four and, mini score in hand, watched and listened as these very different characters gradually made the most wonderfully lyrical sense out of the cold notes on the page. Norbert, larger than life (I once dubbed him the 'Falstaff of the fiddle'), was hugely expressive, as both musician and man. Playing with what sometimes seemed almost dangerous élan (and a wide vibrato), he was a fearless leader. 'Oh, that's awful,' he would expostulate looking pained at one of his colleagues who, Norbert was convinced, had taken too literally and suddenly a *fortissimo* marking. 'It should be more sensitive,' he would plead, going on to play the passage with his own inimitably seductive lyricism. The others would look at each other, recognising his genius and long accustomed to the almost schoolboy petulance with which it was sometimes expressed.

Nissel, usually the least talkative of the four in rehearsal, was the diplomat. As both man and musician, Sigi ensured there was harmony between the colleagues. A brilliantly engaging and witty man (married to the equally talented social statistician Muriel Nissel), it was Sigi who negotiated with the agents, arranged the schedules and generally made sure everyone was happy with what they had agreed to undertake. His subtle musicianship enabled him to emphasise, or de-emphasise, the role of second violin

Daniel with Amadeus Quartet.

Amadeus Quartet book launch. L TO R *Norbert Brainin, Martin Lovett, Daniel, Peter Schidlof, Siegmund Nissel.*

when required and to allow greater priority at any given time to whichever instrument the score demanded. Sitting alongside him, the taller, balding Peter Schidlof embodied a kind of old-world, Habsburg elegance, the subdued but golden sound of his viola melding to perfection with that of the three other instruments. 'Peter could make music out of a cigar box,' said one of his colleagues admiringly. Lovett, the youngest of the four and the only one born in Britain, understandably felt a little marginalised at first as the other three cracked jokes to each other in German. But with his tall good looks, superb musicianship and questioning mind, he soon came to be a fully integrated member of the ensemble.

Watching the quartet up close, I learned something of the problems and fulfilments of their tightly integrated life together. It was not true (as some who claimed to know them liked to say, semi-seriously) that the foursome yelled and screamed at one another in rehearsal. Vigorous discussion, yes; tantrums, no. And once they were on the concert platform, they would launch into whatever it was they were playing with incomparable unity and purpose. All this I tried to describe. It was not easy to write openly and honestly about artists currently before the public. As I explained to them at the outset, I did not wish to hurt people whom I genuinely liked and admired. But nor did I want to write mere hagiography. Under the circumstances, it was courageous of them to agree to take me on, and into their confidence, as they did.

The book was published in 1981 as *The Amadeus Quartet: The Men and the Music*. In some ways it was the seed that grew into all the books I was to write later.

On 5 March 2017, at a reception following the keynote talk I had given at the Royal College of Music to mark the 90th birthday of the one surviving member of the Amadeus Quartet, Martin Lovett, I was approached by a representative of Deutsche Grammophon, the company for whom the Quartet had made the bulk of their recordings. It seemed DG were planning to issue a box-set containing CDs of all their many Amadeus recordings, and they were hoping I might agree to write the accompanying essay about the Quartet, their life and the nature and quality of their music-making. I was delighted, got down to work and, to this day, I treasure the resulting box of musical delights.

Chapter 43

The World of Plácido Domingo

It is mid-morning in New York, June 1981, and the temperature is already creeping up towards the mid-80s. In Central Park there are the usual cyclists, joggers, softball players, dog walkers and, doubtless, muggers and rapists. On the park's Great Lawn, huddled near a huge temporary dais to which workmen are putting the finishing touches, is a group of several hundred opera buffs who have come to stake out territory for tonight's free, open-air performance of Puccini's *Tosca*. Behind the dais, a number of musicians seek shelter from the sun as they await the start of this morning's rehearsal, and gulp down gallons of iced orange juice. Among them is James Levine, Music Director of the Metropolitan Opera since 1975 and Principal Conductor for the past nine years, which must mean since he was about twelve by the looks of him.

The title role tonight will be sung by Renata Scotto and her lover, the romantic painter Cavaradossi, by Plácido Domingo. Domingo, born in Spain and raised in Mexico, is in his element in this heat and his eyes immediately adapt to the glare. He has turned up this morning sporting a long-sleeved, light blue striped shirt and a pair of sparkling white trousers; he looks like an off-duty admiral come to survey his fleet at anchor. Eventually, everyone climbs up onto the dais and the orchestra strikes up the opening notes of *Tosca*, the big, ominous chords associated with the evil police chief Scarpia, sung on this occasion by the big, handsome American baritone Sherrill Milnes.

As the scorching day progresses the initial few squatters are joined by thousands more, all happy to while away the time with food, drink, sunbathing and opera gossip. By 8.30pm, when the performance begins, nearly a quarter of a million people – in sweatshirts and torn-off jeans, with beads and beards, some with tents, most with blankets and many with picnic hampers – have streamed in from all parts of New York and beyond and are by now spread over several acres of parkland ready for things to begin.

It was at that Central Park rehearsal that I first met Domingo. During the decade since I had first heard him in Los Angeles, I went to many of his

Sherrill Milnes, Renata Scotto and Plácido Domingo in Central Park, New York, June 1981, after rehearsal of Tosca.

performances, mostly at Covent Garden. Then in 1981 the *Sunday Times* invited me to write a feature about him for their new colour supplement: it would be tied to Domingo's forthcoming 100th appearance at the Royal Opera House and his 150th performance of *Tosca*, and my piece would be illustrated by the paper's chief photographer at the time, Lord Snowdon, the former husband of Princess Margaret. In June I went to New York and introduced myself to Domingo at that *Tosca* rehearsal and told him about the *Sunday Times* commission, and we agreed we could spend some time together (with Snowdon) the following month when Domingo would be singing *Otello* at Bregenz on Lake Constance.

* * *

Snowdon was one of the most renowned photographers of his day. He came across as a thoughtful, serious, somewhat shy person, fastidious in his tastes, aesthetic to his fingertips, anxious to avoid as far as possible the glamour that had sometimes been heaped too excessively upon him. Small in stature, unassuming in manner, but accustomed to having his way. 'Is that SnowMAN?' he asked, the first time he phoned me; 'this is SnowDON!' During the couple of days or so that he was in Bregenz, word of his presence soon spread and various smooth local grandees began to press their attentions on him. Some even confused us, addressing me obsequiously as 'Lord Snowman'. I think 'Mr Snowdon' was amused too.

'You realise, Daniel,' Snowdon told me drily as we sat down to dinner in Bregenz the night before we were to meet Domingo, 'that you are talking to a man who knows nothing whatever about opera.' 'That's all right, Tony,' I replied, as engagingly as I could, and assured him I knew even less about photography. Conversation remained professional. 'What makes Domingo tick?' he asked. 'What sort of friends does he have? What does he eat? What does he do in his spare time? Is he a happy person? What drives him? Tell me about his family.' I answered as best I could; I had spent the previous few days watching Plácido in rehearsal for *Otello* (not for Bregenz's vast floating amphitheatre but for performance in the classier Festspielhaus) and he and I had also found time to get together over a long, relaxed lunch. Snowdon then fixed his penetrating blue eyes on me and asked equally direct questions about myself, my interests, my BBC work, my home life. I remember feeling a slight resentment that, quite clearly, I was not permitted to reciprocate with any questions about himself.

Around noon the following day, Plácido called to invite us over to the great hillside chalet in which he was staying. I introduced the tall, dark, gregarious Spaniard to the fair, dapper British earl and we all got down to business. After a few initial photos we agreed we'd go into town for lunch: my job was to engage Plácido in conversation while Tony would spend much of the time snapping. I remember wondering, as he took shot after shot, whether the secret of being a good photographer wasn't simply the ability to take hundreds of pictures in the reasonable expectation that at least one or two of them would work out well. After lunch, the three of us trooped off to the huge lakeside theatre where they were setting up for a production of *West Side Story*. Plácido, obeying instructions, stood in front of the gigantic set, arms outstretched in delight as Tony took yet further shots. This was the image the *Sunday Times* used alongside my article when the piece appeared in November. But the photo they placed on the cover of the magazine was emphatically *not* by Snowdon: a great open mouth showing tongue, teeth and prominent epiglottis. They called my article 'The Man with the Golden Larynx'. By the time it appeared I was far away, travelling in Southeast Asia (see Chapter 38).

* * *

Daniel with Plácido Domingo and (left) the BBC's Dan Zerdin.

In the *Sunday Times* article, I wrote at some length about both the man and the artist, and Plácido was kind enough to say he thought it one of the best pieces that had been written about him (though he was less pleased with the cover picture of his full-frontal epiglottis!). Soon afterwards, I was commissioned to write a book in which I described Domingo at work on a wide range of undertakings: rehearsing in the great opera theatres of the world and many that were less known, learning new roles, conducting operas and concerts, recording both opera and a more popular repertoire, filming, collecting a succession of honours and, almost everywhere he went, giving interviews in various languages.

During the course of time, I got to know not only Plácido himself but also his wife (Marta) and family, his personal assistant (Paul Garner), many of his friends and also the agents, managers, lawyers, accountants and professional colleagues around the world who were the inevitable part of his busy life. Whenever I felt I could take time off from the BBC, I spent time watching him at work. The conductor Riccardo Muti told me that he would be conducting Domingo (plus Mirella Freni and Nicolai Ghiaurov) in a spectacular new production of Verdi's *Ernani* with which to open the 1982–83 season at La Scala: a good reason to spend a week or more in Milan, witness all the final rehearsals and attend the opening night. A month in New York in early 1983 enabled me not only to watch Plácido rehearse and perform a number of roles at the Met Opera but also to accumulate material from their archives and record interviews with celebrated operatic veterans for my BBC feature later in the year to mark the Met's 'centennial' (see Chapter 33). In May 1983, Domingo was at Covent Garden working with Kiri Te Kanawa on a new production of Puccini's *Manon Lescaut*. Then there was *Tosca* at the Barcelona Liceu, after which I followed Domingo to Madrid, the city of his birth, where he was rehearsing for a production of Puccini's *Fanciulla del West*. Here I met Plácido's mother who assured me with a laugh that her son 'was always like that, even as a child!' when I remarked on his restless, apparently superabundant energies. That summer, in Ronda in Andalusia, I watched as Francesco Rosi shot the night-time mountain sequences of his *Carmen* movie with Plácido as Don José. While in Ronda, I spent time with the Domingos at the home they had temporarily rented and sat down with Plácido one day to record a lengthy interview, which I later edited into a pair of half-hour programmes for BBC radio: a good, professional excuse for having been absent from my London office for a week or more! Then it was on to *Die Fledermaus* at Covent Garden, which Plácido conducted, performances of *Carmen* at the Vienna State Opera and much else.

* * *

As with the Amadeus Quartet, I tried to describe Domingo at work on a variety of projects while also placing both man and artist in a wider context. Chapters focusing on the New York Met, the Barcelona Liceu, La Scala or Vienna's Staatsoper, for example, would include something about the history and atmosphere of the house concerned, the opera being rehearsed and the colleagues with whom Plácido would be working. What inner drives led him to work so hard, I wondered, to travel so much, to learn and perform so many roles (in his New York apartment he had a cushion embossed with the words: 'If I Rest, I Rust')? By the time I first got to know Plácido he had already clocked up some 1500 performances (twice as many as Callas during her entire career) and close to 50 complete recordings of opera, while he was also keen to do more conducting. The Swedish soprano Birgit Nilsson used to joke that, among his many skills, Plácido was a great linguist: he could say 'Yes' in some half a dozen languages but didn't know how to say 'No' in any of them!

Further questions suggested themselves as I watched this enormously gifted and versatile man at work. Why were so many of the great romantic roles in opera assigned to the tenor voice (and did Domingo ever find himself identifying with the parts he was called upon to play)? And what were the main differences – and similarities – between Domingo and his supposed rival and near contemporary, Luciano Pavarotti? As a young man, Plácido had taken on some of the higher, lyrical tenor parts with which Pavarotti came to be primarily associated, but he had soon gravitated towards the dramatic *spinto* roles more suited to the dark, muscular, almost baritonal quality of his voice; Domingo first sang Otello, arguably his signature role, at the early age of 34. While much of what I wrote was about opera, I also described Plácido at work recording his first crossover albums, including songs by Sammy Cahn, the Beatles, Andrew Lloyd Webber and others. What led him to do these? Was he seeking wider celebrity, more money? Perhaps he just enjoyed the good popular music of his day, just as Caruso, Gigli, Tauber and Ezio Pinza had all done before him.

As I looked (and listened) back over operatic history since the birth of recording, I tried to assess where Domingo stood in comparison with some of his celebrated contemporaries and predecessors. In many ways, his voice quality was reminiscent of the later Caruso, minus the 'protruding jaw' mannerisms and with a cleaner *portamento*. Possibly less 'heroic' than Melchior or that passionate stage animal Jon Vickers, without the easy top of a Schipa, Kraus or Gedda and, for some, lacking the silvery seductiveness of Gigli, the greatness of Domingo, I felt, lay in his capacity to bring together qualities from each of these and to combine and synthesise into his own art a dazzling array of qualities rarely, if ever, found in a single artist. While his sense of lyrical style placed him in a league with Pavarotti and Bergonzi, his voice had the deeper tones of the *tenore drammatico* more commonly associated with Martinelli or Corelli. Probably no other tenor since Jussi Björling had had quite this combination of vocal gifts (and Domingo was a far better actor).

When my text was completed, I sent a copy to Plácido and, a little later, went to his London home just off the King's Road in Chelsea and, after a genial dinner at a nearby restaurant, he, Marta and I spent the evening going through everything and anything that any of us felt might warrant minor revision. I remember Plácido taking gentle issue with comments in my text to the effect that he was something of a workaholic. Of course he worked hard, he said, but reminded me that, while many singers needed to spend time (and money) going to a professional coach when learning to master the details of a new role, he had the basic musical and pianistic skills to teach himself a new role in the comfort of his own home. It was what he enjoyed doing! We checked a few spellings here and there, softened an occasional comment that he or Marta thought might upset a colleague and, in sum, agreed upon a text that we all felt was fair.

I handed in the text on time and suggested to my publishers, The Bodley Head, that they name the book after Otello's joyous exclamation at the outset of Verdi's great opera: '*Esultate*!' They demurred (for good commercial reasons) and it was called instead *The World of Plácido Domingo*. Published in 1985, it sold well and soon appeared in paperback and a number of foreign languages including German, Spanish, Japanese and Hungarian. Over the next few years, I kept in touch with Domingo, attended many of his performances and produced a second book about him, this time to accompany a four-part BBC TV series which I had proposed and co-produced. And then, in 1995, things came to an abrupt halt (see Chapter 46).

Chapter 44
Choral Interlude

'Ladies,' snarled the Chorus Master. 'Please look up at Sir Adrian when you reach your climax!'

Nobody sniggered. Frederic Jackson was not the kind to resort to *double entendre*, except by accident, while Boult, his mind evidently above such

Sir Adrian Boult and the LPC recording at Kingsway Hall – Frederic Jackson, chorus master.
(Photographs courtesy of the London Philharmonic Orchestra)

puerilities and his normally ramrod back bent with the strain of age, glanced at his watch, clearly anxious to get on. But the comment was typical of Freddie Jackson in some ways, at least by the time I joined the London Philharmonic Choir in 1967. I recall his plaintive, slightly tetchy air, eyebrows raised as though in incomprehension at the inadequacies of lesser mortals. I admired him and his musicianship. But I was somewhat in awe of him, terrified that, with his brilliant ear and impatient persona, he would pinpoint my individual failings and humiliate me in front of everyone else.

I joined the Choir almost by accident. At a Christmas 1966 party, I met an American woman called Reymour Rice and we talked about music. I told Reymour about my love of opera, my choral singing at Cambridge and Cornell, and how Sussex had given me time off to write a book about 20th-century American history. I was thinking of spending the time in London I said – moving to London, possibly. 'Why don't you join the London Philharmonic Choir?' Reymour asked, to my incredulity. I wasn't good enough, I protested, I couldn't sightread well enough and had

Concert at the Royal Festival Hall: view from the bass section of the chorus.
(Photograph courtesy of the London Philharmonic Orchestra)

had no proper musical or vocal training. All the usual excuses. But she persuaded me to go to a rehearsal or two and, through the good offices of the Choir Secretary, Miss Norah Cash, I was lined up for audition by the aforementioned terrifying Freddie Jackson.

Norah was, if anything, even more fearsome. Dressed from head to toe in black, her grey hair in a bun in a net, cigarette dangling from lower lip, Norah was a character from Dickens. The RE teacher from Dotheboys Hall perhaps. Her skin, what she permitted you to see of it, was as tightly scraped as her hair. So was her speaking voice – hortatory, with a distinctive touch of cockney. 'Don't sit on those chairs!' she would call across to an innocent bystander, or bysitter. 'Can't you read the notice I've just put up?' Clearly, this was a personage not to be crossed.

I prepared for my audition and, fancying myself a bass in the Pinza or Kipnis mould, brought along one of Sarastro's arias from *Die Zauberflöte*. Freddie seemed to be unworried by the wide vibrato that resulted from my extreme nervousness. But he was not very impressed by the watery bottom F with which my aria ended. He let me join but sent me away for some singing lessons with an elderly lady called Miss Hartnell who lived near Holland Park (fairly standard procedure, I discovered, which made me wonder whether he and Miss Hartnell had an 'understanding' of some kind). A few weeks later, this time with a more sensible piece from *Messiah*, I was re-auditioned, had evidently made progress, and became a fully-fledged member of the LPC. My first concert was *Gerontius* with Boult at the Royal Festival Hall in March 1967.

* * *

By the time I joined in 1967, the Choir was twenty years old. Many of my colleagues were founder-members; some of the older ladies wore hats to rehearsal (and a few keen souls even brought their knitting along to pass the time before the singing began). We were certainly a more formal – and perhaps formidable – lot in those days. Isabelle Cheetham, an alto who joined in 1965, recalled that back in the '60s there was a rigid seating hierarchy. Isabelle didn't dare join those she regarded as the formidable 'front row forwards' (Margaret Driver saw them as 'Prefects') but slipped in towards the back instead where she often found herself next to 'Phyllis the Foghorn'. All of which, I remember thinking at the time, seemed to be reflected in the somewhat churchy way the Choir tended to sing. Rehearsing in the hall alongside Westminster Cathedral, it seemed to me only appropriate that many of the gentlemen wore suits and even young artsy types like me always wore a tie. Most people, I surmised, had probably come into the Choir through the English church tradition rather than via the more exotic operatic route that had propelled me, and they all seemed to know works like *Messiah*, the great Bach Masses and Passions and the Elgar and Vaughan Williams oratorios the LPC sang regularly in those days. I remember a wonderful *Gerontius* we did in Canterbury Cathedral in March 1968, with Janet Baker an incomparable Angel. The performance was filmed (in colour) by BBC TV and included some clever close-ups of the Cathedral's gargoyles, shown as we were singing the Demons' Chorus.

I learned to love the great liturgical compositions that were our bread and butter in those days. I also pined to get my vocal cords around some operatic choruses (which on a few rare occasions we did; for example, we recorded parts of *Carmen* with Marilyn Horne under her then husband the conductor Henry Lewis). But in general, we sang the 'holy' rather than the 'profane' works, and I recall deeply satisfying performances of, for example, the Brahms *Requiem* under the spellbinding Jascha Horenstein, and the *St John Passion* under the reigning Bach expert Karl Richter (this was before the 'Authentic' movement pulled the Bach rug from under our feet). Above all, I remember my first Mahler 'Resurrection' Symphony under the young Bernard Haitink.

Haitink became Principal Conductor of the London Philharmonic Orchestra in autumn 1967 and I have the clearest memories of his early work with the Choir: Britten's joyful *Spring Symphony*, the Bruckner *E minor Mass* – and Mahler. For the 'Resurrection' Symphony, the conductor's piano rehearsal was held in London University's Gordon Square Theatre. We were warming up as Haitink, courteous and pensive, arrived quietly and sat at the side. Personally retiring, evidently uneasy with any kind of pomp or speechmaking, this not especially prepossessing figure, then in his late 30s, patiently awaited his turn and then, with a pencil for a baton, stood before us.

There then occurred the most overwhelming transformation. Arms outstretched, head cocked, eyes alert, left hand shaking with the tense vibrato of a former violinist, Haitink immediately marshalled us to produce the most disciplined yet deeply felt *pianissimo* '*Aufersteh'n*'. Here was a conductor capable of transporting us to levels of musical and perhaps spiritual consciousness of which I would have presumed myself incapable. The idolatry of the amateur? Maybe in part. But it was simply beyond my

Young Bernard Haitink in rehearsal.

comprehension how someone could, at one and the same time, give full rein to the vast, dangerous forces unleashed by the likes of Mahler and Bruckner while simultaneously retaining ultimate intellectual and physical control over them. Some conductors seemed to me to impose too much facile discipline upon the works they performed, while others would yield too easily to maudlin romanticism. Haitink, invariably placing the music ahead of personal ego, seemed again and again to get the impossible balance just right. On occasion, this great, modest man, incapable of silencing the bravos of an ecstatic Festival Hall audience after a shattering performance, would finally pick up the score from his conductor's podium and hold it aloft as though to deflect the applause from himself to the composer. Haitink's personal reticence masked what was clearly a powerful musical mind and personality, and he was instrumental early in his tenure with the LPO in removing Freddie Jackson.

Early in 1968, the LPO Board minutes report that Jackson had been 'invited to retire from the post at the end of this, his 21st season as Chorus Master'. He was succeeded the following year by John Alldis. Alldis was the founding chorus master of the London Symphony Chorus (LSC), and he also had his own highly successful professional choir, the John Alldis Singers, one of the leading professional ensembles of its time. Jackson died soon afterwards, in the midst of conducting a performance of the Verdi *Requiem* at the Royal Academy of Music.

* * *

Once Alldis took over the LPC, we were all re-auditioned. Of the pre-existing couple of hundred or more, about 70 survived the Alldis cull but the Choir was all the better for it, the more so as a number of LSC singers followed him into his new choir. The number of hats in the soprano section was greatly reduced, their places taken by comely youngsters with ringing high Cs and a gearless *passaggio*. Out went large-scale Bach (except for an ethereal *B minor Mass* in 1977 under Giulini), and in came – inter alia – the world premiere of David Bedford's *Star Clusters, Nebulae and Places in Devon.*

The new-style Alldis-trained London Philharmonic Choir now rehearsed in the Bishopsgate Institute opposite Liverpool Street Station: perfect for the City gents who had sung their way successfully through the Alldis audition and bearable for the large cohort of fellow Wimbledonians whom John had apparently brought with him. Under Alldis, the quality of the choir soon rose, as did the numbers of young singers applying to join. At concerts, particularly for weightier works, our numbers and quality were still sometimes boosted yet further by the addition of professional singers, perhaps four or five per section. This caused resentment among some members (and incurred further expenditure by our parent body, the London Philharmonic Orchestra), though it never bothered me. I just wanted to participate in the very best concerts of which we were capable.

In 1970, John Alldis mentioned to me that he felt the Choir needed 'a Chairman figure', someone to represent the interests of the Choir to the orchestra and wondered whether I might be interested. I certainly was – though I did wonder what my responsibilities might be. In the event, all it meant was that I had ready and easy access to top LPO management, was able to pass on any ideas I might have about possible repertoire (I remember suggesting the Verdi *Pezzi sacri*) and could attend all and any LPO rehearsals or concerts that took my fancy. One of my innovations as Chairman was to conduct a social survey of the Choir in order to try to obtain and codify material about the age, background, professional interests and domicile of members. The results proved useful in everything from recruitment campaigns to organising rides home from remote venues.

I loved attending orchestral rehearsals and spent many hours at the Royal Festival Hall watching the LPO under Haitink, Pritchard, Krips, Barenboim and Horenstein – and also, with one excuse or another, at the BBC's Maida Vale studios watching the BBC Symphony Orchestra working with Boult, Bliss, Boulez, Colin Davis and others. And I reported from the one to the other. One day at Maida Vale I sat in on a BBC studio recording of the Strauss *Four Last Songs* with a young soprano from the London Opera School who, despite her long hair and dark, girlish good looks, took me aback with the mature womanliness of her voice. Her name, I learned (from an enthusiastic cellist who had asked for her autograph as an excuse to chat to her), was Kiri Te Kanawa. Next day, at the RFH and during the interval of an LPC rehearsal of the Brahms *Requiem*, I was talking to Haitink and reported on this impressive young soprano. Politely, he asked me her name and I did my best to remember it.

Our soloists in those days tended to be sopranos such as Heather Harper, Sheila Armstrong and the creamy-voiced Margaret Price; mezzos Norma Procter and Helen Watts and, on occasion (including the Canterbury performance of *Gerontius* and the Giulini *B minor Mass*) Janet Baker; the tenors Peter Pears, Richard Lewis and (later) Robert Tear; and the bass-baritones John Carol Case, John Shirley-Quirk, Norman Bailey and Raimund Herincz. Herincz was a character. I remember him kidding with the basses as we rehearsed Handel's *Messiah*. He was about to launch into 'The trumpet shall sound and the dead shall be raised!' But he swore he always sang 'The strumpet shall pound and the bed shall be praised!' and that nobody in the audience ever noticed!

In addition to concerts, recordings continued to provide an important segment of the Choir's activities during the 1970s and '80s. We made many recordings, among them Elgar's *Apostles* and *Dream of Gerontius* under Boult, Tennstedt's Mahler *Eight* and the Brahms *Requiem*, Solti's super-dynamic *Belshazzar's Feast* and Haitink's prize-winning recording of the Vaughan Williams *Sea Symphony* – a work some of us had recorded earlier under Boult.

Sir Adrian Boult was often caricatured, by Gerard Hoffnung and others (and in countless Beecham vs Boult stories), as what we would nowadays call a wimp: the man who drank milk instead of wine, or whose impassivity on the rostrum bred spiders' webs. But in truth he was a lion of a man, a passionate pacifist, a great musical innovator in his day, the archetypal Englishman yet utterly at home in the sophisticated world of Wagner, Brahms and their successors and of his own great professional predecessor Arthur Nikisch. Boult could not abide sloppiness. On one occasion, the bass Forbes Robinson turned up slightly late for an orchestral rehearsal (it was *Gerontius* again). Boult began – dead on time, of course – and as he reached the first entry for the bass soloist he looked up, saw his man rushing in and called out in his stentorian sergeant-major voice: 'Sing it from there, Mr Robinson!' and the poor fellow, shamed in front of 250 people, had to admonish us to 'Go forth!' before even having a chance to take off his coat. But I noticed in the interval that Boult went up to Robinson, smiling, put his arm over his shoulder and made it abundantly clear that the incident was closed.

This was typical of Boult. Discipline, dedication, professionalism were all-important. I saw that at close hand when, in 1968, we made that recording of the *Sea Symphony*. The venue was the old Kingsway Hall: London's Methodist Hall which, while doubtless ideal for the sermons of Donald (later Lord) Soper, was a difficult place in which to record music, since 'takes' had intermittently to be suspended to accommodate the subterranean rumblings of the Tube trains. During one of our sessions with Boult, I jotted down the following dialogue. It seems Sir Adrian had been upbraiding the alto section of the Choir on and off for the past twenty minutes for sounding 'woolly'. Then, finally, they were OK. Boult relaxed at last:

AB Why do you need to be cajoled and shaken and bullied and abused by someone with a wicked tongue (like yours truly) when you can sing perfectly well all the time? Please spit out all the words clearly!

Alto Sir Adrian, may I say something? *(consternation all around)*

AB Yes, please! Say anything you like! Stand up and shout. Clearly! *(nervous laughter from chorus)*

Alto Well, we heard everything you said then, but we often can't hear clearly what you are saying to us. *(VERY nervous laughter . . .)*

AB Congratulations!! But why didn't someone say that to me twenty minutes ago? You deserve a gold medal … but I don't have one to give you!
(consternation relieved; ensued by excellent singing!)

At the end of the final session, everyone applauded Boult, who said: 'You know, I've spent the past four days making nasty noises, while you've spent them making lovely noises!'

One can gain some idea of Boult's methods from a recording made by EMI of one of our rehearsals for a performance and recording of another Vaughan Williams piece: his *Pilgrim's Progress* (in 1970). The Choir was having difficulty with one of VW's syncopations. Boult rehearsed and re-rehearsed us. He was patient yet firm, with not a second wasted. He tapped the rhythm for us several times with his long conductor's stick. We still found it difficult, so he got the brass to play their parallel passage for us. Eventually we got it right, and that was the end of the matter. Once a problem was successfully surmounted, all was sweetness and light. As it happened, I lived near Boult, just off the Finchley Road, and occasionally saw him in the street. Even into his 80s, Sir Adrian liked, on principle I think, to use public transport. Once, I happened to sit near him on top of a bus as it made for his office above the Wigmore Hall and mine in Broadcasting House, and overheard him telling the man next to him how, when he first came to London at the beginning of the century, grass had covered the area on which they were soon to build Admiralty Arch. Then there was the occasion, a few days after the *Sea Symphony* recording, when we both emerged from the same tube train at Finchley Road Station. At the exit I approached Sir Adrian and told him I had been in his Choir and how much I had enjoyed the experience. The old man smiled benevolently, touched his black Homburg hat and agreed that the sessions had been 'absolutely splendid'.

Boult never over-rehearsed, knowing he'd have us eating out of his hand if he let us off early (he'd tell us how Elgar sometimes ended a rehearsal early – but that was usually so that he could go off to the races!). Boult was particularly considerate on the day of a concert. Typically, he'd look at his watch and say: 'Well, ladies and gentlemen, you've all worked jolly hard. There are still one or two places where things aren't quite right. But you are musicians. You know what the problems are and how to solve them, and I'm sure we'll all get everything right tonight.' A brilliant way to ensure we were all on our mettle at the concert. I wish I'd asked him when I had the chance whether Elgar pronounced *Gerontius* with a hard or soft G . . .

* * *

In 1979, Georg Solti succeeded Haitink as Principal Conductor of the LPO. A larger-than-life personality, Solti's enthusiasm and sheer animal magnetism took one over from the start: head lowered, dark eyes alert, elbows and wrists vibrant for action, knees apart like a boxer. His vitality could overwhelm as he would coax, cajole, charm, bark, sing (in the harshest voice of any musician I have ever known) or whistle his commands, call you his 'dears', grip shoulders, rush to the piano, beat out a rhythm with his pencil, tell a risky joke or bend you to his will by sheer force of personality. People used to make fun of him. 'If he's got such a great ear,' people asked in their supercilious English way, 'how come he's still got such a strong Hungarian accent?' His answer was that he'd grasp your shoulder and, his exuberant features inches from your face, say: 'Ah, yes, my deah. But just sink how many langvages I can speak viss ziss accent!' Back in the 1960s, when Solti had been Music Director at the Royal Opera, some critics had found his performances over-energised (and to some in the orchestra he acquired the nickname 'the screaming skull'). But I, as an occasional audience member, had found them exhilarating and was thrilled at the prospect of singing under his ever-watchful eye. The results were incomparable performances that brought out the essential drama of text and music alike: not just the fiery dynamics of Beethoven, Berlioz and Verdi but also the unquenchable optimism of Haydn and Mahler and the sheer elegiac beauty of (for example) the Mozart *C minor Mass*.

John Alldis retired in 1982, his place taken by Richard Cooke, and a year later Solti was succeeded as Principal Conductor of the LPO by Klaus Tennstedt. This extraordinary man, tense, nervous, apparently uncertain of his own tremendous talents or of his physical ability to communicate his wishes, descended on the London scene from nowhere, as it seemed, and yet was to become a mighty tower of musical achievement in the 1980s. Tennstedt's core repertoire was similar to Haitink's, though nothing like so extensive. I recall deeply felt performances under Tennstedt of the Beethoven *Ninth* and Mahler *Two*: 'Already you are too loud!', he would hiss in his droll way at a Mahler rehearsal before we had uttered a sound at our *pianissimo* entry. The Choir also sang a slow, visionary Brahms *Requiem* for him at the 1984 Proms with the exquisite Lucia Popp as soprano soloist (very different from the monumental Jessye Norman with whom we had just recorded the piece), while Tennstedt also led the Choir in a joyous Haydn *Creation* (also with Lucia Popp) and a surprisingly raunchy *Carmina Burana*.

It was with Tennstedt that we recorded Mahler's *Eighth Symphony*, the so-called 'Symphony of a Thousand'. Sessions took place at Walthamstow Town Hall, the only available venue large enough for a giant enterprise involving not only the London Philharmonic Orchestra and Choir but also eight soloists and a boys' choir (from Tiffin School: chorus master, the young Neville Creed). The recording won a Gramophone award.

Klaus Tennstedt made an incomparable impact on the Choir. One of the great occasions was the first time we performed Schoenberg's *Survivor from Warsaw*, a seven-minute piece in which the male chorus sings for a mere 90 seconds. We men had the privilege of sitting behind Tennstedt's orchestra for the rest of the evening: an absolutely riveting performance of Mahler *Five* and surely the broadest, most risk-running performance I have ever experienced. Tennstedt adopted dangerously expansive tempi with massive, idiomatic *rubato*, all communicated via a highly idiosyncratic stick technique, held aloft by his peculiarly unnerving legs-apart-knees-together stance. With anyone else, the interpretation would surely have fallen apart. But – as with Furtwängler or the elderly Klemperer – Tennstedt had such a powerful musical personality that, despite the ostensible infirmity of his beat, the players instinctively knew what he wanted and just how to deliver his interpretation. Poor Tennstedt suffered: physically (throat cancer, hip replacement), and I think psychologically. Seemingly incapable of pacing himself, Tennstedt would throw 110 per cent of his energies into rehearsals, and then yet more into performances. Inevitably, he found himself forced to cancel from time to time. When the London Philharmonic Orchestra scheduled three Royal Festival Hall performances of Mahler *Eight* (the work we had previously recorded with him) for late January 1991, few of us believed he would materialise. As a matter of fact, we weren't sure that *we* would, as the December run-up to those concerts included Walton's *Belshazzar's Feast* under Leonard Slatkin and, a week later, Prokofiev's *Alexander Nevsky* with Kurt Masur, plus the inevitable pre-Christmas carolfest, while we were also rehearsing the Stravinsky *Symphony of Psalms* for a concert with Franz Welser-Möst in February, immediately after the Mahlers.

The three Mahler *Eights* did materialise as planned, and Tennstedt was positively magisterial. After the relentlessly powerful first movement,

Mahler stipulates a five-minute pause. Most conductors wait a decent interval, mop their brow, look round and pick up the stick for the far longer remaining section of the symphony. Tennstedt walked off the platform, and for an alarmingly long time. Had he finally succumbed in mid-concert to one of those illnesses, we wondered? No. He was just making full use of Mahler's long break. I remember being absolutely exhausted around that time and don't suppose I actually sang the Mahler *Eights* very well. But the performances were stupendous and filmed for television (the BBC's first foray into high-definition TV). And Mahler's granddaughter added icing to the cake by gracing us with her presence.

* * *

During the year or so preceding those legendary Mahler *Eights*, my choral colleagues became accustomed to my bringing recording equipment to selected rehearsals. I was making a pair of BBC Radio documentaries about the Choir. In one, I decided to concentrate on three major and unusual events: *Messiah* conducted by Solti, the new recording of Vaughan Williams' *Sea Symphony* with Haitink and Haydn's *Creation* under Simon Rattle. All three conductors agreed to co-operate. Neither Solti nor Rattle (nor the Choir or Orchestra for that matter!) was especially associated with late (or post) Baroque music, and I was able to capture on tape the conductors' strenuous attempts to get us to sing in a more springy, staccato style than we (or, frankly, they) were used to for the *Messiah* and *Creation*. Haitink, meanwhile, was coming to the *Sea Symphony* for the first time but, characteristically, studied the work deeply and (as you can infer from the award-winning recording that resulted) fell profoundly in love with it.

The other programme was about the Choir itself, its history, its members, its *esprit de corps*, and included among other recordings some made during a trip to Snape to perform Benjamin Britten's little known *The Company of Heaven*. In addition, the LPC's long-term secretary Sheila Lewis held a little party for Choir members one evening at her Dolphin Square London flat where I was able to record some uproarious personal memories. Sheila herself recalled the behatted lady in the Freddie Jackson days who regarded 'bellies' (in Britten's *Spring Symphony*) a rude word, even though it was set to rhyme with 'shellies', and she always sang 'tummies' instead. Then there was the time Norah Cash, with utter insouciance, ordered everyone to hand in their *Unknown Regions*.

I suppose we were still at our best in English music from the church tradition; certainly our reviews, of a recording of Elgar's *King Olaf* under Vernon ('Tod') Handley for example, emphasised the 'incandescent' quality of our singing, especially the sopranos. What was allegedly lacking, at least according to critics, was a more 'continental' sound, a phrase seized upon by the youthful Franz Welser-Möst when in 1990 he took over as the LPO's Music Director in succession to Tennstedt.

* * *

After the departure of chorus master Richard Cooke in 1991, the London Philharmonic Choir and Orchestra both went through difficult times. Political philistinism and/or economic recession meant that Arts Council money was tight and sponsorship opportunities limited, and the LPO found itself starved of adequate funding. This was not helped by the fact that the London critics did not take to Welser-Möst (a talented young man in a job that was too big for him, they implied) while for a couple of years the Choir had no permanent chorus master. They eventually found him in the person of Neville Creed, former head of music at Tiffin School (whence he had collaborated with us on the Mahler *Eight* recording) and conductor of the Bournemouth and Guildford choirs. Neville's high musical standards, accurate ear and beat, allied to an attractive, upbeat public persona, succeeded in bringing a flagging LPC out of the doldrums just in time to give creditable performances with the LPO of the Britten and Verdi *Requiems* under Welser-Möst, Berlioz concerts with the ever-exuberant Roger Norrington, Beethoven's *Ninth* and the great Bruckner *Te Deum* with Haitink and, most memorable of all, two stunning concert performances of Verdi's *Aida* under the charismatic and, as always, scoreless Zubin Mehta.

Then in 1996 came the divorce between orchestra and chorus. The hard reality was that the LPO could no longer afford to provide work for the Choir; henceforth, the LPC would have to sell its services in the marketplace if it was to continue to exist. But for every snake there is a concomitant ladder, and the Choir found itself performing in a host of new, unfamiliar venues: Guildford Cathedral, Petworth, the Milton Keynes Bowl and many another. There were collaborations, too, with other London orchestras in similar difficulties: concerts, starting in the later 1990s, with the Royal Philharmonic Orchestra, the London Symphony Orchestra and the Philharmonia. And around the same time, the impresario Raymond Gubbay started promoting concerts of popular classics aimed at a wide general audience, for which he would often engage the LPC. We soon found ourselves signed up for evenings of little-rehearsed opera choruses, Christmas carols and the occasional Beethoven *Ninth* for Gubbay at the Royal Albert and Barbican Halls. As an unreconstructed opera lover, I could hardly complain about having to sing, several times a year (and sometimes twice in a day!), some of the great surging choruses of Verdi & Co that still touch my heart.

Then there were foreign tours. Back in August 1979, with Alldis still at the helm, the Choir had visited Wilhelmshaven in northern Germany to sing with a local wind ensemble. Then in 1998 and 2000 it undertook two tours to Spain where, inter alia, we sang at Madrid's magnificently restored Teatro Real. Don't think foreign trips are a doddle. On these two Spanish trips we performed two of the more difficult works in the choral repertoire. Tippett's *A Child of Our Time* was the composer's response to the assassination by a young Jewish boy of a Nazi official in Paris in November 1938 that led (in the very week I was born, as it happens) to the obscene horrors of *Kristallnacht*. It is a searing work, a kind of musical equivalent of Picasso's *Guernica* (which many of us went to see while in Madrid), containing some almost unsingably fierce fugal themes rendered bearable by the balm of the 'Negro spirituals' Tippett incorporates. The Beethoven *Missa Solemnis* is the craggiest peak of them all, a relentless, 90-minute masterpiece by a wilful genius apparently oblivious to human limitation. Performing the *Missa* is a constant encounter with risk, a jagged journey across musical and vocal terrain that sometimes feels almost impassable. Yet alongside passages such as the rapid fugal setting of 'Et vitam venturi' in the Credo, which is almost beyond the capacity of mere human beings to sing at high speed with total accuracy, Beethoven also has passages of transcendent delicacy. In Spain, we performed both works under the baton of the hugely talented conductor García Navarro who, sadly, was to die not long afterwards.

Trips abroad were very good for recruitment. The LPC had a wonderful few days performing the Verdi *Requiem* at the Canary Islands International Music Festival in January 2003 with soloists of the quality of Petra Lang and René Pape. The Choir was housed in the most sumptuous hotels – absolutely palatial in Tenerife – and members obtained special pleasure, as they sipped cool wine out on the terrace, from gloomy reports of sleet and snow in London.

A year after the Canaries, in January 2004, the Choir was in Rome performing Mahler's *Resurrection* Symphony for Pope John Paul II at a Vatican 'Concert of Reconciliation'. This was in many ways a political rather than an aesthetic occasion. Coming in the wake of the controversial US-led war in Iraq in 2003, the concert brought together a Turkish (i.e. Muslim) choir, one from the Polish Pope's former home town of Krakow (Catholic), the LPC and an American orchestra (the Pittsburgh) and Jewish conductor, Gilbert Levine, in a work of spiritual reconciliation and resurrection. The Mahler was preceded by the world premiere of a short choral work by the US composer John Harbison about the biblical Abraham, a father figure to Jews, Christians and Muslims alike. Maestro 'Sir' Gilbert Levine (a Vatican knighthood) clearly relished the occasion, demanding excessive rehearsal time, some of it in full evening dress, largely for the sake of the ubiquitous cameras. The eventual concert was filmed, and the resulting video reveals our knightly maestro coaxing a towering performance of Mahler *Two* from his monumental forces. However, respect for the truth requires me to report that the video was inter-cut with footage from all those earlier sessions for, in the concert itself, several of Levine's punctiliously rehearsed details came out far from perfect while, out of deference to the age and fragility of the Pope, only the first, fourth and fifth movements of the Mahler were actually played!

None of this dampened the symbolic significance of the occasion. I had been in the immense Audience Hall before, when making my series of BBC programmes about the Vatican in the mid-1980s. On the occasion of our papal concert nearly 20 years later, the hall was filled with dignitaries, amongst whom were not only a sea of red-capped cardinals but also the leading rabbis and mullahs of Italy. When the Pope was wheeled into the hall, everybody applauded and, like the celebrity he was, the ailing, ageing pontiff smiled, waved and clapped back. I thought he looked ruddier and less shaky than of late as he sat, attentively enough give or take the occasional surreptitious yawn or glance at his watch, through the (foreshortened) performance. At the end, Levine mouthed something to his orchestra that looked like *Aufersteh'n*, lifted his baton and plunged into an encore. This was something that, for all our days of rehearsal, we had not been warned about. Gradually, the choir cottoned on to the alarming fact that he had begun from the fortissimo climax of the piece so, bar by bar, we gathered courage, joined in and, by the end were singing full throttle. Someone said it was like watching a giant airliner cruising down the runway, gathering speed until, eventually, it decided it had the guts to fly. It was a great occasion, much reported by the world's media. At the conclusion, the Pope had himself wheeled up alongside our multi-cultural, multi-faith choir to wave and smile his thanks. Afterwards, at a grand reception, the LPC Chairman Peter Taylor, still in black tie and dinner jacket, carried a tray of drinks over to some colleagues; as he passed, a cardinal helped himself to a drink, presuming our Chairman to be one of the waiters!

Book 9

Fin de Siècle

1989–95

Chapter 45

Past Times (and Good Company)

If my extended visits to the hot and cold places on the planet led me to reflect on its possible future, I remained at heart a historian, keen above all to understand how things had come to be the way they were. In the run-up to the bicentenary of the French Revolution in July 1989, I was invited to produce the BBC's prestigious Reith Lectures. Originated in 1948, these were named after the Corporation's founder John Reith and intended to embody the highest ideals of public service broadcasting.

I went to France to find my lecturer. In Paris and beyond, I met a number of the leading French intellectuals and historians of the day, and my succession of contacts led me to the literary critic, poet, translator and cultural polymath Jacques Darras. Unlike many of his compatriots (and British Francophiles), Jacques was a resolute northerner. Not for him the dewy-eyed romanticisation of Provence and the Midi. Born not far from the Channel, Jacques first learned his English in Scotland and he had a love of Celtic art and Flemish architecture, long shadows, thick clouds, heavy cakes and rich autumnal colours. Author of a book entitled *Le Génie du Nord*, his translations into French included the poetry of Walt Whitman, Ezra Pound, David Jones and Basil Bunting while his conversation would be peppered, quite unselfconsciously, with references to Dufay and Josquin, van Eyck, Erasmus or the political benevolence of Philip the Good of Burgundy.

From the outset, we agreed that his lectures would focus on the multi-layered historical and cultural connections between France and Britain and, building up our ideas, we travelled together to some of the locations that had meant most to him both personally and intellectually, recording material as we went for an introductory documentary programme. We drove to Artois and Picardy, to the picturesque city of Laon (a 'City of Light' during the Dark Ages) and to the acres of war graves commemorating the mindless massacres of the First World War. We visited Brussels and, in particular, the Grote Markt or Grand-Place, and I took Jacques across the highlands and islands of north-western Scotland. The first time we sat down to go through the Reith Lectures in some detail was on the sands of Iona one

With Jacques Darras.

bright morning in May. On this rocky little outpost, once the seat of Celtic Christianity, we talked of St Columba and of Robert Burns, of heroism and failure, and of the destructive passions of Louis XIV and Napoleon. At the time, the British and French were collaborating on a project that people on both sides of the Channel had long dreamed of (or feared): a tunnel linking the two nations. The French had developed such a plan back in Napoleonic times. Now at last it was happening. Jacques and I developed a series of programmes that we entitled *Beyond the Tunnel of History*.

In those days, the Reith Lectures still took their original form of a six-part weekly series of 45-minute scripted monologues. With Jacques (and the agreement of my BBC superiors), we broke the traditional mould. In a succession of studio sessions in Paris and London, I sat opposite Jacques as he spoke in his accented but idiomatic English from carefully prepared notes. Occasionally, I would intervene, ask a question, suggest a further point or possible example, and then remain silent as he backtracked and then continued uninterrupted. The results were edited into what became a series of passionately delivered and clearly unscripted monologues enabling this committed cultural pluralist to reach a wide audience with his reflections on the symbolism of the great city-squares of northern

Daniel at work in BBC studio.

Lucie Skeaping learning Bangladeshi music.

Europe, its rivers and transport systems, its war graves and, in an era of rapid change and much talk of a 'common European home', its shifting ideologies. It was surely time, argued Jacques, that the narrowly national histories on which we were all nurtured were replaced by a greater emphasis on our shared European past. As he spoke, Soviet Russia was experiencing the exciting yet challenging process of what was dubbed *Glasnost*. And shortly after the lectures were first broadcast, the Berlin Wall came down. As I said in my introduction to the book arising from the series, Jacques Darras was 'a poet, professor, historian, citizen of Europe and, like all good poets, something of a seer.'

* * *

My love of history and of music came together in a number of programmes in the later 1980s and early 1990s, many of them featuring the versatile singer, instrumentalist and broadcaster Lucie Skeaping. Best known at the time for her two groups, 'The City Waites' and 'The Burning Bush', Lucie and her colleagues (and husband Roddy Skeaping) had researched and revived the popular ballads and street songs of early modern England and also those of both the Eastern European and Hispanic Jewish traditions.

In 1989, Lucie and I visited Spain, a nation just then struggling to revive something of a rich multi-cultural historical legacy that had for decades been brutally suppressed under the Francoist dictatorship. Everybody was conscious of the approaching quincentenary of that all-important year 1492: to some Spaniards that of the heroic unification of their nation under the 'Catholic Kings' Ferdinand and Isabella as well as the triumphant transatlantic voyage of Columbus, to others the year that marked the final, brutal expulsion of Spain's hitherto peacefully co-existent Jewish (Sephardi) and Muslim populations. During our visit, through meetings with a wide variety of scholars and musical groups in and around Madrid (and nearby Toledo), Lucie and I were able to construct a richly evocative portrait in sound of what we called the *Songs of Sepharad*.

A year later, she and I collaborated on a series of Radio 4 programmes (*Songs my Mother Taught me*) each of which featured the music of one of the national and ethnic groups that had settled in various parts of Britain, among them a Bangladeshi community in Edinburgh, Latvians in Leeds, Greeks in Birmingham and a Chinese group in the Wirral. Later, we made a further series (*On the Road for a Song*) exploring traditional music in different regions of the British Isles. Every one of these programmes ended with Lucie herself learning and performing a song in the appropriate language and style, to relevant instrumental accompaniment which she also learned but was primarily provided by the community concerned.

I also included the City Waites in a number of documentaries, notably a major feature in 1991 to mark the 500th anniversary of the birth of Britain's King Henry VIII. This programme included a substantial contribution, recorded as we visited appropriate sites, by the up-and-coming young Tudor historian David Starkey, and I named the programme after the most famous of Henry's own musical compositions (superbly performed by the Waites) *Pastime with Good Company*. Altogether, and with interruptions for other work, production of this programme took about six weeks. Ten years later, my successors at the BBC were under pressure to produce a high-quality feature or documentary programme of this kind in a matter of just a few days.

* * *

Other projects at the time included a series of Friday evening introductions to some of the operas that Radio 3 was scheduled to relay the following night. Aled Jones, whom I invited to present the series, was formerly a celebrated child singer and now, in his mid-20s, keen to get himself established as an adult broadcaster. Aled was not particularly expert on opera. But I made sure that the programmes included not just the story of the opera concerned but something about the historical context in which it was created, and Aled read his scripts with a cheery enthusiasm that undoubtedly helped attract wider audiences to Radio 3.

I also produced a number of programmes with the opera historian Roger Parker, notably a powerful feature he had written about the death of Gaetano Donizetti. One of the most talented and creative of opera composers, Donizetti sank into serious mental decline as a result of progressive syphilis and died when just 50 in April 1848, his passing scarcely noticed as it coincided with the outbreak of the revolutions that were spreading across Europe at the time. The programme included quotations from letters to and from Donizetti, as well as plenty of musical examples. The soprano Susan Bullock, soon to become a major international star on the operatic circuit, joined us when we made the programme and generously offered to play the piano excerpts Roger had prepared so that he could concentrate on recording his linking commentary.

Chapter 46
Plácido Redivivus

For a while, in the early 1990s, I found myself living something of a double life (I speak here purely professionally). In addition to performing my day job as a radio producer, I was also heavily involved, on a freelance basis, in a major television project which I proposed, helped to produce and for which I wrote the accompanying book.

In 1992, I went to Seville with Dennis Marks of BBC Television and the independent producer Martin Rosenbaum. Domingo was in town (appearing in *Carmen* of course!), and we had set up a meeting with him. I introduced my colleagues to Plácido and explained that our idea was to film him at work on a number of forthcoming undertakings. 'What are the most challenging projects in your diary?' I asked him. The famous brow darkened and furrowed as Plácido seemed to sense opportunities and dangers. 'Everybody has seen your performances on television,' I went on, 'and many people presume you can just fly in and perform to a near-perfect standard every time, just like that.' Domingo nodded. 'What people don't realise is just how much hard work goes into the preparation of one of your roles.'

This interested him. He disliked the way the world's press were by then portraying him as part of an international operatic jet set, flying around the world to perform 'his' Canio, Don José, Rodolfo or Cavaradossi and gaining all the plaudits. Here was a chance at last to show people something of the effort and commitment that underpinned his legendary portrayals. During the discussions in Seville, and a series of subsequent meetings with Martin and myself, Plácido told us of a *Ballo* here and a *Carmen* there. There was a TV *Tosca* to be shown live all over the world from the original locations in Rome, and did we know about the new Plácido Domingo competition ('Operalia') to be launched in Paris? We learned of the *Tabarro-Pagliacci* double act, when he would be singing at both of Vienna's opera houses on the same night, and about early plans to reunite the 'Three Tenors'. What we had in mind, Martin and I emphasised, was something even more ambitious: not so much the glamorous events as the artistically demanding ones, and we began talking about new roles

Domingo was planning to learn, new productions that would stretch him to the limit, and of his secondary career as a conductor. Eventually, we settled on four truly challenging undertakings over the course of the next couple of years in four opera houses in four different countries.

In December 1992, Martin and I (with the director Donald Sturrock) set out for Vienna. Here, we watched as Domingo learned and mastered the challenging role of Siegmund for his first appearance in Wagner's *Ring*. He was able to teach himself the basic score and text at the piano, but he needed linguistic coaching in order to render his German pronunciation more idiomatic, and we also filmed him (and his Sieglinde, Waltraud Meier) throughout the long and demanding production rehearsals. By now, it was becoming clear that Domingo was the only tenor from the Latin/Mediterranean world capable of making a serious impact in the Wagnerian repertoire. In late summer 1993 we went to Los Angeles to watch (and film) as Plácido prepared to conduct *La bohème* and to New York in September where, back in his accustomed role as singer, he rehearsed a spectacular new production of Verdi's *Otello* at the Met by Elijah Moshinsky. And the following June to Bonn where he undertook the title role in *Il Guarany* (a Latin American 'Indian' complete with flowered headdress) by the 'Verdi of Brazil', Carlos Gomes, in a production by the controversial film director Werner Herzog. The TV series that resulted was quite unprecedented and showed, for the first time, the huge expenditure of time, effort, money, energy and sheer artistic skill and imagination upon which the entire operatic edifice depended. The programmes were first aired, and my accompanying book published (by BBC Books), in autumn 1994.

A year later, in September 1995, I was invited by Los Angeles Opera to give a lecture in the Dorothy Chandler Pavilion as part of an education day to inaugurate their 1995–96 season. This was scheduled to begin a few days later with Domingo starring in Verdi's *Stiffelio* for which rehearsals were taking place on stage while the education day continued in another part of the building. When my lecture was done, I crept into the main auditorium and sat in on the end of the rehearsal after which I knocked on Plácido's dressing room door to pay my respects. Marta was there with him. She greeted me with an icy stare and proceeded to upbraid me for the way I had 'used' my friendship with Plácido over the years for my own selfish purposes. I was taken aback. True, I had only approached Plácido when working on a book or article or radio or TV project about him, and never felt I had a right to the kind of access normally given only to a close

Werner Herzog with Plácido Domingo (in Il Guarany*).*
(Photograph courtesy of the BBC and the photographer Emma-Louise Ogilvy)

personal friend. I asked Marta what I had done wrong and her answer suggested I had revealed things about the family that were no business of the outside world. I recalled having written in *The World of Plácido Domingo* that it could not always have been easy being the wife (or sons) of a busy peripatetic star like Plácido, though I had added that, conscientious as he was, Plácido always did his best to keep in touch with the family and that often (as here in Los Angeles) Marta would accompany him on his travels. During the conversation I got the distinct impression that something awkward was going on between the two of them at the time (indeed, I had a shrewd idea of what it might have been), and I began to sense that I was being caught in the crossfire. As it happened, I had come to know a great deal more about Plácido than I revealed in my writings about him. Twenty-five years later, everybody knew.

Chapter 47
End of an Era

Many of my BBC productions continued to include something of a historical focus. *History Now and Then* was the title I gave to a series of Radio 3 discussions, first broadcast in late 1993 and chaired by Roy Porter, on current issues of historiography. Roy was a social historian, a protégé at Cambridge (like Simon Schama and David Cannadine) of Sir Jack Plumb, and he had subsequently become something of a pioneer in his chosen field of medical history, with a senior post at London's Wellcome Institute. But he retained an insatiable interest in all things historical, and the programmes examined many of the pivotal issues currently rumbling through the profession. Thus, we invited Jonathan Clark, Miri Rubin and Raphael Samuel to consider the (then) very hot topic of whether and how far history should be viewed from the 'top down' or the 'bottom up'. Linda Colley and others considered the ways in which the historical role of women, and gender more generally, were coming to be regarded, while Lyndal Roper spoke of witches and witchery. In one programme, Asa Briggs and Jeremy Black debated the pros of cons of writing 'big history' (what do you include and what do you leave out?), while Ronald Hutton, Conrad Russell and Barry Coward came to grips over how far the English Civil War was really fought over religion. Throughout, Roy proved a wonderful colleague and a superb interviewer, and we became firm friends. A genial workaholic, he would pour his energies into whatever was currently preoccupying him, public or private! Sadly, but not entirely surprisingly perhaps, Roy Porter died in 2002 in his mid-50s.

* * *

Something of the spirit that had inspired the programmes with Roy led to what was one of my last broadcasting projects and in some ways one of the most ambitious: a six-part series for Radio 4 commissioned by the always open-minded Controller Michael Green which I originally dubbed *Fins de Siècle*. If my title deviated slightly from the impeccable French of which the Académie Française would approve, the entire undertaking certainly had a 'hook': the run-up during the 1990s to the end of not only a century but also a millennium, and the widespread sense that we were approaching a major historical turning point. Had something of the same been true in the past each time a century was approaching its end?

I had always been intrigued by the artificial if convenient periodisation so often imposed upon the past. We talk of 'Ancient History' and the 'Middle Ages', the 'Renaissance' and 'Early Modern' times on the comforting assumption that everyone understands and agrees with the categories thus cited. And, of course, about centuries and decades. We talk of the 18th-century 'Enlightenment', for example, or of the imperialism or family values of the 19th and, regarding more recent times, of the Depression of the '30s or the affluence or counter-culture of the '60s.

Of course, history does not really move according to such convenient temporal categorisations, but I have sometimes, in provocative mood, tried to argue that what we call centuries and decades have often in fact begun a few years after their official calendrical commencement. Thus, some of the truly great transitions in European history, for example, occurred in 1715 (with the death of Louis XIV), 1815 (end of the Napoleonic wars) and 1914 (outbreak of the First World War). As for decades, consider the election of FDR to the American presidency in 1932, the advent of Elizabeth II to the British throne in 1952, the death of Stalin a year later and the assassination of Kennedy in 1963. Maybe each century (and decade) needs a breathing space to get settled, I would sometimes suggest. In which case, I wondered, when exactly were the ends of centuries?

* * *

By the mid-1990s, there was already much discussion in Britain and elsewhere about various almost apocalyptic possible endings that seemed to lie in wait for us: nuclear annihilation, world population explosion and accompanying famine, an AIDS or other epidemic, genetic manipulation and abuse, global warming resulting from the greenhouse effect. 'The End of the World!' the headlines had screamed in November 1992 as sober scientists identified a comet, dubbed Swift-Tuttle, that looked set to collide with the earth in the early 2000s. For those of a more optimistic frame of mind, the British government established a commission whose remit was to take an estimated 1.5 billion pounds of National Lottery revenue and hand it out to imaginative projects that would mark our graduation into the third millennium.

There was thus a great deal of 'futurology' in the air. But my proposal was to try and capture the *fin-de-siècle* mood by looking not forward but backward, to use the full panoply of sounds available to radio to evoke the atmosphere in these islands at the ends of previous centuries. As in *The Long March of Everyman* 25 years earlier, I aimed to evoke the experience of ordinary people, where they lived, what they wore and ate, their beliefs, fears and hopes as well as the great public events which would also be present as points of reference. There are of course no inherently magic or metaphysical qualities in the turn of a year and, in any case, calendrical time is man-made and until two or three hundred years ago most people normally identified the passage of time by reference to the seasons, religious festivals or regnal years and were largely indifferent to the date as we understand it. But as I looked back over the British past, as one century ended and another began, I was struck by how a 'sense of an ending' not dissimilar to our own seemed increasingly to have had an impact upon the way people came to perceive their own place in history.

I decided to concentrate on the last six centuries, going back as far as the era of Richard II – which (as though to make my point) culminated with that unfortunate king's ousting by the first of the Lancastrians in 1399 and his murder in 1400. Jumping forward a century at a time, I noted that Henry VII, acquiring the throne of England in 1485, put down firm roots for his regime (and subsequent Tudor dynasty) over the next 20 years. Elizabeth I died in 1603 to be succeeded by the first of the Stuarts; William and Mary ousted James II and became joint monarchs in 1689; George III went mad, and political power fell to his Prime Minister (William Pitt the Younger) around 1790 and Queen Victoria died after what was then the longest reign in British history in January 1901. Virtually every 'end of century' thus saw the end and/or beginning of effective power for a monarch, minister, regime or dynasty.

Many other great public landmarks stood out during these periods, too. The last 15 years of the reign of Elizabeth I, for example, were darkened by the shadow of successive armadas from Spain and recurrent wars in Ireland and the Low Countries, while the wars that erupted in the 1690s and 1790s were among the longest and bloodiest in English history. Many important social and cultural transitions also appear to have occurred as one century gave way to the next: the English rather than the French language seems finally to have been adopted as the tongue of daily discourse at court and in the church as well as among merchants and yeomen farmers between about 1380 and 1410, while the first infiltration into England of Renaissance humanist ideas occurred a century later during the reign of

Henry VII. Between the 1680s and 1720s, a society that had long believed in the magic of the monarch's touch and had burned people for heresy and witchcraft underwent a rapid conversion (if that is the right word) to a more tolerant, rational – or cynical – set of values that vigorously embraced the stock exchange, the political pamphlet and the newspaper.

There were some striking parallels, too, between earlier ends of centuries and the one we ourselves were undergoing. What was being dubbed 'Euroscepticism', for example, far from being a purely modern phenomenon, had clearly been evident in the resentment of Lombard and Fleming workers in London in the 1390s, while many in late Elizabethan England talked darkly of a crime wave and regarded the urban homeless with a complex mixture of compassion, fear and contempt. As for the modern tabloid preoccupation of the peccadilloes of hot young bluebloods, this had not-too-distant parallels in the later years of both Elizabeth and Victoria. And as these two reproachless but ageing monarchs approached the end of their lives people were wont to whisper, just as they were also beginning to do in the 1990s of Queen Elizabeth II, 'she's fine, but heaven knows what will happen when she finally goes.'

I set to work on the past six *fins de siècles* of British history and started by recording interviews with some forty historians, among them friends from the *Long March* days such as Asa Briggs and Theo Barker, their mid-career successors like Linda Colley, David Cannadine and Roy Porter and rising young stars such as Daniel Pick. Originally, I had hoped to record each in an appropriate location, but this proved impossible to arrange – with one notable exception: Professor William ('Bill') Fishman whose informed *in situ* enthusiasm as he guided me through late-19th-century Whitechapel proved a model of the kind of 'actuality-based' interviews I had had in mind. As in the *Long March*, each programme was carefully constructed to take the form of a continuous collage of speech, sound and music. There was no scripted linking material or overall 'authority figure' or narrator. Rather, the wide range of material, carefully structured, was allowed to make its own points.

Perhaps the boldest decision was to broadcast the programmes 'backwards', starting with the 1890s and following a week later with the 1790s and so on until we reached the final programme, that on the 1390s. There were two principal reasons for this, one practical and the other historiographical. First, I thought more listeners would tune in to a new series if it began with a programme featuring Gilbert and Sullivan, Oscar Wilde and the Diamond Jubilee and death of Queen Victoria than one about the ousting of Richard II. But I also felt that there was virtue in telling history in this 'neo-Whig' fashion: pointing to something comparatively familiar and then, in effect, saying that if you want to know how things came to be like this, tune in next time. I have occasionally taught social history this way to student groups ('What did you have for breakfast today? How did you get to the classroom? How is your tuition paid for?' followed by similar questions about what your parents and grandparents used to eat when they were your age, their means of transportation and finance etc.), and it seemed to me that a radio series might follow the same principle.

The programmes, bound together as *Fin de Siècle,* were first broadcast on Radio 4 on Wednesday evenings in June and July 1994. Despite all the counterattractions of a series of warm summer evenings (not to mention such television distractions as the World Cup soccer matches from the USA and an interview with Prince Charles by Jonathan Dimbleby), the series attracted an appreciative audience and outstanding press coverage. 'If only all history lessons were as vivid as Mr Snowman's *Fin de Siècle*' wrote the generous critic of *The Times* while the *Telegraph*'s Gillian Reynolds thought that Radio 4 should clear its schedules for a day and repeat the series end-to-end. Whatever the merits of the individual programmes, it was clear that the basic idea had 'hit the spot'. A couple of years later, Asa Briggs and I turned the concept into a richly illustrated book, published by Yale University Press, in which each 'fin de siècle' was given its own chapter. That on the 1790s was by Roy Porter.

Chapter 48
'Producer Choice'

I used to joke (and have done so above) that I dated the decline of the BBC from the moment I joined. In practice, I was there during its great days and certainly, as a producer, was offered every opportunity and encouragement to create, and control right through until transmission, a great range of programmes. But there is no disguising the fact that, during my time there, dark clouds began to gather in broadcasting heaven. There were signs of it as early as 1970 with the policy document 'Broadcasting in the Seventies' in which management announced its intention to streamline the new radio networks, thereby (many of us felt) betraying the fundamental Reithian mission of educating by stealth (see Chapter 34).

Things became appreciably worse in the 1980s when the Thatcher government placed the Corporation firmly in its sights. As a publicly funded institution committed to 'balanced' presentation of complex issues, the BBC was anathema to an assertively Conservative government committed to a free market philosophy in not only matters economic but also in culture and the arts. To the Government, the BBC's attempts at balanced reporting on, for example, the Falklands War of 1982, the miners' strike of 1984–85 or the ongoing Troubles in Northern Ireland could sometimes look suspiciously left-wing, if not overtly subversive: just the sort of thing you'd expect from an organisation that did not have to compete in the marketplace for its funding. In September 1986, Marmaduke ('Duke') Hussey, long-time chief executive and managing director of Times Newspapers and a darling of the Conservatives, was appointed Chairman of the BBC Governors; three months later, in January 1987, he summoned the Corporation's Director General, Alasdair Milne, and precipitately forced him to resign.

Milne had risen through the ranks as an innovative programme maker in BBC television news and current affairs, and his sudden departure from the top job sent shock waves through the Corporation. The Controller of Radio 4, David Hatch, made a rapid tour around the radio departments telling us the news – along with the realistic message that, henceforth, none of the valued corporate continuities we had hitherto taken for granted was necessarily there in perpetuity. If the Director General's job could suddenly be terminated, so – henceforth – could that of any of us. It was understandable, said Hatch, if our sense of loyalty to the Corporation we served had been seriously dented. But our job was to continue to produce programmes of the highest quality, as we had always done, and to retain the standards of which the BBC was rightly proud. And he wished us all luck, as we wished him, in the stormy waters that would undoubtedly ensue.

The waters in fact proved fairly placid for a while, as Milne was succeeded as Director General by Michael Checkland, an amiable man with an accounting rather than a programme-making background. Then in 1992 he was himself succeeded by John Birt, a former programme maker for commercial television. By now, Thatcher had been ousted from office, but attitudes towards the BBC continued to be hostile in some Conservative (and conservative) circles. There were rumours that the BBC might be broken up, some of its more 'popular' outlets perhaps earning their keep from the commercial sector rather than the License Fee. Birt's job was to retain at least the outer garments of BBC integrity and respectability and some felt he achieved this at a difficult time. Others lambasted him for throwing out its essentially Reithian values and imposing instead a ruthlessly commercial atmosphere upon an organisation that had once embodied the highest cultural values.

One of the things that disturbed (and occasionally amused) me was the new 'management-speak' that was imposed by the Birt regime. Everything we did seemed to be subject to cost-benefit analysis, the qualitative was superseded by the quantitative, the expression of ideas by the enumeration of bullet points. Thus, the annual reports written about staff members by their immediate superiors came to include lists of 'aims and objectives'. And I recall surveys assessing our satisfaction level with the work environment (the results duly reported in the staff magazine *Ariel*). Was I very happy/satisfied/dissatisfied/miserable about, for example, the accessibility or communication style of my line manager? I was perfectly satisfied. I liked my boss, Ann Winder, and always felt I could talk to her whenever I felt the need. What *dis*satisfied me – and what the survey did *not* ask – was some of the policies she now found herself having to supervise. Thus, programme proposals, instead of being discussed openly at regular meetings chaired by the relevant Controller, now had to be placed on a Procrustean computer matrix named 'Trivium' then undergo a series of formal online assessments before acceptance or rejection. For 20 years I had thought of the programme idea as being paramount; now it was the cost, the duration, the number of 'producer days' it would require and the nature of the proposed audience profile and 'TX' (transmission) slot and date that were given priority. Couldn't you get a better-known presenter, I'd be asked: maybe someone from television – perhaps a woman? I remember offering a one-off, a brilliant idea as I thought (though I can't for the life of me remember what it was!). And the response? Great idea, Daniel; couldn't you think of six more so as to make a seven-part 'strand'? This, I was told cheerily, would help build up audience expectation.

Worst of all was the adoption of the Orwellian-entitled policy of 'Producer Choice'. This was a system of total costing enabling producers to decide how best to make use of the programme budgets assigned to them. Where the expense of using in-house actors or studios, for example, was hitherto regarded as being 'below the line' (facilities, that is, provided by the benevolent BBC for the use of those who worked there), such resources were now made available at market rates to any producer wishing to purchase them. If you could get similar studios for a lower price outside the BBC, you were entitled to do so.

Perfectly reasonable on the face of it; it cannot be wrong in an organisation under some political and economic pressure to encourage its staff to become more cost-conscious. And you can forget most of the silly stories about paperclip costings and the proliferation of paperwork. The new system doubtless helped peel away some needless layers of fat. However, as a belt-tightening culture took hold, the temptation everywhere was to make what were sometimes false economies. Thus, a music producer would be tempted to call upon contacts in the record industry to supply him or her with press samples rather than borrow CDs from the increasingly beleaguered BBC Gramophone Library. A producer of talks and documentaries, similarly, might befriend a freelance recording engineer and the two of them offer a series of interview programmes costing far less than if they had been produced in house.

This kind of thinking became widespread among producers, despite the loss of facilities and posts entailed: an indication of one's rugged, non-nonsense approach to the job – even if, as a direct consequence, fewer records were bought by the Grams Library and staff had to be laid off.

Why borrow books from the BBC Library, much less browse in the stacks, when you could get the basic facts you needed by what we were learning to call E-mail? Why, indeed, go to the bother and expense of a scripted programme when a studio discussion would fill the proposed slot just as easily? Why incur travel expenditure when you could contract a local freelance to record your material at a fraction of the cost? Why book a studio and studio manager for an interview which you could record yourself on a portable machine and edit in your office? Why record and edit a programme at all when it would be cheaper to put it out live?

Producer Choice meant, in practice, having *less* choice. As mentioned above (Chapter 31), I had become accustomed in the past to decide on my own initiative if I felt it might be useful to buy a particular book, attend a certain play or invite a distinguished intellectual out to lunch at the BBC's expense. And it was entirely up to me to assess whether there might be some future programme-making to emerge as a result. But by my last few years at the BBC, every expense had to come out of a budget already assigned to a previously accepted programme. I well remember wanting to meet a famous historian while I was developing what eventually materialised as *Fin de Siècle*. In order to invite him out for lunch, I had to pretend the expense was in connection with another programme on which it looked as if I would underspend. 'Producer Choice' thus encouraged me to lie.

Much that I had loved about the BBC was by now eroding. Not only were in-house institutions such as the BBC's studios and libraries undermined by the newly ascendant commercial philosophy. So were its own production staff as programmes came to be increasingly solicited from independent production companies. By opening the system to outside competition, argued the Birt regime, the range and quality of what was on offer would surely become enhanced. 'Choice' – one of the buzzwords of the time – was automatically assumed to present the opportunity for 'Better': a philosophy that became increasingly widespread over the next few years. I don't want to demonise John Birt. Indeed, it is arguable that, by re-focusing the BBC along contemporary managerial lines, he helped save it from possible breakup and even destruction. His policies, harsh as they sometimes seemed, were consistent with the style of the times. This was also, of course, the dawn of the digital age in which traditional 'top down' culture increasingly gave way to a culture emphasising individual 'choice'. One way and another, Birt arguably helped a much-beleaguered

BBC reclaim something of the political status it had been in serious danger of losing. Was it guilty of 'dumbing down' as a consequence? Or did its output become more 'accessible'? Choose your cliché…

* * *

I watched all this from what, I have to say, was something of a privileged position. I had a permanent, pensionable post with a good salary (by BBC standards) and, along with a few senior colleagues such as Piers Plowright, Rosemary Hart and Judith Bumpus, was still encouraged to come up with ideas for the kind of substantial features and documentaries that won headlines and prizes. When Nick Kenyon, the Controller of Radio 3, proposed a multi-programme Festival in 1995 to mark the 300th anniversary of the death of Henry Purcell (to be named *Fairest Isle*), I was delighted to contribute several costly and labour-intensive features, including one on 'Pretty, Witty Nell (Gwynn)' and another about that early entrepreneur of the English ballad, Thomas D'Urfey. New, younger producers were increasingly likely to be placed on short-term contracts (without the prospect of a pension) and pressed to play their part in pre-existing 'strands'. And I found myself more and more likely to be asked by a (rather younger) line manager if I would kindly agree to take my place among the list of those scheduled to produce such regular slots as *Pick of the Week*. Of course, I agreed to do so. But this was no longer the creative and innovative job it had once been. I was in my mid-50s and began to think of taking early retirement. I figured that if I stayed on until my obligatory retirement at 60, I would be regarded as too old to launch myself into other work. But if I left at 56, I might be able to do some more writing, lecturing – and perhaps (on a freelance basis) broadcasting…

One day, I went to see Ann Winder, my head of department, and asked, in the friendliest way, whether she might like to sack me. I didn't want to leave 'voluntarily' because this would jeopardise the severance pay the Corporation would be obliged to give me if I were forced out. Ann understood perfectly and, as I had anticipated, felt that my departure would enable her to abolish my post and release funds with which she could pay the salaries of two younger producers. All very amicable. It was agreed that my employment with the BBC would cease at the end of 1995. Thereafter, I would receive a monthly pension based on my final BBC salary.

Early in the new year, the BBC threw a farewell party for me. I made a brief speech and then launched into a poem I had written to mark the occasion. Or, rather, a Hamletian soliloquy in which I tried to suggest the dilemmas I had faced when contemplating my departure.

To leave or not to leave, that is the question.
Whether 'tis nobler, quiet like a mouse,
With petty pace to quit Broadcasting House.
To breathe the air of freedom, to rejoice!
Or stay, and struggle with 'Producer Choice'.
To grunt and sweat, to beg from empty coffers,
To write with patient merit rejected offers:
'User-friendly, cheerful, cheapest, sweetest
Fresh, accessible and non-elitist'!
To suffer slings and arrows of oblivium,
To fall asleep while struggling with Trivium.
To sleep. Perchance to dream – oh lucky creature.
For in that dream – a documentary feature!
A consummation devoutly to be seen.
But by whom? By Brian, or Michael Green?
Duration, genre, strand code, price? Now here is
That manager's delight, a six-part series,
An enterprise of greatest pith and plot,
Awaiting merely manning, cost and slot.
It's put on ice, and for its slow defrosting –
The backburner for its total costing.
The slots are held – they change the TX day!
Oh whips and scorns of time, the law's delay.
Take arms against a BB – C of troubles?
It's tempting. But opposing first redoubles
The heartache and the thousand natural shocks
We used to whinge about in Talks and Docs!
So fill a glass – if only to stop fidgeting
As you pass from analogue to digiting
(The kind of thing much written up in Ariel*)*
While I, for reasons largely actuarial,
Trade in my earphones, leave my mike inert,

Hand in my blue ID and quit John Birt.
Farewell to Ps as Bs, Producers' Estimates;
Farewell to meetings, full of all my best'-o-mates.
An undiscovered country lies ahead
No talk of Charters, Strategies. Instead
I dream of lectures, books, TV and travel
And contracts only agents can unravel
Unless you think retirement unassailable
Your freelance friend assures you – he's available!
Enfin: je ne regrette rien, you may now heckle
For it's au revoir: my personal 'fin de si-eckle'!

* * *

For a while thereafter, I found myself being invited to present and/or produce occasional broadcasts on a freelance basis. One project, loosely linked to the run-up to the centenary of the death of Verdi (2001), was a succession of programmes based on interviews with famous performers on (respectively) 'Singing', 'Conducting' and 'Directing' the works of the great composer, while I also presented a five-part series about Puccini. The rebuilding and renovation of London's Royal Opera House in the late 1990s led to documentaries about parallel projects being undertaken at the time in Venice, Barcelona and San Francisco. In 1998, I produced a feature programme about Vienna and its cultural history and spent a week in the Austrian capital collecting material with my presenter, the former TV producer (and briefly manager of London's English National Opera) Dennis Marks. It was during these years, too, that I recorded my series of conversations with Evelyn Barbirolli about 'Glorious John'. Like Verdi, Queen Victoria had died in January 1901, and to mark the centenary of her death I presented a Radio 4 series that focused on her multifarious progeny and the widespread influence they were to have on subsequent history.

The most ambitious of my post-BBC broadcasting projects were linked to two books I had undertaken during my so-called 'retirement'. In 2002, shortly after the initial publication of my study of the cultural impact of the Hitler émigrés, I was invited to present – live – an entire evening on Radio 3 devoted to the subject. And in 2007, Radio 3 broadcast a succession of interval features I presented, using material gathered in many parts of the world, outlining the social history of opera.

Book 10

'Retirement'

1995–2013

Chapter 49

The Hitler Emigrés

As mentioned above (Chapter 47), I have tended to regard somewhat sceptically the idea that periods of historical change could be conveniently boxed into 'centuries' or 'decades' (arguing, perversely, that these always seemed to begin a little later than the calendar would seem to dictate!). And I don't suppose that important turning points occurred in my own life at decennial intervals. But it is not difficult, looking back, to see something of a pattern:

1949–52	Secondary school, Bar-Mitzvah, onset of puberty
1958–63	Cambridge, Cornell
1970–73	Joined BBC staff; year in California
1981–82	First meetings with Domingo; undertook BBC's *World in Common* ('hot places')
1988–92	Polar projects, Reith Lectures and early programmes with Lucie

And a further decade on, around the turn of the millennium? Many things, actually. In 1998 my book about the cultural impact of the Hitler émigrés was commissioned and I became accepted as a lecturer for NADFAS, giving my first lectures the following year. 2001 saw the epoch-changing assault on the Twin Towers in New York, and it was in that year that I led the first of what turned out to be over 50 tours to many of the major cultural centres of Europe (and the USA). And in September 2002, following publication of *The Hitler Émigrés*, I set off on a two-month lecture tour to Hong Kong, across Australia and New Zealand and thence to Los Angeles, Vancouver and Toronto.

* * *

By the mid-1990s, there was much talk of the Covent Garden opera house having to undergo major renovation and it occurred to me that, in anticipation of the reopening in the early new century, I might be well equipped to write a book outlining the history of the Royal Opera. I had long been something of a Covent Garden regular and was frequently there – front of house and backstage – especially while working on my book about Domingo in the early 1980s. I discussed this with my agent Dinah Wiener and, through her, with a number of potential publishers. The kind of book that would sell, several emphasised, would be one revealing the larger-than-life personalities and behind-the-scene dramas that were widely believed to characterise the world of opera. I had heard all this before. Back in 1985, over lunch in New York with my American publishers, I was asked whether, having done a book about Domingo, I might like to undertake one about Pavarotti. Or perhaps about the two of them – the great rivals? What did I know about their respective private lives? Or what they thought of each other? Recent revelations about the personal lives of the conductor Leonard Bernstein and the pianist Vladimir Horowitz had proved mildly sensational; think how much I could make with a book revealing the personal secrets of supposedly 'temperamental' operatic superstars!

I was sceptical. The reality, I knew, was that for 99 per cent of the time most opera houses were busy, hardworking factories in which everyone had to turn up on time and fulfil to the best of his or her ability whatever it was they were required to do. Callas didn't pull fits all the time or cancel performances on a whim, nor did Toscas bounce or orotund prima donnas burst out of their costumes. When Pavarotti made a recurrent error (as I saw at La Scala in 1987 during rehearsals for a performance and recording of the Verdi *Requiem* with Muti at the helm), he simply had to work at it until he got everything right. When Domingo was uneasy about a stage movement required of him when rehearsing his first Siegmund in Vienna in 1992, when we were making our TV documentary about him, he quietly asked the Director if they could try something slightly different until, in the end, a mutually acceptable compromise was reached. Opera is a complex multimedia art in which, if it is to succeed, everything has to cohere. If the sets begin to sway, the lighting fails or the chorus is slightly out of sync with the conductor, the performance will suffer.

* * *

If I was not the right person to embark upon a celebrity-packed book about the modern history of the Royal Opera, I began to think about something more substantial I might undertake which could perhaps incorporate some aspects of the Covent Garden story. I thought back to an evening at the opera in June 1965. I had managed to obtain a seat, high up and somewhat to the side but with a good view of the orchestra. The papers were full of how this production (by Peter Hall) was going to be something of a scandal, with naked virgins and a human sacrifice. Not the sort of thing the Lord Chamberlain would normally permit on stage in those days. But then this was 'high art'. In the stalls I was able to pick out Claus Moser, Berlin-born and a passionate music lover. Moser was on the faculty of the London School of Economics and would soon be appointed Director of the Central Statistical Office. He was also on the Board of the Royal Opera House and became Chairman in 1974. George Weidenfeld was in the audience, too. A prominent publisher and bridge between readers and the great authors of continental Europe and beyond, Weidenfeld had adored opera since his childhood in Vienna and would not miss an occasion like this. Present, too, was the composer and musicologist Egon Wellesz, once a protégé of tonight's composer. Wellesz had written an introductory note in the programme in which he quoted something he remembered Mahler saying in 1907. Karl Rankl, first Musical Director of this company, was there too, returning to his old house for the first time in many years and sitting hunched in near obscurity. Tonight's composer was once his professor, too.

The lights dimmed and there was a ripple of applause. Into the pit, angular elbows and shoulders pugnaciously forward, darted Georg Solti, this evening's conductor and the Royal Opera's controversial Musical Director. Sometimes too demanding for the phlegmatic English temperament, Solti was one of those Hungarians who (they would joke behind his back) would enter a rotating door after you and come out ahead. Some openly disliked Solti, finding his energy excessive. On one notorious occasion the 'Get Rid of Solti' campaign led to his car being vandalised. But everybody acknowledged his formidable musicianship and his kindness to the talented young singers he constantly sought out and encouraged. With Solti at the helm at Covent Garden, and especially when he was in the pit, everyone sensed that something important was going on. Especially on a night like this. Without him it would have been unthinkable for the Royal Opera to have mounted Schoenberg's *Moses und Aron*.

Rankl, Moser, Weidenfeld, Wellesz, Solti and Schoenberg himself: all (like three-quarters of the Amadeus Quartet) had been refugees from Nazism. What I came to call the 'Hitler Emigrés'.

* * *

Despite my strange surname, I am not a German '*Schneemann*'; my forebears came from various parts of the 'Pale of Jewish settlement', the region on the eastern borderlands of imperial Russia (nowadays the Baltic states, parts of

Poland, Belarus, Ukraine, etc.) in which Jews were permitted to live in Tsarist times. But I was raised in Jewish northwest London and grew up to respect, almost revere, all who had German names and accents. When we planned a holiday, we got into the habit of consulting the latest volume of *The Buildings of England* by someone mysteriously called Nikolaus Pevsner while the art history book of choice was by one Gombrich. In time, I became acquainted with the work of the philosopher Karl Popper and historians such as Eric Hobsbawm and Geoffrey Elton. My mother, meanwhile, was much taken by psychoanalysis and felt honoured to have had a correspondence with Anna Freud, daughter of Sigmund. Above all, there was music. When I went to a concert, the conductor might have been called Boult or Sargent; but I knew it would be something special if he was called Otto Klemperer, or Szell, Susskind or Schwarz. Many years later, I still remember joking as a youngster that anyone called 'Schmidt' was bound to be cleverer than anyone called just plain 'Smith'!

But was this true? If so, why? Maybe here was the core of a book I should undertake. What was it about the refugees from the Third Reich that had enabled them to make such a disproportionate contribution to British intellectual and cultural life, and what was the nature of that

Otto Klemperer (left) and Hans Keller (right) by Milein Cosman.
(Both images courtesy of The Cosman Keller Art and Music Trust)

contribution? I had vivid memories of Radio 3 meetings at the BBC when sparks would fly between the Viennese-raised Controller Stephen Hearst, the Hungarian-born Head of Drama Martin Esslin and that assertive and witty musicologist Hans Keller, all of whom seemed far more knowledgeable and articulate about current trends in British cultural life than the rest of us around the table.

All migrations involve some degree of cultural transfer, and what primarily interested me was how elements of the culture of pre-Hitlerian Central Europe came to influence, or to be integrated with (or rejected by), the pre-existing culture of their new home country. What happened when English *rus in urbe* (Garden Cities, the architecture of Lutyens or the Tudor-inspired pastoralism of Vaughan Williams) encountered the musical modernism of Schoenberg and his pupils or Bauhaus-style architecture? My intention was not to praise the achievements of the émigrés but to assess their cultural impact.

In order to do the subject full justice, I knew I would have to learn a great deal about the social and cultural history of pre-Nazi Central Europe: the Vienna of Freud, Mahler, Kraus and Klimt, 'Expressionist' film, Weimar-era theatre and cabaret, 'Modernist' architecture and music and much else. I would also have to upgrade my detailed knowledge and understanding of the cultural history of my own country, the Britain in which the émigrés settled. And though my work was to concentrate on the British experience, the subject was part of a wider international phenomenon and this involved some knowledge of the parallels elsewhere, notably in the USA; think of all those Hitler émigrés who gravitated to Hollywood, for example.

With the encouragement of Dinah, my agent, I drew up a proposal. It was accepted and the book commissioned by Chatto & Windus. Over the next few years, I read voraciously, pored over documents in research libraries, notably the Wiener (no relation to Dinah!), and made several visits to Germany and Austria. Most rewardingly, I was able to record lengthy interviews with some 60 or more distinguished émigrés, most of them by then elderly, each of whom had made an important cultural or intellectual impact on Britain. Many told me, movingly, that they had never before spoken so openly about all they had experienced in their early years. Many of these recordings are now lodged in the sound archives of London's Imperial War Museum.

* * *

What I emphatically did not want to write was a sentimental chronicle lauding the wonderful achievements of one famous Jewish refugee or 'exile' after another. For a start, many of the people I intended to consider were not Jewish: the artistic founding fathers of Glyndebourne, the director Carl Ebert and the conductor Fritz Busch, for example. Nor were the artists Oskar Kokoschka or Kurt Schwitters Jewish, or Fritz Schumacher, author of *Small is Beautiful*, or the architect Walter Gropius or the dance choreographer Rudolf Laban, both of whom tried to make some accommodation with the Nazi regime in its early years but soon found this impossible.

Many of the Hitler émigrés *were* of course Jewish, but only nominally so. 'To my father,' (this was Claus Moser talking) 'being German came first. He thought of himself as a German, and only then as a Jew.' Lord Moser's father was a wealthy Berlin banker. He had fought in World War I and he and his wife, like so many others in their position, considered themselves proud and patriotic Germans. Claus Moser's memory was shared by many other refugees from Nazism who came from Jewish backgrounds. 'This terrible thing cannot last. Germany is a civilised nation and these barbarians will soon be out.' This was the father of the artist Milein Cosman (wife of the musician and broadcaster Hans Keller). And here is Fred Uhlman in his semi-autobiographical novella *Reunion* about a young Jewish boy brought up in the 1930s:

> 'I know my Germany,' says the father. 'This is a temporary illness, something like measles, which will pass as soon as the economic situation improves. Do you really believe the compatriots of Goethe and Schiller, Kant and Beethoven will fall for this rubbish?'

The cultural references are significant. Again and again, it was music, art, literature, that refugees from Nazism mentioned when reflecting on what had made them and their families so proudly German. Moser told me in a sentiment shared by countless others, 'In Britain, culture was the icing on the cake, whereas we were raised to think it *was* the cake!'

Furthermore, not all those I wanted to write about were necessarily refugees. Friedrich Hayek (the free-market economist whose work helped influence Margaret Thatcher) did not come to Britain as a refugee. Nor, for example, did the film producer Alexander Korda or the art historian Ernst Gombrich. These, in each case, initially came to Britain to work. Then, as the situation in Central Europe deteriorated, it became increasingly obvious that this was the place to stay. The Vienna-born biochemist Max Perutz came to Britain as a student, while the historian Eric Hobsbawm arrived from Hitler's Germany as an adolescent, not as a refugee but with a British passport and under the care of an uncle who had work here. Some were refugees elsewhere during the war before later settling in Britain: Georg Solti, for example, or the philosopher Karl Popper. And a tiny handful of people arrived in the UK after the war having miraculously survived the worst horrors of Nazism, among them the musicians Rudolf Schwarz and Anita Lasker Wallfisch and Rabbi Hugo Gryn.

* * *

While not all the Hitler émigrés had Jewish origins, many did, and this led me to wonder whether there was anything specifically Jewish about what they went on to achieve. There were probably both positive and negative answers to that complex question. Throughout Jewish history, from ancient times, great emphasis had been placed on learning. From the Biblical Moses to Moses Maimonides to Moses Mendelssohn, it was often the prophets and philosophers, the scribes and the scholars who were the role models. In the old *Shtetl*, the Rabbi was not so much a preacher or prayer leader as a teacher and scholar, the person responsible for the education of the next generation, the only figure in town capable of solving difficult questions of Jewish law. Even Jews who were not particularly conscious of their Jewish ancestry, or believed they had transcended or disavowed it (such as Marx, Mahler or Freud), tended to gravitate towards achievement in the intellectual and cultural worlds. Devotion to learning is a constant theme throughout Jewish history, and it was much in evidence in pre-Nazi Middle Europe. In *fin-de-siècle* Vienna, Jews made up about 10 per cent of the population, but they accounted for something like 30 per cent or more of the pupils enrolled in those elite grammar schools, the *Gymnasien*.

There was a negative side to all this as well, of course. If you were a young Jew in early 20th-century Vienna or Berlin, you would have been unlikely to aspire towards a career in the army, diplomacy, politics or (obviously) the church. These professions tended to lend themselves to the sons of the social elite, and a young Jew, however gifted and ambitious, would probably have been courting rejection if he had set serious sights on them. It was partly a question of anti-Semitism; one only has to read the prose works of Wagner or the political speeches of the mayor of Vienna at the turn of the century,

Karl Lueger, or to recall the fate of Alfred Dreyfus, to be reminded that anti-Semitism was not invented by Hitler. Far better to gravitate towards those fields in which Jews (with all that *Gymnasium* education behind them) tended to be more widely accepted: the law and medicine, economics and philosophy, art, music, literature, journalism and publishing.

So: the reasons why so many Jews moved into such fields probably included both the traditional pull towards learning as well as the push of exclusion from the upper reaches of the army or politics. Culture, in other words, provided a gateway to social mobility.

Was there nothing specifically Jewish as such about the later achievements of the Hitler émigrés? Ernst Gombrich, to the end of his life, denied that his Jewishness had anything to do with his art history. Who cares, he would ask, whether this or that historian or philosopher happened to be Jewish? – adding, pointedly, that such questions were more the domain of the Gestapo. From the opposite corner, as it were, Chief Rabbi Lord Jakobovits told me with equal vehemence that he too could see nothing in the ideas of Marx or Freud (or Mahler or Trotsky or Einstein for that matter) that arose in any way from their Jewish backgrounds. As an orthodox rabbi, Jakobovits regarded the historical importance of such

Karl Popper and Ernst Gombrich.

people as lying outside Jewish history and therefore neither influenced by it nor contributing to it.

I wondered about this. Mention of Trotsky brought to mind another writer who tried to grasp this thorny issue: his biographer, Isaac Deutscher. Deutscher, in an essay he entitled *The Non-Jewish Jew*, considered what he called the great Jewish 'heretics' – he added figures such as Spinoza and Heine to the familiar litany – and wondered what, if anything, they had in common. To Deutscher, it was not a question of race or religiosity. He argued that these people, and others like them (doubtless including himself), gained their special strength from the fact that they dwelt on the borders of various civilisations, religions and national cultures, and were born and brought up on the borderlines of epochs. 'Their mind matured where the most diverse cultural influences crossed and fertilised each other,' wrote Deutscher. 'They lived on the margins or in the nooks and crannies of their respective nations. Each of them was in society and yet not of it.' Steven Beller, writing about the Jews of Vienna, showed how they inhabited 'the centre of culture but the edge of society'.

In other words, the very fact that Marx and Mahler and the rest transcended their Jewishness and reached out to cross boundaries of mind, place and even time, arose – paradoxically – from deep within Jewish history and tradition according to Deutscher. Jewish achievement was therefore, at least in part, that of a people on the move, a scattered diaspora, a cosmopolitan people linked by a shared legacy of settlement, upheaval, flight and temporary *re*-settlement; the idea that provides the key is that of 'living on the frontier', in Sander Gilman's phrase. A view of Jewish history that puts a modern, rather positive gloss on the old image of the Wandering Jew. In Judith Kerr's semi-autobiographical novel *When Hitler Stole Pink Rabbit*, the little girl asks her father when they are on their way to exile in Britain, 'Do you think we'll ever really belong anywhere?' The father replies gently, 'I suppose not… But we'll belong a little in lots of places, and I think that may be just as good.'

In my own research, I repeatedly came across this sense of homelessness as being regarded almost as a virtue, that the only true culture is one that crosses boundaries. 'The bags are always packed' – at least intellectually. And indeed, many of the Hitler émigrés gravitated towards international, multicultural or cross-disciplinary areas of interest. I think of journalists (such as Hella Pick) who gave British readers a broad international perspective on the stories of the day, publishers like Weidenfeld or Deutsch who consciously tried to act as a bridge between languages and cultures, historians (Hobsbawm is a classic example) who helped us to study historical processes across national boundaries. Gombrich brought to art history insights from psychology and anthropology, while the musical compositions of Joseph Horovitz, for example (whose father founded the Phaidon Press which published Gombrich), showed again and again how traditional stylistic boundaries in music could be creatively crossed. The biography of Arthur Koestler by David Cesarani was entitled, revealingly, *The Homeless Mind*. Isaac Deutscher was not, I suspect, alone in believing that this very process of travel (and travail) across constricting boundaries was one of the things that, in part at least, has defined Jews – and Jewish achievement – from time immemorial.

* * *

Well into the 21st century, refugees were continuing to knock at the door asking for asylum in Britain, by now primarily from the war-torn Middle East and north and central Africa, while large numbers of young people from the poorer, eastern nations within the EU – legal immigrants in their case – also headed for the UK. Throughout history people have attempted to migrate from impoverished, dangerous and unstable territories to those that were healthier and wealthier and, in modern Britain and elsewhere, a succession of governments struggled to find policies that they hoped would appear wise, just and politically acceptable: a difficult juggling act, not helped by a popular press happy to fuel rampant xenophobia. So 'What's new?', you may think. Immigrants everywhere have always appeared to present a threat; they are by definition foreign, alien, 'other'. Anarchists, terrorists, foreign spies: yes, immigrant groups have traditionally contained these too, and the new Churchill government in summer 1940, fearful lest there might be some lurking among the Hitler émigrés, infamously 'collared the lot', interning artists and architects, musicians and mathematicians, filmmakers and physicists on the Isle of Man and elsewhere.

In Britain, ambivalence towards the 'other', the outsider, ran deep. On the one hand, the traditional panorama of British history tended to highlight this country's insular independence from the continent, how Britain had never been successfully invaded since 1066, how 'we' beat off the Armada, Napoleon and Hitler. But when it came to 'culture' – well, the British had often regarded foreigners from Europe as being rather good at this. Think of the continental scholars at the court of Henry VII or the Venetian musicians or Holbein at that of his son Henry VIII. Think of Rubens, Van Dyck or Handel. In the 18th century, no gentleman was considered properly educated unless he spoke French and had undertaken the Grand Tour; in the 19th and into the 20th, any British musician worth his salt had to study in Germany, while any decent artist needed exposure to Paris.

The story of the Hitler émigrés could thus be seen as, among other things, one chapter in that long story of British ambivalence towards arrivals from the continent, similar in a way to the story of the Huguenots who had fled Louis XIV and came to Britain in the late 17th century. Some in Britain were hostile, questioning the wisdom of letting them in. But in retrospect the British were happy to acknowledge how the latest arrivals added greatly to the cultural mix which later generations were able to inherit. After all, as everybody knew, the Huguenots had brought high quality silk-weaving and silverwork to London and left a legacy of superb domestic architecture.

Was it possible for me to generalise about the legacy of the Hitler émigrés? By mixing their labours with what they found when they got here they probably helped *professionalise* aspects of British cultural life. I considered, for example, the transformation of art history from a genteel, Sunday-afternoon pursuit a century earlier, preoccupied with questions of aesthetics and connoisseurship, into the highly professionalised academic subject of more recent times as pioneered by Gombrich and his colleagues at the Warburg Institute. Or the somewhat amateur atmosphere at the Royal Opera House that upset George Solti when he arrived as Music Director and which he swore he would eradicate. At his first press conference, Solti said he'd turn the place into the finest opera house in the world, which I think it probably was by the time he left in 1971.

In addition, the presence of the Hitler émigrés helped *cosmopolitanise* the still somewhat insular culture of Britain, acting as a bridge between British cultural life and that of resurgent continental Europe. Nikolaus Pevsner introduced the ideas of Gropius and the Bauhaus to a generation raised on Tudorbethan revival and the Garden City ideal, while Martin Esslin at the BBC introduced the work of Central European playwrights to British audiences. George Weidenfeld strove to bring a truly international perspective to his publishing list. 'I always saw myself as somebody who bridges and who straddles worlds,' he told me proudly, someone who thought of himself as being at home everywhere – though not, perhaps, completely rooted anywhere. When George talks about 'we', Weidenfeld's friends would joke, you never quite know if he means the British, the Europeans, the Jews or the whole of humanity!

In some ways the Hitler émigrés were an unusual group of asylum seekers. Many were from educated, well-connected (and reasonably moneyed) middle- or upper-middle-class families: not, by and large, your huddled masses yearning to breathe free. But, like many groups of migrants before and since, they did want to do whatever they could for their country of adoption. I heard countless touching stories of people who, having found refuge in Britain, made Herculean efforts to become as British as possible: to hide their foreign accent and speak good English, roll their umbrellas, eat porridge and put milk instead of lemon in their tea, and learn to love cricket. One man was said to have waited years to get British naturalisation. Finally, his papers came through – and he promptly burst into tears. 'But why now of all times are you crying?' his friend asked. 'I know I should be happy,' blubbed the new British citizen; 'I am crying because – why did we have to lose India!'

In the 1930s, many émigrés found they could comfortably doff one nationhood and enthusiastically embrace another. In the Britain of more recent times, however, earnest expressions of patriotic unity became unfashionable, people tending to emphasise not what united but what differentiated them. Region, religion, colour, ethnicity, sexual orientation or age bracket – these came to be asserted, with accompanying demands for appropriate respect and cultural provision. Nowadays, as people tell you they are black or Asian, Welsh or Scottish, straight, gay or lesbian, senior citizens or single-parent welfare claimants, it almost seems there are as many Brit*ains* as there are Brit*ons*. Thus, many of the more recent arrivals to these shores seemed almost to identify more closely with the culture they and their parents had come from rather than the one they have come to. It would have been wrong to blame them if they were less inclined than the Hitler émigrés to identify themselves as essentially English or British; this was no longer the fashion. But if the Hitler émigrés made a contribution to the life and culture of their new homeland, this was undoubtedly eased by the fact that most tried to identify with its values, speak its language and subscribe to its civic structures and traditions.

The Hitler Emigrés: The Cultural Impact on Britain of Refugees from Nazism, was published in 2002 and a year later it appeared in paperback. Today, almost all the Hitler émigrés have passed away and the subject is moving from memory and becoming history. My children, now well into their 40s, are not particularly interested in the legacy of Expressionist film or Modernist architecture or the work of Kokoschka or Koestler, Popper, Pevsner or Perutz. They and their contemporaries live in a 21st-century digital world of Facebook, tweets, blogs and e-books, of Black and Multi-Ethnicity (BAME) and Me-Too feminism. Nor, frankly, was the contribution of the Hitler émigrés the be-all and the end-all of the immensely rich and varied cultural world of 1950s and 1960s Britain in which I was raised. I was brought up in a world of Laurence Olivier and Peter Brook and Peter Hall, of Michael Tippett and Benjamin Britten, of Bridget Riley, Francis Bacon and Henry Moore, of Fonteyn and Nureyev, of Braine, Wain and Kingsley Amis.

But the work of the émigrés, and the ways it intermixed with what was already here, did provide an important additional ingredient, one that immensely enriched my own intellectual and cultural life and that of many others of my generation. And I am glad to think that I caught it when I did. Fifty years ago, it would have been impossible to have undertaken a book like *The Hitler Emigrés*. Most of the people I wrote about would have been in mid-career and wouldn't have been prepared to reflect on their early lives as candidly as they were to do later. Fifty years from now, of course, the story, like all history, will have gone.

Chapter 50
Arts Nouveaux

Shortly after I had formally left the BBC, I was chatting with my former colleague Judith Bumpus. Judith had made something of a speciality of producing programmes about the arts and artists (and wrote a regular column in *Arts News*). She suggested that I might like to consider lecturing for NADFAS, the acronym, she told me, for the National Association of Decorative and Fine Arts Societies. 'But I don't know anything about the arts,' I replied, 'certainly, compared with you!' But Judith explained that NADFAS took a very broad view of what was meant by the arts, adding kindly, 'You are a wonderful public speaker!' And I had indeed found myself frequently invited for some years to lecture to Music Societies about, for example, the world of Plácido Domingo, and had undertaken several mini tours of Scotland, courtesy of the Royal Scottish Geographical Society (RSGS), to talk about the Arctic and Antarctic.

I duly got in touch with NADFAS and asked about becoming a lecturer. I encountered an impressive, formidably professional organisation. They wanted to know what experience I had had as a public lecturer, what I currently had booked and where one of their committee members might come and watch me. All this was eased by the kind encouragement of the RSGS, who also agreed to write a reference. Some months later I was summoned to NADFAS House in London's Guilford Street for an audition. My instructions were to prepare a 15-minute talk to present before a small judging panel.

NADFAS liked lectures to be image-led so, building on my recent book about ends of centuries, I put together a series of slides portraying various *fin-de-siècle* monarchs (Richard II, Henry VII and so on up to the aged Queen Victoria) and variegated cultural figures, topped off with a few germane quotes from Dryden, Wilde et al. On the day, I found myself one of some eight or ten applicants, each of whom would have his or her moment of nervous glory before being informed whether or not they had passed muster. This, I learned later, was the notorious 'trial by tweed'.

As I knew next to nothing about NADFAS, I was not particularly nervous when my turn came to speak or during the question period that followed. When asked what other subjects I had that might interest NADFAS audiences, I mentioned my interest in opera, and I recall the vigorous discussion that followed about whether or not music and opera should be accepted as a lecture subject by an organisation devoted to the 'decorative and fine arts'.

Reader, I was accepted. Sometime later came a second inaugural ritual: the annual 'Directory' meeting at which two representatives from every NADFAS Society (there were by then well over 300 of them) had a chance to meet their lecturers. As a new boy, I was given my two-minute opportunity to say a few words to the assembled multitude about what I would be happy lecturing about: 'Art and Culture in Britain at ends of centuries, 1400–2000' – the perfect topic, I emphasised, as we approached the new millennium. In due course I found myself booked to speak to over 70 societies around the country the following year, 1999, and another 30 or 40 in 2000. Then, as the new millennium set in, the *fin-de-siècle* lecture clearly had to be augmented by something new, the obvious subject being that on which much of my attention was currently focused: the cultural impact on Britain of the 'Hitler émigrés'. This provided the basis of a lecture I was invited to give over 50 times in 2002 (the year the book appeared), and continued to be booked from time to time ever since.

By 2020 I had given over 650 lectures and study days to branches of NADFAS (by now renamed 'The Arts Society'), mostly around the UK but including visits to affiliated societies in parts of Germany, Spain, Belgium and the Netherlands as well as two lengthy lecture tours (in 2002 and 2006) across Australia and New Zealand. Then, in March 2020, Coronavirus struck; all lectures ground to an end.

* * *

NADFAS was far more than a lecture agency. Founded in the early 1980s, it was a network of societies whose members would, among other things, act as local heritage volunteers, offer their services to record and preserve the artworks in local churches and encourage the arts in local schools. They would also arrange group tours in Britain and abroad to places of cultural interest. One day, after I had been lecturing for NADFAS for a year or two, I was approached by a member of the national committee who told me about the international tours they helped organise, mostly under the expert aegis of a major travel company such as Cox & Kings, and asked if I would consider leading any of them. If so, where might I be interested in going?

There are some invitations you just don't turn down! At the time, I was deeply immersed in my work on the Hitler émigrés, and in October 2001 I led my first tour: a group of about 25 people with whom I spent a few days and nights in Berlin. This was followed not long afterwards by visits to Dresden and Leipzig, then Budapest, Munich, Prague and Vienna. I soon found myself doing four or even five trips every year, increasingly for what many considered the finest or most sophisticated of the cultural tour companies, Martin Randall Travel, for whom I led over 30 opera tours. Venues for MRT included several annual Christmas visits to New York and summer trips to the Puccini Festival in Torre del Lago, plus tours to the music festivals in Aix-en-Provence and Savonlinna (Finland) as well as to Barcelona, Madrid, Milan, Munich, Naples, Paris, Prague, Riga, Rome, Turin, Valencia and Vienna.

Randall (the man and the company) could occasionally seem a little earnest, or old-fashioned if you prefer. Lectures had to be of the highest academic quality, and a little levity with clients, who were after all on

Daniel and tour group at Savonlinna Festival (Finland), 2008.
(Photo courtesy of Kathryn Hampton)

holiday, tended to be frowned upon by the management. Eventually, we parted company. Looking back, I suspect this was partly because Randall had cottoned on to the fact that I also worked occasionally for other (rival? lesser?) companies. One of these was ACE, a delightful charity on the outskirts of Cambridge with whom I collaborated on an early tour to Poland and later led a couple of trips to both Stockholm and Venice as well as to such old favourites as Prague and Riga.

Everywhere I went, and for whichever company, the routine was pretty much the same. Most mornings, after breakfast, I would give an introductory lecture about whatever or wherever we would be visiting later that day, after which we would usually be taken by a local guide to a museum or other place of cultural or historical interest and then, in the evenings, go to a concert, opera or good local restaurant. Before long, there was scarcely an opera in the international repertoire or an important opera theatre anywhere in Europe with which I was not familiar – a cumulative experience that was hugely to enrich a major book on the social history of opera that I was already beginning to write.

Altogether, I led over 50 tours until, in 2014, my friends at ACE told me regretfully that they were no longer able to obtain corporate insurance for a tour leader over the age of 75. I could hardly complain. I had had a good run.

* * *

I had long been a regular reader of (and since the early 1990s a frequent contributor to) the excellent magazine *History Today*. When preparing my BBC series about ends of centuries, I remember turning to the magazine's editor Gordon Marsden for advice about possible contributors and he had been his usual helpful and supportive self. In 1997, Gordon was elected an MP and his place at *History Today* taken by Peter Furtado. Peter and I got together and developed a project that would continue on a more-or-less regular basis for several years: a series of quarterly feature articles in which I would write about the life and work of many of our most important and best-known historians. The procedure was that I would read all the books of the next historian on our list and then, with Peter, have lunch with him or her and spend the afternoon recording a lengthy interview, after which I would go away and, over the course of the next two or three weeks, write a considered feature for the magazine of around 2,500 words. The first to be published, in October 1998, was with David Cannadine,

Daniel and Geoffrey Hosking at a History Today *party.*

an old friend from the time I used to invite him to participate in some of my BBC programmes. David had recently been appointed Director of the Institute of Historical Research (IHR) at London University, and I recorded my interview with him in his office in Senate House. In due course, I did pieces about Asa Briggs, Eric Hobsbawm, Peter Burke, David Starkey, Roy Foster, Linda Colley, Natalie Zemon Davis, Simon Schama, Antonia Fraser, Niall Ferguson, Richard Evans, Ian Kershaw, Lisa Jardine, Geoffrey Hosking and others – some 30 in all.

In 2006, the entire collection was published as *Historians* by Palgrave Macmillan (who went on to re-issue the book in paperback a decade later). Meanwhile, my knowledge of history and historians was extended further by another project Peter Furtado invited me to undertake at the time: an anthology of some of the best pieces to have been published by *History Today* to mark the magazine's 50th anniversary in 2001. This appeared as *PastMasters* published by Sutton Press. One way and another, I found myself around the turn of the millennium reading literally hundreds of books and articles and, in the process, absorbing a great deal of history and historiography that had hitherto passed me by.

* * *

All this, plus my concurrent work on the Hitler émigrés, led me to reflect more than before on the ways we regard – and perhaps disregard – the past.

How, I wondered, can people understand the present and plan intelligently for the future without a sense of how things got to be the way they are? Through my contacts with Sutton Press, I was commissioned to undertake a short book about the importance of history and the ways we use and abuse it. The working title (taken from *The Tempest* and the US National Archives in Washington) was 'The Past is Prologue'. I began drafting chapters about the widespread popularity of history, the issues raised by historical 'heritage', the mythologisation of the past, links between history and the arts, the role of the individual in historical change and how and why history comes to be re-written. This was clearly a substantial undertaking and, after a year or so, I asked if my contract could be extended. I did not want more money; just more time to do a better book. It seems Sutton was undergoing a difficult time and my request was eventually turned down and I repaid my (small) advance. In due course, Sutton became transmogrified into The History Press, with whom I was to have much more amenable dealings in 2012. And a few years later still, my ideas about history and historiography were to find an outlet through a succession of high-profile public seminars at London University's Institute of Historical Research (see Chapter 54).

More immediately, I reluctantly consigned my project about 'The Past' to the past. Something even more enticing had come my way: an invitation to draw together my lifelong interest in social history and my love of opera. 'Has there ever been a book about the social history of opera?' I was asked in August 2004 by Toby Mundy, a former aide to George Weidenfeld and recently appointed CEO of Atlantic Books. I owed my contact with Toby Mundy to our mutual friend David Cannadine. In 2003, David had invited me to deliver the IHR's annual Scouloudi Lecture in the Beveridge Hall in Senate House: a lecture which I devoted to reflections on some of the wider resonances of the story of the Hitler émigrés. This had gone down well, and David was evidently keen to enlist me, or at least encourage me, as I pursued my interest in linking the arts and culture to broader historical trends. When I found myself withdrawing my involvement with Sutton, he suggested I contact Toby at Atlantic. I did so, and we had a long and engaging talk together, and it was towards the end of this meeting that Toby asked whether anyone had written the social history of opera. I was not aware of such a book, I replied. 'Then you're the person to do it!' he said. I left his office elated if somewhat daunted. Over the next few weeks, I worked out a detailed proposal, put it to Toby through my agent and, lo and behold, the book was commissioned.

Chapter 51

The Gilded Stage

Most histories of the arts concentrate on revered creators and their works; there are many excellent studies of famous operas and their composers, just as there are of Baroque architecture or the art of the Impressionists. But what interested me was to go beyond this and to place opera within the broader historical context in which it had been created, financed, produced, received and perceived. There is a wonderfully exuberant letter from Prague written in 1787 by Mozart to a friend back home in Vienna in which he says: 'Here, nothing is played, sung or whistled but Figaro. No opera is drawing like Figaro. Nothing, nothing but *Figaro*.' But was everyone in Prague really playing, singing and whistling Mozart's music? If so, how would most people have known it, or even known who he was, in an era before photography, recording, radio, TV and a mass press? In London earlier in the century, Handel's operas were produced in a theatre (the King's, Haymarket) capable of holding an audience of under a thousand; did crowds of people stare at him in the streets and point him out with awe to their children? And was it really true in mid-19th-century Italy that everyone hummed the latest Verdi arias and choruses and revered the composer as a national hero? What I undertook to tackle in my new book was not only the 'supply' but also the 'demand', not just the production of opera but also its consumption: the many chains of connection linking opera houses and impresarios, monarchs and money makers, art, artists and audiences.

Throughout much of my adult life, I found myself gravitating towards projects that would impel me to undertake work that I knew I would enjoy but for which I had to invent, or invoke, some kind of external pressure. I had always loved opera and had been busy learning and lecturing about it when writing my Domingo books or, latterly, leading opera tours abroad. And by now I had been to well over 1,000 performances of opera, in London and around the world. But here was a major new undertaking for which I simply *had* to become seriously expert on the entire history of the subject, with a contractual deadline just a few years hence. It was also a project that required me to read widely across the political, economic and social history of the past four hundred years and more.

All this would necessitate easy and direct access to countless books, academic articles and the like for which, as a freelance writer with no official academic post, I would presumably have to pay. I discussed this one day over lunch with David Cannadine and he generously suggested he propose me as a Senior Research Fellow at the Institute of Historical Research, of which he was still Director. This would give me free access to not only to the IHR's own extensive library but also the entire University of London Library system (including a huge collection of books and papers right there in Senate House). Perfect, I thought, but asked David what being a Fellow of the IHR would require of me in return? Nothing in particular, he replied with a laugh, adding that I should just be around, perhaps attend some of the events organised by the IHR and share my interests and enthusiasms with those I encountered.

The IHR Fellowship came into effect in 2004 and was renewed regularly thereafter. But it was some years before I felt I was able to pay back my debt and contribute something substantial to the Institute that came to mean a great deal to me.

* * *

As I set to work on my ambitious new project I tried to keep in mind a number of broad historical themes, all of which would figure in the eventual book. I came to think of them as 'PESTA'.

The first was **political**. When a Gonzaga or Wittelsbach duke or a Bourbon monarch promoted opera, the aim was usually to impress someone (a rival ruler, perhaps), while 'popular' opera could often be more subversive. Mozart quit the secure employ of an archbishop to freelance in and around the court of an emperor where he encountered his finest librettist, a Venetian Jew who landed up in John Quincy Adams' America. Napoleon appeared at the opera to show himself to the people whose cause he was supposedly fighting in foreign lands. In the wake of the French Revolutionary wars, much of central Europe gradually became immersed in a rising tide of cultural nationalism, a theme that many of the producers and consumers of opera embraced and which survived well into the 20th century, notably and notoriously under the Third Reich. In our own times, public debate about the supposed elitism or popularity of opera has sometimes taken a fiercely political turn.

Alongside politics was **economics**. It was impossible to talk about an art form that aspired to combine all the others – and was therefore liable to be the most expensive – without discussing money and management. Detailed historical information was sporadic about, for example, the wages paid to members of early choruses or orchestras. But we do know something about the sums paid to celebrated soloists and, here and there, the cost of buying a box at the opera for a season or the cost of tickets for individual performances. Opera has rarely managed to be self-financing, and if there is one issue that recurred like a rondo theme throughout the story it was the question of who paid or, rather, who picked up the deficit. The story of opera was therefore in part that of a succession of dukes and monarchs, risk-running impresarios, syndicates of bountiful bankers and industrialists, grants from local or central governments, and latterly of various ingenious, more or less tax-exempt schemes to raise money from sponsorship and private donation.

Opera was a **social** phenomenon, too. The shift in the nature of the operatic audience clearly paralleled other historical changes as power and money moved from the aristocracy, church and higher soldiery to the emergent bourgeoisie and, latterly, to a wider social spectrum. This shift was evident in everything from the physical shape of the opera house itself (the relative absence of boxes and other social distinctions in most modern opera theatres), the way audiences behaved and dressed at the opera, pricing policy, the style of playbills and programmes, and the food and drink on offer. Equally remarkable was the changing social status of those in the operatic professions – especially, perhaps, among talented female singers to whom opera at times offered a rare opportunity for substantial social and economic improvement.

Changes in **technology**, too, transformed the nature of opera. From earliest times, opera flaunted magical stage effects as Eros flew overhead, Jove or Juno descended from heaven or the plot's wicked miscreant was dragged down into a fiery hell. 'Scenes and machines' were as much remarked on as the music or drama. Indeed, the latest scientific wizardry often featured, sometimes in parodic form, in operatic plots (for example, the caricature of Dr Mesmer in *Così fan tutte*). During the course of my narrative I wrote of candle, gas and electric lighting, of gauzes and swimming machines and of the arrival of laser lighting and surtitles. But the story also included the development of new means of spreading the word (and sounds and sights) of opera beyond the confines of the theatre: music publishing and copyright laws, and the successive invention of photography, recording, film, TV, video and the latest satellite and digital technologies.

Finally, of course, opera is an art form, and the book was therefore, in addition to all else, a cultural history. Here, several historical arcs emerged. One concerned the people who actually made opera happen. The singer had always been important, and the story was replete with the supposedly extravagant behaviour, funding and achievements of operatic superstars. But everyone else's relative weight on the scales of significance shifted radically over time as the story lurched from what might loosely be labelled 'Patrons' Opera' (the courts of the Gonzagas to that of Joseph II), 'Composers' Opera' (from Gluck and Mozart to Puccini and Strauss), 'Conductors' Opera' (the Mahler/Toscanini era) and 'Directors' Opera' in more recent times. Who, or what, is the principal attraction when *you* decide to go to the opera?

As for the **art form** itself, two broad strands wove their way in and out of my narrative and these, too, changed over time. The first, which was encountered in the courts of late-Renaissance Italy, in Handel, Wagner, Verdi and Benjamin Britten, was what might be dubbed 'serious' opera, usually through-composed and dealing with heightened emotions, situations and characters. The other, a more popular style of music theatre with catchy tunes and vernacular dialogue, emerged in everything from Venetian commedia dell'arte, *The Beggar's Opera* and *The Magic Flute* to Viennese operetta, Gilbert and Sullivan and beyond.

In earlier times, opera goers liked to attend something new (rather like the cinema audiences of later times). By the early 20th century, however, it was becoming clear that they preferred to revisit a standard repertoire of acknowledged classics, an emerging canon to which few new works were subsequently added. Running alongside this fundamental change was the way operatic plots and productions altered focus over the centuries from high authority and quasi-mythical heroes towards ordinary people and victims. The music of operas, similarly, tended to shift from stylised aria and recitative towards more integrated music-drama, thence perhaps to psychodrama and, in parallel, the popular musicals of recent decades.

* * *

Over the next few years, I found myself chronicling what proved to be an intoxicating operatic odyssey during which I feasted on a rich diet of art, architecture, music, literature and drama: a magnificent 'grand tour' of the mind that required me to stop over in the courts of Renaissance Italy, Louis

XIV's Versailles, the London of Hogarth and Handel, Habsburg Vienna, the Paris of Delacroix and Chopin, Verdi's Italy, Wagner's Germany and much else. By the mid-19th century, opera was no longer a European monopoly; out on the American frontier, gold rush millionaires flaunted their flamboyant claims to high culture while New York's *nouveaux riches* set up the Metropolitan Opera and established a vogue for high-quality opera that continued to thrive right across the USA. In the 20th century, opera managed to survive and surmount the tragedies of two world wars to become a truly global art form: latterly, the most famous building in the entire southern hemisphere was the Sydney Opera House.

During the course of my journeying, I found myself confronting a huge range of challenging questions. How far had opera been influenced by the sources of its finances? How did the *prima donna* get her fiery reputation? Which had proved better for opera (and the arts in general), dictatorships or democracies? How had a supposedly 'elite' art form taken root in such self-consciously egalitarian societies as the USA or Australia? When did theatre audiences start to give more attention to the stage and less to their fellow audience members? And why, during the 20th century and into the 21st, had there grown such a wide divergence between the desire to perform the music as authentically as possible and the frequent determination to stage familiar operas in ways often wilfully different from anything seen before?

And the biggest question of them all: what did I mean by the word 'opera'? The word (plural of opus, meaning 'works' or 'oeuvres') was simply an Italian catch-all term for a complex, multimedia art form that had originated as an attempt to combine all the arts (a '*Gesamtkunstwerk*', to adopt Wagnerian terminology). Should I include the history of 'operettas', 'comic operas' and 'musicals'? If not, why not? In general, I aimed to be inclusive in my analysis and to avoid too narrow or precise a definition of what was meant by the word opera. Indeed, I suggested at one point that it might be a good idea to ditch the emotionally loaded 'O-word' altogether.

* * *

As I looked back over the entire story, it was hard to avoid the conclusion that 'opera', at least as widely construed, was an art form that had reached its acme between about the time of Mozart and the death of Puccini and that, in this sense at least, what I had been documenting was the rise, triumph and gradual decline and fall, and possible eventual demise, of a once great but now receding art form. When I saw my first Puccini opera, the composer had been dead for less than thirty years, and his final opera, *Turandot*, remains to this day part of a universally acknowledged standard repertoire, produced right across the operatic world in its original language, like *Zauberflöte*, *Rigoletto* or *Carmen*. No opera since *Turandot* (premiered in 1926) could be said to come under this category. That was not to deny the quality of much that was produced later. But even a masterpiece like *Peter Grimes* or *Billy Budd*, if put on in Sweden, France, Germany, Italy or Japan, has almost always had Anglophone guest artists rather than native singers playing the principal roles. Maybe what I was witnessing was a process whereby opera was becoming a museum art, a kind of old-fashioned religion re-enacted inside great temples before an ageing audience of the devout. I am not against museums. On the contrary, I love them, I'm a historian and have always enjoyed a good, contemplative look at a Greek vase, a Rembrandt portrait or whatever is on display. Similarly, my heart will leap up at the sight of a restored old castle or thatch-topped house or a skilled wigmaker at work. Perhaps opera was slowly entering similarly historic territory.

Opera lovers, like myself, found themselves going again and again to what was in fact a tiny, recurrent core repertoire of perhaps 50 works, almost all of them dating from the 'long' 19th century, out of the many thousands that had been composed over the previous 400 years and more. One way and another, as I worked towards the end of the book (with the economies of the western world plunging into recession), I found myself facing a recurrent, somewhat mournful question: does opera as we understand it have any future – or merely a past?

* * *

But then, in more optimistic mode, I recognised that, while the core repertoire of the world's opera theatres may not have expanded greatly over the previous half century or so, there had been welcome additions. It was no longer uncommon to catch a production of Monteverdi's *Orfeo*, say, or *l'Incoronazione di Poppea*, while the operas of Handel, widely thought unstageable a century ago with all those supposedly boring A-B-A arias, had in recent decades gradually entered the mainstream. As for the modern end of the spectrum, not just Britten but more recent composers such as Philip Glass, George Benjamin, John Adams and others were being staged around the world.

What about the often controversial modern productions to which traditional opera was increasingly subjected? It had been common currency since the 1980s, if not earlier, to deplore *Regietheater* ('Director's theatre') in which the supposedly perverse ideas of the director often predominated over and frequently swamped those of the composer he or she was supposedly there to serve. Any opera goer would tell you of awful productions that had ruined what could otherwise have been a wonderful evening. Why dress Wotan like a lollipop lady, have Verdi's conspirators in *Ballo* sitting on toilets or Lucia visibly bonking her lover or having an onstage abortion? Some things are more powerful if left to the imagination; a glimpse of an ankle beneath a crinoline is often sexier than a naked lady parading across the stage.

And yet, and yet. Many imaginative directors, taking full account of the work they are presenting, have greatly enriched the experience of opera. Jonathan Miller's *Rigoletto* worked superbly when set in New York's mafia-packed, 1950s-style 'Little Italy'. An opera like *Carmen* or *Bohème* can make perfect sense if portrayed as young people in today's world as they struggle with powerful but potentially damaging erotic relationships. Why not set *Tosca* in Fascist Rome or show the prisoners in *Fidelio* emerging from a Nazi concentration camp? Such ideas can work well if those playing the parts are capable of not only singing but also acting their roles. The idea of a stage director (like that of the orchestral conductor) didn't really become established in the opera theatre until the later decades of the 19th century (much to the irritation of people like Verdi and Wagner who, from much earlier, would often sit in on rehearsals and tell their performers not only the kind of sound they wanted them to make but also how they should look, where they should move etc.). Even as recently as when I first started going to opera, press reviews commented primarily on the singing and only then if at all on the production, while audience members (such as my father) attended almost entirely for the voices, with little complaint as this or that tubby tenor or bosomy soprano belted out a phrase or an aria and then waited, more or less immobile, until it was time for their next utterance. If you had a gramophone recording of Gigli or Björling singing a bewitchingly beautiful aria, this was what attracted you to the theatre when they were billed to perform. By the time I was going to opera, a number of versatile singers were emerging (Callas, Gobbi, Christoff, Vickers) whose very ability to act persuasively was sufficiently unusual to draw comment.

By now things had moved on further. The record industry was in decline and few people were likely to become familiar with the latest celebrity opera singer merely through listening to a CD or a radio station. More likely, they'd have caught a clip on YouTube, sampled highlights on a videodisc or perhaps enjoyed a night out in the cinema watching a live relay from the New York Met or Covent Garden. Through these, plus a variety of social media, opera had come to be regarded far more as a visual art form than it had been a couple of generations earlier. The great opera houses of the world were unlikely to cast an ungainly looking singer as Tristan or Otello unless he was capable of the rare soaring power demanded of a true *Heldentenor* or, in *bel canto* roles, the beautiful, breathless lyricism of Pavarotti or Caballé. Better if you could sing, act *and* look the part – like Fleming, Netrebko, Gheorghiu, Kaufmann or Flórez. And if a director had a cast of versatile singer-actors (along with the latest kinds of digital lighting), there was no limit to the kind of production to which the inventive mind might give rise.

When attending the opera, you might feel you want to *hear* the original score, the version the composer intended (itself a contentious issue; think of the many versions of, say, *Tannhäuser* or *Simon Boccanegra*). But the only possible reason for wanting to *see* an old opera as originally produced would be to sample not art but history. I'd love to know what *Lucia* or *Lohengrin, Trovatore* or *Thäis* looked like first time around. But I suspect they would look risible to modern eyes, accustomed as we have become to meticulous stage production, digital lighting and singers who make serious efforts to act the parts they are playing. In this respect, too, opera – far from being a dying art ready for the museum of human experience – was alive and well and undergoing a degree of aesthetic rejuvenation.

* * *

There was one other respect, too, in which opera, far from retreating into the past, might have been undergoing something of a revival. By the time I was writing my book, more opera was performed, financed, seen, heard, filmed and broadcast than ever before. There were opera companies and opera theatres right around the world, including new houses opened in Dallas, Copenhagen, Oslo, Tenerife, Tel Aviv, Dubai, Moscow, Beijing and elsewhere. Many of the leading operatic tenors of recent decades had emerged from Latin America (Domingo, Villazón, Cura, Flórez, Marcelo Álvarez and Javier Camarena) while it became common for a major role

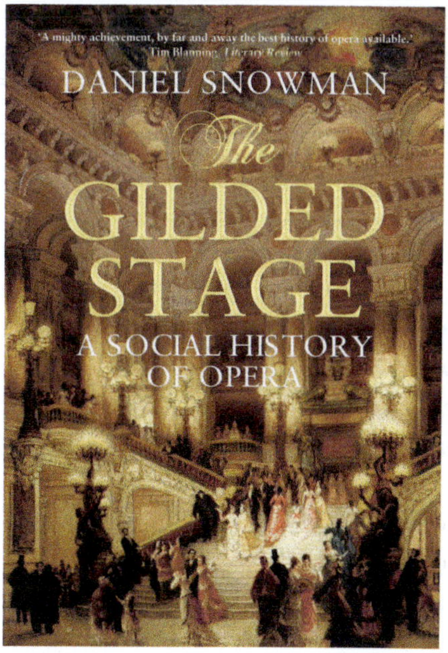

The UK paperback and Chinese editions of The Gilded Stage.

Bangkok Opera's 2006 production of Das Rheingold *with features drawn from Southeast Asian myth.* (Photo courtesy of the Bangkok Opera)

in one of Europe's leading houses to be played – in excellent, idiomatic French, German or Italian – by a singer from Russia or the nations of Eastern Europe or, indeed, from China, Korea or elsewhere in Southeast Asia. While working on the book I was in email correspondence with Somtow Sucharitkul, the Thai director who was working on a production of Wagner's *Ring* in Bangkok.

Maybe what I had been chronicling was the 'globalisation' of an art form that, having made its initial tentative steps as a court entertainment in northern Italy 400-odd years ago, was by now genuinely popular right across the world. As, perhaps, was its supposed 'democratisation' as opera managements talked increasingly of bringing opera to a wider (and younger) public, set up workshops and educational projects, insight and outreach events, and opportunities to attend rehearsals and 'meet the stars', and promoted come-as-you-are performances in parks and other popular venues. In order to guarantee funding for this most expensive of art forms, managements also had to retain a residue of the old-fashioned elite image of opera, the idea of opera's exclusivity, that traditionally appealed to those with wealth and a sense of social status. The trick was to find ways of bringing the two brands together: to encourage those with money and status to play a pivotal part in an enterprise that, at the same time, was doing all it could to widen its appeal across the social scale. And across the world. Overall, and on balance, I felt that there were perhaps more reasons to celebrate than to mourn the state and status of opera in the early years of the 21st century.

Book 11

'New Worlds'

2013–20

Chapter 52

Viva Verdi!

Yet again, life seemed to go through one of its more or less decennial changes. During the latter half of 2012, I undertook to write a brief biography of Verdi. My personal life was by now in something of a turmoil and I felt a profound and welcome sense of distraction, and perhaps identification, as I launched into that of the Italian composer. The following year, my wife and I decided, sadly, to live separately. In 2014 I led what proved to be the last of more than 50 tours to the cultural capitals of Europe (and New York). In 2015, after 48 years and 436 concerts, I finally left the London Philharmonic Choir – and went on to organise and chair an ambitious series of public seminars at the Institute of Historical Research. By then, a rich new life had opened up to me.

* * *

The Verdi biography was commissioned by Tony Morris, an old friend from the publishing world, and it was one of a series of *Pocket Giants* launched by The History Press (alongside similar volumes on Jane Austen, Henry V, Pope John Paul II and others). Verdi was one of my heroes, the Shakespeare of opera, the artist who had probably given me greater pleasure than any other. He was also one of the very few to have had an active and sophisticated interest in the politics of his times, becoming after the achievement of Italian statehood in 1861 a member of the first all-Italian parliament. It would be hard imagining Mozart or Puccini as an MP!

Verdi could be a difficult character at times. Far from being the passionate, romantic figure he evoked in so many of his operas, he could appear to the outside world as a little distant, calculating even, especially when in his later years he repeatedly turned down invitations to compose further operas, preferring to immure himself and his wife Giuseppina behind the gates of their extensive farmlands. Yet inside this set exterior, Verdi proved to be one of the few great artists who, remaining active into old age (Titian was another, perhaps, and Picasso), refused to live off the memory and reputation of a few early works, continuing instead to strive, to struggle, to grow, to transcend. His crowning glory, *Otello*, was premiered when the composer was already in his mid-70s; after a great performance you can emerge quite drained, sensing that you have experienced the ultimate pinnacle of Italian opera, the greatest integration of drama and text, vocal and orchestral music ever penned and, if you are lucky, sets, props and acting of the highest quality as well. Then, when Verdi was nearly 80, the great operatic tragedian produced a bubbling comedy (*Falstaff*). Truly the Shakespeare of opera. Verdi died on 27 January 1901, a few days after Queen Victoria, and I still remember maintaining a vigil to mark the 50th anniversary of his passing.

* * *

Verdi died in the Grand Hotel et de Milan, just up the road from La Scala. During his final decline, the city authorities covered the streets outside his hotel room with straw to dull the sound of horses' hooves, and people began to congregate nearby as their beloved maestro sank gradually towards his inevitable demise. On the day of the funeral, as the cortège wound its way across Milan, the largest crowds the city had ever witnessed lined the route and, gently and spontaneously, began to sing the chorus 'Va pensiero' (from his opera *Nabucco*), Verdi's paean to his beloved homeland penned nearly 60 years earlier as a coded anthem yearning for a united, independent Italy.

Thus, the legend. And, like most legends, or clichés, it contains an element of truth. In fact, Verdi's actual funeral was, as he had instructed, a relatively modest affair and he was initially buried in Milan's *Cimitero Monumentale*. But a month later, to great pomp and circumstance, his body was transferred to lie (alongside that of Giuseppina) across town in the crypt of the 'Casa di Riposo', the home for retired musicians Verdi himself had founded and funded. As the cortège was about to leave the Cimitero, Arturo Toscanini, the 33-year-old principal conductor at La Scala, led a huge choir in a performance of 'Va pensiero' and many of those within earshot doubtless sang along. As for the suggestion that this chorus was a surrogate national hymn, this may have been a common perception by 1901, but was hardly that back in 1842 when it was composed.

Much that happened in Verdi's life remains clouded by myth or uncertainty, and the man himself, like many ageing celebrities, was not above adding to the mystique. 'I am just a peasant, rough-hewn' he would chuckle to visitors, seeming to forget that his father, Carlo Verdi, ran an inn, kept efficient accounts and, in a society in which many were illiterate, could read and write and afford to send his son to school. True, the family background was provincial, living as they did in a tiny village near what was a smallish town. But that was true of most Italians in those days. Different parts of the vast Italian peninsula were ruled by a series of remote, often foreign-based authorities whose writ tended to impinge upon village life far less directly than that of the landowners and priesthood of the vicinity. Life was, essentially, lived in the locality with local people, local diet and local dialect. Even into old age, long after Italy had been united and its national language standardised, Verdi spoke and wrote Italian with occasional imperfections deriving from the regional dialect he had learned as a youngster. 'Just a peasant'? No. But one can see why the wealthy celebrity of the 1870s and 1880s, fêted in cities like Milan and Paris, might have said so when reminiscing about the remote flatlands of his early childhood.

The Verdi mythology starts with the date of his birth and the home in which he was raised. For over 60 years the composer told people that he was born in Le Roncole ('the scythes'), a little village in the Po Valley near Busseto in the Duchy of Parma, some 65 kilometres or so southeast of Milan, on 9 October 1814. That, at least, is what his mother Luigia had told him. In fact, as his birth certificate attests, he had been born a year earlier, in October 1813 but (according to the ecclesiastical record in the local church as well as the civic record) more likely on 10 October. He was certainly born in Roncole; but not it seems in the house with the slanting roof that, to this day, remains the official birthplace of the great man. The family did live there, but probably not until the boy was older. And his baptismal name was not Giuseppe but Joseph; in 1813 the region was still under French rule and it was another couple of years before the baby could become Giuseppe in the eyes of officialdom.

Every age has to recreate its own version of the past, seen through the agenda of a constantly changing present. We now know that some of what has long been believed about Verdi may be the result of subsequent mythologisation, helped along in part by the ageing maestro himself. But none of this in any way reduces the greatness of the man. On the contrary, the very fact that Verdi has long been regarded as one of the supreme visionary heroes of Italian unification and statehood, a genius who used his art to help better the fate of his compatriots, has itself long been incorporated into the narrative of Italian history. In my book, I tried to separate demonstrable fact from resonant fiction, while allowing an important place for both. And, throughout, I felt it important not to forget

ABOVE *Daniel lecturing for NADFAS.*
ABOVE RIGHT *Daniel lecturing about the 'Hitler Emigrés' (Royal College of Music, February 2014).*
RIGHT *Chairing conference panel, Royal College of Music, London, 23 February 2014. With Daniel is Sir John Tooley, former General Director of the Royal Opera House, Covent Garden.*
BELOW *Interviewing Daniel Barenboim at the Royal Academy of Music, London, 3 February 2010.*

that Verdi was a human being with his own needs and desires, fulfilments, frustrations and failings. This, to my mind, rendered his achievements – as musician and man – all the more impressive.

Most creative artists are known to posterity by their artworks alone and, perhaps, by something about the lives they led. We may admire the works of Leonardo and Michelangelo, Shakespeare and Tolstoy, Mozart, Beethoven and the rest, and return to them again and again. None of these was ever regarded, in his own time or since, as a virtual embodiment of his nation, let alone a pivotal figure in its very foundation. Yet this was how Verdi was mourned on his death in 1901 and how many continue to see him to this day.

* * *

Culture, the arts, music (especially opera) – and the historical interrelation between them – came to be among my central preoccupations as the new millennium progressed. In the wake of my books about the cultural impact of the Hitler émigrés and the history of opera I found myself invited to present lectures, conduct interviews and chair conferences on these and related subjects before an ever wider variety of academic and general interest audiences: to countless NADFAS societies, to Jewish and immigrant groups as well as at London's various music academies, the Royal Opera House, English National Opera, Glyndebourne and further afield at, for example, New York's Juilliard School of Music and the New York Metropolitan Opera Guild. Meanwhile, I continued to sing with the London Philharmonic Choir.

Chapter 53
Choral Evensong

By the early 2000s, the LPC was undergoing an undoubted 'high' in its history. A couple of months after its Vatican visit, the Choir spent a week in Hong Kong, a trip largely planned by my fellow opera lover, Hin-Yan Wong, a popular member of the Choir's bass section (the trip had been postponed from the previous year because of the SARS scare). At Hong Kong's Cultural Centre, we delivered a pair of (I have to say) virtuoso performances of Haydn's *Creation*, packed with high-octane, highly disciplined pizazz – and plunged, the day after the long-haul flight home, into final rehearsals with Mark Elder of *La damnation de Faust*. A matter of days later came Mahler *Two* with the Philharmonia and Esa-Pekka Salonen, and a month after that we scaled the mountain of Beethoven's *Missa Solemnis* under the London Philharmonic Orchestra's Principal Conductor, Kurt Masur. Then, a month later, the *Glagolitic Mass* in what was the 150th anniversary of Janáček's birth, conducted by that incomparable expert Sir Charles Mackerras. For many Choir members, the LPC virtually took over their lives for much of 2004, something of an *annus mirabilis* in the Choir's history.

* * *

Why are so many of the great works masses for the dead? The Britten *War Requiem* is a piece I sang many times with the Choir, including under Haitink in 1976, shortly before Britten died, and latterly with Paul Daniel, John Eliot Gardiner and Kurt Masur. In 1983 we did the piece with the great Russian cellist and conductor Mstislav Rostropovich. 'Slava' spent much of his piano rehearsal regaling us, in his thick Russian accent, with wonderful stories only he could tell. Britten had given him a copy of the score to take to Shostakovich who, looking at the 'Agnus Dei' – so deceptively simple yet so ineffably moving – apparently shook his sad head and said in wonderment: 'How does Ben do it?' We saw a tough, earthy side of Rostropovich, too. When we launched into a doubtless too careful, polite rendition of Britten's savage 'Dies irae', Rostropovich told us to imagine the KGB tearing out fingernails. That did the trick! And I remember the orchestral rehearsal during which Slava spent much of the time arguing, sometimes quite petulantly, with his soprano soloist, Galina Vishnevskaya – who just happened to be not only the person for whom Britten had written the part but also Rostropovich's wife!

In May 2005, at London's Royal Festival Hall, the Choir sang the Britten *War Requiem* under Kurt Masur, the LPO's Principal Conductor for the previous five years. It was the last great choral concert before the Hall was closed for refurbishment. More significantly, the concert also marked the 60th anniversary of V-E Day. At the initial piano rehearsal, our distinguished German conductor told us how, 60 years before, he had been a teenage soldier trying to save his country from defeat – which, he said, thank God he hadn't. He talked about the destruction of Coventry, and of Dresden. 'Imagine,' he said, 'that your city, one of the most beautiful in the world, has been destroyed.' As I struggled to enter the spirit of this deeply felt choral work, I reflected on the career of a man who had lived under both Nazism and East German Communism and who, from his base in Leipzig (where he was Chief Conductor of the Gewandhaus Orchestra), had emerged as a pivotal figure in the peaceful transition to democracy and German reunification.

* * *

In 2006, the LPO announced Masur's successor as Principal Conductor: Vladimir Jurowski. The charismatic young maestro, already for several years the Artistic Director at Glyndebourne, was familiar to the LPC from performances of *Alexander Nevsky* and the Mozart *Requiem*. But the relationship was put sternly to the test shortly after the LPO's announcement as the choir prepared itself for an exceptionally demanding concert: a Prom containing not only Rachmaninov's *The Bells* (sung jointly with the Philharmonia Chorus in what was Jurowski's native language) but also the UK premiere of a lugubrious composition by that ageing *enfant terrible* of British music Mark-Anthony Turnage entitled *A Relic of Memory*. This piece proved to be the most achingly difficult to master that I had encountered in my (by then) nearly 40 years with the Choir. Packed with uncomfortable leaps, often hair-raisingly syncopated and set against utterly unrelated harmonies, it was clearly going to be something of a vocal Everest to climb. Yet we also knew that our entire future relationship with Jurowski, the LPC's Maestro-in-Waiting, could depend upon how we acquitted ourselves in this particular concert.

There was only one way of tackling the problem, and that was head on. Extra rehearsals were arranged, including an all-day Saturday workshop while the LPC's pianist, Iain Farrington, recorded the piece four times, each giving emphasis to one of the voice parts, and the CDs were distributed for home learning. On the night, the Royal Albert Hall was packed. For the Turnage? The Rachmaninov? Perhaps for the Prokofiev piano concerto. Anyway, the concert the audience heard was a *tour de force*. The Turnage was far from perfect (and I would not like to hear a close-miked recording of my personal contribution!). But it was as good as any non-professional choir could ever achieve, a real performance. And by the time the Philharmonia joined us for *The Bells* we were ready to rip the roof off the RAH. At the end of the evening, the audience erupted with applause. Jurowski, his face framed by a rich head of black hair, was beaming. So were we.

By the time I had been in the LPC for 40 years and more, people began to ask what had kept me in the Choir for so long. I loved the music, of course, though there was probably also an element of inertia, of habit. Many a time, tired at the end of a busy day, I was aching for a quiet evening at home. But it was a rehearsal night. So off I went, in bad grace and probably in bad voice. Why? For the boring reason that that's what I did on Monday and Wednesday evenings. Then, almost invariably, the miracle occurred, and I returned home three hours later with body and mind revivified by music, companionship and the uplifting physicality of singing.

But the Choir was more than a visit to the gym, or a club. Through the LPC I became intimately acquainted with some of the great musical masterworks and made revered friends whom, every now and then, I had the huge pleasure of re-encountering. I sometimes joked that the reason I joined the Choir was in order to go to lots of free concerts. Not true, of course. But over the years, before or after singing the assigned choral composition, I heard at close range countless performances of (for example) the symphonies and concertos of Mozart, Beethoven and Brahms or wonderful orchestral showpieces by Stravinsky, Ravel and others – works that everyone out in the hall had had to pay to hear.

Above all, membership of the Choir enabled me to get to know some of music's great masterpieces from the inside, as it were. I think of such profound intimations and evocations of life, death, war, peace and eternity as are encapsulated in (for example) Haydn's *Creation*, Mahler's *Resurrection* symphony or the requiem for the dead as set by Mozart, Berlioz, Verdi,

Brahms and Britten. In my daily life, I am not much given to spiritual reflection. But great music superbly executed can touch the soul and change lives. Like most in the LPC I suspect, I relished above all the great occasions when a major work, with outstanding soloists and an important conductor, was given with our own 'mother' orchestra after proper rehearsal time in a packed hall to a discriminating London audience.

A decade or so into the new century, under the leadership of Jurowski, the LPC found itself increasingly invited to perform works from the later 20th century rather than the traditional classics. During the Southbank's *Rest is Noise* project in 2013, we moved from early 20th-century works to pieces by Poulenc and Pärt to John Adams' *El Niño*: all fine pieces, but progressively harder to master. Finally, by early 2015, I felt the time had come to quit. In the past, I had usually sailed through the regular re-auditions to which all Choir members were subjected. But these were by now coming to be a cause of some anxiety. And, in any case, I no longer had the vocal resonance or the breath control of the vibrant young men amongst whom I found myself sitting. I decided to go – and that the decision should be mine and not that of our long-time Chorus Master, Neville Creed.

Daniel in choir rehearsal. And in surplice for Mozart Requiem *concert (2015).*

I looked through the Choir's programme for the next few months and noticed much of the usual esoterica. But I also noted that, prior to various Proms performances and an autumn *Carmina Burana*, we were scheduled to do two popular concerts, both of which featured a Requiem: the Fauré in May and the Mozart – for which the Choir were required to wear surplices – in June. How appropriate, I thought, to go out on two masses for the dead!

I duly sang in both and, at the final rehearsal before the Mozart, made a short speech of gratitude and farewell to the choir that I loved so much. I ended with a little poem, a toast to the LPC, in which I tried to encapsulate something of what the Choir, its members and its music-making had meant to me over nearly half a century. I ended like this:

Right now I'm winding down. No awkward, tricky compositions
To struggle with; no nerves about approaching re-auditions!
But I miss you all already, and my pain is all the keener
As you gear up for the Proms, and after that Carmina.
But I'll relax with drink in hand on choir rehearsal nights
At home – or in Taberna*! – new life of sensuous delights!*
– But my thoughts will fly in your direction. So (do keep this discreet!)
If my spirit hovers over you, please keep an empty seat!
So Alle Menschen, Hallelujah! Auferstehn – Arise!
Let's sing aloud and make a joyful noise! For I surmise
That forty-eight more years from now my dominant and tonic
Will e'er remain my thanks to the choir of the London Philharmonic!

I knew I would miss not just the music, but also many good friends. In a way, the LPC had been my 'club'. But I had already found another; by the time I left the choir I was deeply immersed in a new project at the Institute of Historical Research.

Chapter 54

History Now and Then

Throughout my adult life I found myself repeatedly immersed in matters historical. I was interested in history, had lectured, written and broadcast about it. And I often found myself returning to the past as a welcome distraction from an occasionally difficult present.

Shortly after the various disruptions in my life during the mid-2010s, I joined the Pepys Club (Secretary: Lucie Skeaping). The Club had been founded in 1903, the 200th anniversary of the death of the diarist, Head of the Admiralty (and MP) Samuel Pepys. Pepys had lived in turbulent times, witnessed the execution of King Charles I, the restoration of the Stuart monarchy under Charles II and the subsequent flowering of theatre and the arts, the great plague and fire of London, a succession of naval wars against the Dutch, the fierce anti-Popery of Restoration times and the 'Glorious Revolution' of 1688 and its consequences. The famous diary covered only nine years, from Pepys's mid-20s until his mid-30s, and Club members were not for the most part obsessed with the minutiae of his life. But many had an informed interest in various aspects of the times and, as in any good club, the opportunities it provided for interesting and enriching sociability.

The Club had a membership of around 130, among them a number who had been judges and barristers, top civil servants, parliamentarians, naval commanders, medical experts, historians and other leading academics. Every year the Club held a variety of events which included guided visits to locations associated with Pepys and his times, an annual lecture by a distinguished historian, a Memorial service in Pepys's old church at St Olave's (where he is buried) and a grand formal dinner held in one of the great historic halls of the City and presided over by John Montagu, Earl of Sandwich, a direct descendent of the original Earl who, in company with his cousin and *protégé* Pepys, accompanied Charles II back from the continent in 1660 thus restoring the Stuart monarchy. All these events, plus a variety of book reviews and other relevant articles, would be written up in the Club 'Newsletter' which, under Lucie's editorship, expanded to become a substantial, richly illustrated magazine.

Members of the Pepys Club at the National Portrait Gallery, London (7 March 2019, following the Annual Lecture presented by Claire Tomalin). DS on left, Sir David Latham extreme right.

By 2020, the Club was positively flourishing, its chairman by then being the former Lord Justice of Appeal, Sir David Latham, son of Robert Latham who was the first to edit and publish the complete Pepys diaries. Then in March, the Pepys Club like so much else essentially went into furlough, struck down by the advent of the Coronavirus pandemic. Many members sought comfort by re-reading what Pepys had written about the Great Plague of 1665. All Club dinners, meetings and outings had to be cancelled, and lectures and Committee meetings conducted henceforth via Zoom.

* * *

Much the same, sadly, was true of the Institute of Historical Research. But looking back (my favourite pastime during the Covid-19 pandemic), I realised that I had enjoyed a busy and productive time at the IHR since becoming a Senior Research Fellow back in 2004. From the outset I had attended conferences, presented papers from time to time and sat in on occasional seminars chaired by a succession of IHR Directors. Was there anything more I could do to help the work of the Institute, I would regularly ask? In 2010, much to my delight, I was invited by the Director Miles Taylor to deliver the annual Fellows' Lecture.

I used the occasion to argue, as I had essentially done in my recent book *The Gilded Stage*, for closer links between what I called 'mainstream history' and that of the high arts. History, I said at the outset to my fellow practitioners, was surely the discipline above all that invited cross-fertilisation with others, if only because everything that had ever happened was, as we say, 'history'. Yet I sensed that much arts history (particularly the study of so-called 'classical' music) continued to be largely preoccupied with its own in some ways esoteric subject matter while much mainstream historical research tended to marginalise the arts (again, Western art music in particular, perhaps), preferring to leave it to the experts. Surely it was time that historians should bring music and the arts in from the cold and incorporate them, like any other historical data, into their deliberations.

This was a theme that had run right through my professional life, I told my IHR audience. Back in the early/mid 1960s when I was a Lecturer at Sussex, we had no academic departments; rather cross-disciplinary 'Schools of Study' and an interdisciplinary course structure. At the BBC, similarly, it was the opportunity to seek links between ostensibly separate intellectual territories that had always appealed to me. And it had continued to do so in the years since. I explained how, in my book about the Hitler *émigrés*, I had tried to examine the cultural transfer resulting from a wave of migration, while *The Gilded Stage* was avowedly an attempt to link two very different historiographies: that on the history of opera, mostly by people trained as musicologists, and a (far larger) corpus of material on political, economic and social history.

As a case study to illustrate my theme to the IHR audience I spoke of the fire which destroyed the Covent Garden theatre (the 'Royal Italian Opera') in 1856. Part of opera history, of course, but a topic that touched on many aspects of life in Victorian London, among them architecture, insurance, finance, theatre management and a range of legal implications. Frederick Gye, the man in charge of the theatre, was in France when the fire occurred, and his diaries record how he came to be informed and the efforts he made to find his way back to London as speedily as possible. As for the social status of opera, this was well illustrated by press reports of the opera-loving Queen Victoria visiting the burned wreck of the theatre at the earliest opportunity to offer her condolences.

The fire of 1856 was the second time the Covent Garden theatre had burned down (the first was in 1808). But it was by no means the only theatre to suffer this fate: virtually every important opera house burned down during the 19th century, including those in Barcelona, Berlin, Dresden, Moscow, Munich, Naples, New York, Paris, Prague, St Petersburg, and Venice. Such events were certainly part of opera history. But they told one a great deal more about the history of the times. I argued in my IHR Lecture that the history of the high arts should no longer be regarded as a kind of sugary decoration on the outer edges of the main historiographical cake but as an essential ingredient and therefore incorporated into our study of the past like all other data, that what historians should ultimately aspire to produce might be a kind of Wagnerian *Gesamtkunstwerk*: a bringing together of everything. We historians, I said, should try to find a view of the past that incorporated the arts into something broader: a kind of Hegelian synthesis drawing together the sometimes rather specialist insights of the history of art and music and those arising from the political, legal, economic and social focus of most 'mainstream' historical research in the hope that a new all-embracing synthesis might emerge.

* * *

The IHR had a large and active website which included not only a list of recent and forthcoming events, but a great many online news items, articles, book reviews and the like. In December 2013, I recorded an interview for the website with Miranda Seymour: the first of what became a series of interviews with well-known historians. Miranda was the author of a wide range of cultural histories and biographies, most recently a book she had entitled *Noble Endeavours*. In this she outlined, in almost novelistic form, the long history of Anglo-German cultural interconnections from the 18th-century love of Shakespeare among German literary and intellectual figures, through the 'Grand Tour' that took many leading Britons down the Rhine, the mutually affectionate links epitomised by Queen Victoria and her husband Albert, and the love of Goethe and Schiller, Schubert, Heine, Weber and Wagner shared by so many Britons right through until the onset of War in 1914. Her object – and this is what had attracted me to the book in the first place – was to transcend the simplistic, cliché-ridden British view of the Germans that saw them almost entirely through the prism of two World Wars.

Miranda proved an excellent interviewee, and I subsequently added a number of further interviews with, among others, Claire Tomalin, Antonia Fraser, Ian Kershaw, Roy Foster, Peter Burke, Peter Hennessy and Margaret Macmillan.

I enjoyed working at the IHR and in 2015 was able to undertake a substantial new project for the Institute: a series of six public seminars in Senate House at which panels of distinguished historians were invited to discuss before a wide general audience the often controversial ways in which people tended to use – and abuse – the past.

I outlined the idea in autumn 2014 to the incoming IHR Director, Lawrence Goldman (previously director of the Oxford Dictionary of National Biography). I told him of the intellectual weight and content I intended the series to contain, the kind of names I hoped to entice to sit on the panels and the opportunities the series would present – if energetically publicised – to bring to the IHR a larger and broader-based audience than generally attended the events it promoted. Lawrence gave the project the go-ahead and I spent much of the spring and summer of 2015 preparing the details of an ambitious undertaking that we launched in October.

* * *

In some ways, the project took off from the apparent paradox that had been central to the book I had started some years earlier for Sutton. On the one hand, what we call 'history' seemed to be in many ways more popular than ever: in schools and universities, on film, television and the internet, in sales of historical novels and biographies, in visitor numbers to heritage sites, family history, re-enactment societies and the like. In Britain, millions watched TV costume dramas such as Downton Abbey or Wolf Hall; books and TV programmes abounded on historical anniversaries (Magna Carta, Agincourt, Waterloo and the First World War) and there was the huge popular interest aroused by the recent rediscovery and re-interment of the bones of King Richard III. There were parallels elsewhere, too: in the USA, for example, where the 150th anniversary of end of the Civil War and the death of Abraham Lincoln were marked by a flurry of new books and TV programmes.

Yet at the same time we also seemed to live in a culture that could be disturbingly lacking in historical awareness. Press and politicians liked to alarm us by reporting polls revealing that (for example) only one British teenager in six knew that the Duke of Wellington led the British army in the Battle of Waterloo and only one in ten could name a 19th-century

IHR poster, 2015–16.

British Prime Minister. Or that 33 per cent of respondents in a US poll did not know when the Declaration of Independence was adopted and 80 per cent had no idea who was President during World War I.

It was not just a question of not knowing the facts. More profoundly, important current issues were frequently discussed with little regard for the backstory. Of course, people often turned to a version of history or a pivotal personality or event in the past when addressing contemporary concerns. But it was often highly selective history that was sought and cited: a simplistic invocation of the past to help bolster present-day attitudes (for example, the way one foreign 'hate' figure after another, from Nasser and

Idi Amin to Saddam Hussein and Osama bin Laden, was lazily compared with Hitler, or how British advocates of overseas military intervention routinely invoked supposed analogies with 1939). In practice, genuinely complex problems all too often tended to be discussed in immediate, present-day terms, with little or no serious regard for their longer-term roots: migration policy, for example, or continued British membership of the EU, Russian involvement in Ukraine or continuing war and violence in the Middle East. I was reminded of the wise words of the French historian Marc Bloch (who was murdered by the Nazis in 1944):

'Misunderstanding of the present is the inevitable consequence of ignorance of the past.'

* * *

I decided to call the IHR seminar series *History Now and Then*, a title I had used over twenty years earlier for my BBC series with Roy Porter but which seemed particularly apposite now. And we started with the disturbing paradox outlined above: that there was a lot of history about and yet, at the same time, many people seemed to live in a bubble of the immediate present.

One manifestation of this, it seemed, was the widespread appeal of what had come to be called our 'Heritage': the topic of the second Seminar. There had always of course been those, in Britain and elsewhere, concerned to conserve or renovate valued remains from the past (this was the day job of Prosper Mérimée, better known as the author of *Carmen* in 19th-century Paris, and of his protégé Viollet-le-Duc). But the reverence for Heritage (with a capital 'H') had become more widespread than ever in recent decades, perhaps alongside a growing sense that much of our historic fabric was in danger of being lost. The traditional corner store was being elbowed aside by the shopping mall and pedestrian precinct, while fading aristocrats were forced to vacate their country houses, often seeing their crumbling townhouses replaced by concrete tower blocks. Euston station lost its classical arch and nearby St Pancras was only reprieved from demolition at the last moment. It has been said that history becomes especially important at times of danger. Here, it was the very physicality of the past that seemed under threat. Pressure groups and governmental authorities began to take action (English Heritage was set up in 1983). Who could quarrel with the idea that, while there was still time, a nation's 'Heritage' had to be saved?

Well, there *were* critics. Some, while sympathetic to the fundamental idea of preserving the legacy of the past, were disturbed by how they saw it being done. Patrick Wright, for example, argued that history was in danger of becoming enwrapped in quaintness and antiquarianism, that a sanitised narrative of national history was being harnessed for basically political purposes. David Cannadine worried that the very idea of a national 'Heritage' was in danger of encouraging what he dubbed 'a picture-postcard version of Britain', while Robert Hewison wrote a powerful polemic about what he called the 'Heritage Industry', arguing that the past was becoming commercialised and commodified. The sort of thing that had been wittily evoked by Alan Bennett in his play *People*, produced at London's National Theatre in 2012.

The idea of 'Heritage' was and remained controversial. What exactly should be conserved and what scrapped? Why this building but not that? Wasn't it, some argued, false to history to restore a crumbling building back to its 'original' state? Uppark, a magnificent 17th-century country house in Sussex, was devastated by fire in 1989 but superbly restored and, in 1995, reopened to the public. And who could deny the magnificence of Dresden's *Frauenkirche*, painstakingly rebuilt (partly with British help) exactly as it was when destroyed by Allied bombing in February 1945? Yet I often wondered whether, had St Paul's Cathedral been badly hit during the war (which it nearly was), it would subsequently have been re-erected as a replica of Wren's masterpiece on the old site. More likely, I suspected, something 'modern' (like Liverpool's Catholic Cathedral, perhaps, or Spence's Coventry). And I had some sympathy with the apparently perverse argument that, in the interests of 'authenticity', the great tower in Pisa should be engineered back to its intended perpendicular position (or allowed to fall) rather than to remain permanently, artificially, propped up at an angle akin to the one it assumed sometime after its original construction.

So: why renovate Uppark, the *Frauenkirche* or the Pisa tower at all while continuing to clear away surviving industrial-era slums or factories? To its critics, 'Heritage' was in danger of becoming something of a sentimental, rearguard movement that arguably overvalued the aristocratic (and often slavery-financed) past and could all too often allow the supposedly 'beautiful' to take precedence over the merely 'historic'. Maybe it was a symptom, in Britain as elsewhere, of a resurgent quest for a shared national identity. Wasn't there a danger of the real past becoming anaesthetised, every ancient site endowed with theme-park prettiness and an obligatory lavender-tinted retail outlet? I understood such arguments. Yet, at the same, I felt we could not hope to learn from the past unless every effort was made to preserve and conserve those valued material manifestations of the past that had survived. One way or another, the idea of 'Heritage' was a topic capable of arousing powerful passions.

So was the relationship between history and myth, another of the themes discussed in the IHR seminar series. What do you know – and how, and from what sources – about Boadicea (or 'Boudica') and her knife-endowed chariot, King Alfred and the cakes or Drake playing bowls before defeating the Spanish Armada? Or about the Trojan Wars, or of Joan of Arc trouncing the English (if you are French), George Washington and the cherry tree (if you are American) or the Emperor Barbarossa (if German)? Who were the heroes and villains of history? Many widely repeated historical myths concerned the origins, creators and subsequent continuity of nation states. As a child growing up in London, I proudly repeated that 'we won the war' and how we'd had a continuous monarchy (and never been successfully invaded) for something approaching a thousand years. True? At best 'true-ish'. But the very repetition of certain mythologies, from those of Homer or Virgil, via the 'cake' anecdotes associated with Alfred the Great or Marie Antoinette to the preternaturally unsmiling Queen Victoria, remind us of the historical resonance such stories can acquire.

Any self-respecting historian would of course avoid repeating myths about the past as though they were true. Then why, I wondered, did no work of historical research ever seem to be definitive, the final word on the subject (the theme of another of the IHR seminars)? Was there even such a thing as historical reality? I sensed that, despite protestations to the contrary, we all see the past through the shifting perspectives of the present, with each generation seemingly constrained to re-interpret and even (dare I say it?) re-mythologise the past. Often, the myths and distortions of the past are essentially political. Thus, the Japanese had recently been re-writing their school history books (particularly the sections about World War II), and they were doing something of the same in Ukraine and Poland as they made attempts to distance themselves from Russia. Did the British Empire help educate millions around the world into the benefits of democracy or was it primarily a form of ruthless (and racist) commercial exploitation? How, I found myself wondering, did one regard – and label – the mass murder of Armenian Turks a century before, or the evacuation of Arabs from Palestine in 1947–48? Did Lincoln fight the Civil War in order to free the slaves or primarily to prevent his nation from falling apart? As I began to set up the seminar series, I began to think ahead: to the centenary of the Dublin uprising in Easter 1916 and, the following year, that of the two Russian Revolutions: plenty of scope there, I surmised, for new bouts of historical re-writing.

Then there was the role of artworks as a supposed source of insights about the past (the focus of another of the seminars). The first I knew about Henry V and Richard III and other historical figures came from Shakespeare. His portrayals of the Plantagenets and the rest certainly misrepresented some of the facts, and we might say the same of the picture of a battle on a Greek vase, a painting or statue of Louis XIV, an opera by Lully, Schiller's (or Verdi's) portrayal of Philip II of Spain or Rodin's *Burghers of Calais*. Can artworks, however much they may mythologise the past, nonetheless help provide a pathway towards our understanding of it? As authentic products of their own time and place, they can surely tell us something of how people in a previous era regarded those of a still earlier period, thus providing data like any other for the historian to use.

While preparing the Seminars, I was struck by how we had nowadays come to expect more exacting standards of historical accuracy from creative artists, that works such as Hilary Mantel's Tudor novels (or their TV dramatisations) were liable to arouse criticism if found to be in any way historically misleading. In the light of the extraordinary to-do about the re-interment of Richard III, I took another look at the 1955 Olivier film of the Shakespeare play. The fact that the Bard was no historian was acknowledged in the opening titles where an imitation late-Medieval illuminated manuscript informed viewers that, while the play may not be a work of historical scholarship, it was none the worse for that:

> *The history of the world, like letters without poetry, flowers without perfume, or thought without imagination, would be a dry matter indeed without its legends, and many of these, though scorned by proof a hundred times, seem worth preserving for their own familiar sakes.*

* * *

One way and another, I had no doubt that what we loosely called 'history' was widely popular. But what, I wondered, did 'history' mean to all those who so avidly consumed it, used it (and abused it)? To you? Or to me? For some, especially amongst older history lovers perhaps, history could no doubt provide a heart-warming element of nostalgia or of consolation while others might find themselves experiencing a sense of shared pride or vindication. Some history lovers doubtless sought affirmations of personal identity as they sifted through the past (think of the popularity of national and family history, and of histories touching on gender, ethnicity or nationhood) while who has not, at one time or another, relished learning more about a much-loved hero of earlier times or a much-despised villain? History means many things to many people. But its focus had moved on since I first learned about its kings and generals and political leaders to an emphasis on economic and social history, then to cultural history, a much heralded 'return to narrative', a burst of post-modernism from some historians and, more recently, a powerful re-emphasis on ethnic minorities and gender history. What new historiographical turn, I wondered, should we be anticipating in the years to come? How, as the digital era took increasing hold, would people seek their historical 'fix'? Already when the IHR series was launched, many were increasingly inclined to turn to the Internet or iPlayer than to lengthy books; museums and heritage centres flourished as bookshops and publishers faltered. As the series came to an end, I expressed the hope that, in what was said to be an increasingly present-oriented age, debate about the present and future would be properly buttressed by an informed awareness of all that had preceded it.

The six seminars, one per month, ran from early October 2015. Inevitably, over the course of the six months, a few changes of cast had to be made (notably in response to the sad and premature death of David Cesarani, whose place at the third seminar was kindly taken at short notice by Adam Sutcliffe). But in general, all went as planned and the seminars proved a great success. So much so that Lawrence Goldman asked me to organise and chair a follow-up series for 2016–17.

The new series was, if anything, even more adventurous in its reach than the first. Panelists included many of our best-known historians and the series began with the issues raised by the controversy over the Rhodes statue at Oriel College, Oxford. A militant student movement ('Rhodes Must Fall') demanded the removal of a statue said to represent a man by now regarded by many as a symbol of white, racist imperialism. There was much in the press around this time about student groups (not only in Britain) demanding 'safe spaces' where subjects causing 'offence' should be banned. Thus, visiting speakers arguing or representing a currently unpopular view about race, religion, empire, sexuality, Israel and much else were likely to

IHR poster, 2016–167

have the invitation withdrawn or, if they kept the engagement, to be noisily boycotted by those who disapproved of their stance.

It seemed to me (and to Lawrence Goldman and most mature academics I knew) that this was precisely why such issues should be open to public discussion at universities and elsewhere: coolly, calmly, rationally, with opposing views courteously but openly expressed. If the statue of Rhodes should be removed, why not that of Robert Clive at the Foreign Office (or of Churchill, glowering just across from Parliament)? And if Rhodes should be retained on the grounds that, whatever you might think of him, he was an important figure historically, shouldn't Munich have one of Hitler? In general, should memorials to figures of whom we might now disapprove be removed and street names altered to suit the times – or was this kind of thinking false to history? What about the creation of prominent new memorials to people from the past whom we had come to know about and admire only recently? Mary Seacole, for example, whose statue was unveiled in June 2016 and stands at St Thomas' Hospital, directly across the Thames from the Houses of Parliament. Was it appropriate for people today to apologise for supposed wrongs committed by their ancestors in the distant past? How far, in sum, should history be re-written in accordance with current values?

These were the issues I planned to raise at the opening seminar in October 2016, with a panel of distinguished historians, including the brilliant (and often outspoken) David Starkey. As the date for this opening seminar approached, the IHR was informed that a student group was planning a possible protest: the very topic was evidently anathema to some, while controversy was doubtless exacerbated by the presence of Starkey on the panel. In the event, the evening was sold out and, despite promise of police protection, no disturbance was reported (and David gave us a characteristically witty contribution to the proceedings).

A second seminar focused on the nature and causes of historical change. Why does so much history tend to concentrate on great discontinuities in

Daniel introducing IHR Seminar, 2 November 2016.
SEATED L-R *Margaret Macmillan, Gareth Stedman Jones, Andrew Roberts.*

the past, and how far have major changes been brought about by individual leaders?

From there, we moved on to ask what should be the proper focus of history. Many historians choose to concentrate on the nation state, though some have preferred to focus on the locality, or maybe the wider world. And should 'history' have a short, precisely defined temporal focus, or a longer *durée*? A month later, the spotlight fell on the question of how far history could be said to repeat itself and, more generally, what kind of lessons (if any) one might learn from the past. What about the 'ifs' of history – the topic I had covered in my book of 1979 (see Chapter 41)? Could the past have been different if, for example, Wellington had lost the Battle of Waterloo or there had been no Hitler? In the fifth seminar, we went on to examine the historical role of religion. Has religion, with its sometimes charismatic leaders and powerful ideals, provided a fundamental motivating force in history – in the Crusades, for example, or the Thirty Years' War or British Civil War? Or has it primarily reflected deeper socioeconomic trends and priorities?

In the sixth and final seminar, I decided we would attempt to look at 'the future of the past' and I asked my panelists to travel forwards through time and imagine themselves looking back, half a century hence, on the here and now. What would future historians consider we had over-emphasised or under-emphasised as they examined the first decade or two of the new millennium and came to judge the ways you and I currently try to look back at earlier times? What impact would new digital technologies have on how the past is regarded? More generally, what new historiographical turn should we be anticipating? Maybe, I suggested, the IHR could re-run this entire series of seminars a few decades hence so we could all find out!

Chapter 55
Opera Resurgens

One day in 2012, I received an invitation to attend an exploratory meeting at the Victoria and Albert Museum, London, at which members of the V&A and Royal Opera House management teams would explore the possibility of a major exhibition on the history of opera. The meeting took place on 9 August and was chaired by the V&A's recently appointed Chief Executive, Martin Roth. I was evidently invited on the strength of my book *The Gilded Stage* and, as those around the table discussed the possible scale and style of such an exhibition, costs, visitor numbers and whether and where it might tour after London, I found myself – the only 'unattached' person present – advocating the widest historical focus: not merely a collection of memorabilia of great composers and singers, but something about the cities and theatres in which opera took place, audiences and ticket prices.

In due course – and I like to think I had some influence over this – the plan was for the exhibition to concentrate on seven European cities, each of which hosted an historically significant operatic premiere:

Venice (Monteverdi's *L'Incoronazione di Poppea*, 1642/3)
London (Handel's *Rinaldo*, 1711)
Vienna (Mozart's *Le nozze di Figaro*, 1786)
Milan (Verdi's *Nabucco*, 1842)
Paris (Wagner's *Tannhaüser*, Paris version, 1861)
Dresden (Strauss's *Salome*, 1905)
St Petersburg (Shostakovich's *Lady Macbeth of Mtsensk*, 1934)

The aim was to examine each of these through three perspectives:

the broader social/cultural history of the city concerned
more specifically, the theatrical and operatic context
the particular composer and featured work

The exhibition was planned to open in September 2017 in the V&A's new wing on Exhibition Road – which would only recently have been inaugurated. Originally intended to remain in London for three months, it was later decided that the exhibition warranted a longer residence at the

V&A, remaining there through the new year until the end of February 2018, after which it was hoped it would travel to all or most of the other six cities in turn over the course of the next two or three years.

During the run-up to what was clearly intended to be a major international exhibition, I found myself not only called upon periodically as opera historian/consultant but also invited to write one of the essays for the exhibition catalogue (on Handel and the London of the early 18th century) and then to undertake a 12-week course of lectures to accompany the exhibition from September–December 2017. Meanwhile, the publishers of *The Gilded Stage*, evidently impressed at the potential marketing opportunities provided by the exhibition, decided to do all they could to add further foreign language editions of the book to those already obtained (Italian, Spanish and Chinese) in good time for the show's journeyings across the map of Europe.

The exhibition opened to great acclaim at the end of September 2017. Curated by the V&A's Kate Bailey, it essentially took the form of a great pie cut into seven slices. Thus, the first slice introduced you to the luxurious joys of 17th-century Venice, a commercial republic especially enticing to the wealthy visitor between Christmas and Lent, the months of 'Carnival'. Venice in the 1630s and '40s was home to the first commercial opera theatres, and it was here that Claudio Monteverdi composed his final great stage work *L'Incoronazione di Poppea* which was packed with those operatic mainstays, sex and death. The exhibition utilised a wonderful, state-of-the-art earphone device whereby the music moved with you. Thus, as you edged your way out of the Vienna-&-Mozart section and into Milan-&-Verdi, an ensemble from *Figaro* gave way to the chorus from *Nabucco.*

For the accompanying lecture course I had three one-hour sessions to fill every Friday for 12 weeks (September–December): 36 one-hour sessions in all. This, in turn, was the first third of a year-long V&A course on 'The History of Performance' with colleagues speaking on dance history during January–March 2018 and theatre history in April–June. I gave most of the opera history lectures myself, making sure to emphasise the wider historical context of this most multimedia of art forms. But I also invited a number of expert guests from the academic world and the operatic professions to speak to the class from time to time as well as John Allison, editor of *OPERA* magazine, my cousin Nicholas who had of course run opera companies and an old friend, Stephen Brown, who until recently had been Company Manager of the Metropolitan Opera, New York. All went well and, before my term was over, the V&A asked if I would repeat it a year later, in autumn 2018, long after the exhibition had departed. Not a bad way to pass one's 80th birthday, I figured!

In February 2018, shortly before the exhibition closed, I was invited to give a lunchtime 'pop-up' lecture in one of the V&A galleries: an event advertised to people who happened to be visiting that morning. All very casual. I suggested giving a talk about Verdi and Victoria: a topic that seemed neatly to encompass both the Museum and what was its principal current exhibition. We had a good turnout as we gathered around a bust of the great lady herself. All good fun. I was flattered (amused? not sure…) to see the talk promoted that day as being presented by the 'inimitable' Daniel Snowman!

Daniel at the V&A, 2018.

The 'Inimitable' Daniel Snowman!

Book 12

'Over and Out'

Chapter 56

Back to the (possible) Future . . .

Another turn of a decade and I found myself involved in another project: Consultant to what was planned to be a year-long festival celebrating the artistic contribution of the refugees from Nazism. The festival, named *Insiders/Outsiders,* was the brainchild of the art historian Monica Bohm-Duchen. Daughter of the refugee photographer Dorothy Bohm, Monica had curated an exhibition as long ago as 1986 at the Camden Arts Centre (Arkwright Road) on *Art in Exile in Great Britain, 1939–45*, and over the years we had met from time to time. In 2013, around the time I was launching a new NADFAS lecture on 'War and the Arts', I reviewed her latest book *Art and the Second World War* published by Lund Humphries. By then, Monica was a fellow NADFAS lecturer and (also like me at the time) led cultural tours for the Martin Randall Travel company. I was delighted when she invited me to act as consultant to the festival and to

'Refugees' *by Josef Herman (Cover of* Insiders/Outsiders, *2019).*
(I am grateful to publishers Lund Humphries, and to David Herman, son of the artist, for permission to reproduce this image)

write the introductory chapter in the book (also published by LH) that accompanied it.

When I wrote my book about the Hitler émigrés back around the turn of the century, many of the most distinguished of the refugees were still alive, by then in their late 70s and 80s and even older, and were at that stage in their lives happy for me to interview them. Indeed, the book could not have been undertaken without their cooperation. As time passed, sadly most of them died, my interviews with them lodged in the sound archives of London's Imperial War Museum, and the whole subject gradually passed into history. Then, somewhat to my surprise, it returned to prominence once again with the approach of the 80th anniversary of the outbreak of the War in 2019, and the 75th of its conclusion a year later – just at a time when the British press and political world had become preoccupied once more with the urgent question of how to deal with an upsurge of migrants and asylum seekers. It was in this atmosphere that the *Insiders/Outsiders* festival was conceived and launched.

The Project opened in spring 2019 and was planned to last a full year or more. It proved a huge success, was linked to galleries and museums across London and the length and breadth of Britain and included countless exhibitions of artworks (many of them by women) as well as a concert of works by refugee composers and a number of lectures. By early 2020, Monica and the team (myself included) were talking about how we might be able to prolong the legacy of the festival and further events we might like to set up. I was keen to highlight not just the refugee composers but also such musical performers as Klemperer, Solti and the Amadeus Quartet, and we also talked of a possible event commemorating some of the great cultural entrepreneurs: Claus Moser, Paul Hamlyn and Victor Hochhauser, for example, and publishers such as Deutsch, Weidenfeld, Phaidon, Thames and Hudson and others. We thought we should approach London's Southbank about the forthcoming 70th anniversary of the 1951 Festival of Britain, at which many of the major buildings and artworks had been designed or engineered by refugees from Nazism. Then, in March 2020, just a few days after Monica and I had spoken at a conference at Cambridge to mark the contributions of the Hitler émigrés to the university, Britain was struck down – virtually closed down – by the arrival of Coronavirus.

* * *

Daniel on Anti-Brexit march (opposite Parliament), June 23, 2018.

Despite my personal good fortune, I had begun over recent years to find myself increasingly concerned about the apparent erosion, in Britain and beyond, of the values to which I had been committed throughout much of my life. It had been unimaginable to me that the people of Britain would choose, in a referendum, to leave the European Union. Or that Americans would vote for a President Trump. The short-term thinking, or lack of thinking, that led to these results shocked me. How could anyone in Britain with even the slightest historical awareness vote to quit the EU, an institution set up in the aftermath of two appalling World Wars in the hope of developing a new era of international cooperation? In order to 'win our sovereignty back'? When was Britain ever 'sovereign'? When, that is, was Britain ever in a position to govern itself unimpeded by the requirements and demands of other nations, to feed its population primarily on home-grown food, limit its involvement in foreign trade, travel and indeed war? And when did Britain – an off-shore island, for centuries drawing waves of people from across the Roman Empire, Angles and Saxons, Normans, Huguenots, the Irish following the Famine, my own ancestors from Jewish Eastern Europe, refugees from Nazism and beyond and immigrants from across the largest empire in history – when was this little island ever a bastion of sovereign exclusivity?

As for the crudity of the 2016 US presidential campaign, with victory going to a zillionaire airhead whose policies were proclaimed via self-aggrandising sound-bite slogans and tweets, this truly seemed to threaten an international system from which most had benefited. Would Trump really exclude all Muslim immigrants to the USA, build a wall across the Mexican frontier (and tariff walls against many of America's principal trading partners), disregard the basic tenets of NATO and the attempts to bring Iran (and Cuba) back into the comity and congeniality of nations? Did 'liberty' mean anyone in America could do anything, more or less unimpeded, in order to try and become rich, while leaving those who were poor, including in the slums of America, to rot unaided on the social scrapheap?

Trump and Brexit were signs of the times. I could understand that, for nearly a decade following the financial crash of 2008, many in Britain, America and around the world had come to feel themselves denied what they considered their due and increasingly irate with the 'establishment', the governmental authorities that had seemingly led them so inadequately. Selfishly, indeed, feathering their own nests at the expense of 'we the people'. As the visionary Czech leader Václav Havel said to America's new young President, Barack Obama, when they met in spring 2009, the global economic crisis was helping strengthen the forces of nationalism and populist extremism right across Europe and beyond.

Increasingly, I sensed a growing desire for leadership that would put 'us' first even if at the expense of the 'other'. Among followers of Britain's UKIP and the American 'Tea Party', for example, and in France with the rise of Marine le Pen's *Front National* and Austria where the neo-fascist Freedom Party candidate, Norbert Hofer, had come close to winning the Presidency in 2016, a contingency only avoided by holding a second referendum. There were similar stirrings, too, in Germany with the emergence of the AfD party, and in Italy with the oppositional Five Star movement and the Netherlands with Geert Wilders becoming an icon to many. In Poland and Hungary self-assertive nationalist parties and leaders proved widely popular while there were parallels in the ever-stronger Islamic nationalism of Erdoğan's Turkey and the Hindu-led government of India under Prime Minister Modi - and I haven't even mentioned Putin's Russia or Xi Jinping's China. Like Boris Johnson in the UK, all seemed to be proclaiming their own national versions of the simplistic slogan adopted by Trump and his followers: 'Make America Great Again!'

One manifestation of this widespread and growing political mood was that many of the great institutions of international collaboration were increasingly undermined, not just the European Union but also NATO, the World Health Organisation and the United Nations and its various agencies, plus a host of cross-national agreements covering trade, travel and the like. None was perfect any more than were most international treaties, such as that signed with Iran in 2015 by (mostly) Western powers, promising improved trading relations if Iran would limit its defence system to non-nuclear weaponry, or the Paris Agreement signed by most of the world's nation states a year later aimed at limiting the rise in global temperatures. To my mind the way to deal with inadequate cross-national or cross-party agreements or institutions was to make the most of them, to try to improve them, not simply to pull out and restore a potentially dangerous *status quo ante*. I found myself thinking back to the optimism of the 1990s, the emergence of a potentially democratic Russia, the end of Apartheid in South Africa, the Oslo agreement between Israel and the Palestinian leadership, the Good Friday Agreement between the warring parties in Northern Ireland and the adoption by many of the states of continental Europe of a shared currency, the Euro. None of these put an immediate or total end to the problems they aimed to solve. But all helped to alleviate them.

I am not given to false historical analogies. But as I watched the apparent dissolution of the optimistic internationalism of previous decades and the rapid rise in political circles of a crude and often angry nationalistic, self-regarding rhetoric, it was hard not to reflect on some parallels with the German world in the later 1920s. Germany, after just a few decades of national sovereignty followed by military humiliation in the Great War, had plunged into severe economic recession and millions of people, resentful of mainstream political leadership, became increasingly transfixed by the fiery yet redemptive rhetoric of a young National Socialist leader born across the border in Austria.

* * *

Here in Britain, as in Trump's America and elsewhere, the popular political rhetoric was becoming more divisive, more concerned with protest than with possible solutions. What did smug political leaders (or the 'experts' who advised them) know, people asked, when none of them had personally experienced the tragedies and deprivations they were supposedly paid to resolve? After the high-rise Grenfell Tower block of flats in London caught fire in 2017, with many lives lost, a widespread reaction was not so much a communal determination that such a catastrophe should never become possible again but, rather, recurrent anger at the inadequacies of the local council, the fire service and the people who had installed the external cladding.

A similar response was aroused by other issues. 'Institutional' racism and sexism, for example. I had always supported the idea of equality of opportunity for all – black, white, male, female, heterosexual or homosexual or whatever – and fundamentally agreed with the principles underlying the emergence of such movements as 'MeToo' feminism and 'Black Lives Matter'. And, as demonstrated in my IHR series of public Seminars, I was all in favour of public discussion about, for example, whether a memorial to Colston in Bristol or Rhodes in Oxford (or a Confederate general in the USA) should be removed or re-labelled. Or for that matter how best to deal with the oil industry at a time of climate crisis or with such controversial foreign nations as Saudi Arabia or Israel. But such issues came increasingly to be discussed with anger, demonstrations and even potential violence. Or, at the other extreme, to be closed down altogether lest they cause 'offence' in what came to be dubbed the 'cancel culture'.

Another controversial phrase arose with the growth of 'identity politics': not least in the UK where people, who might earlier have thought of themselves primarily as British, came increasingly to identify themselves with others of similar race, colour, gender, region or religion. No problem with this. We all have multi-identities and these are among them. But the new trend often seemed to take a negative turn. It was not so much that you identified yourself as black, female, transgender, disabled, a 'northerner' or whatever. Alongside this was a growing and often outspoken resentment towards those labelled as being prejudiced against you. Demands were made, quite understandably, for more black actors or women to be cast in film and tv roles, more members of ethnic minorities to be represented at universities and for special music or literary prizes exclusively for black or female artists. But that could result in the opposite prejudice: the exclusion of people of talent who happened to be male or white.

Something of the same resulted from the emergence of what came to be called 'cultural appropriation', the idea that if someone in a film or play was supposed to be Jewish, gay or disabled (or black, like Shakespeare's Othello) the part should be given to someone of the same identity, not 'copied' by an outsider. Whatever happened to the idea that the job of an actor was to 'act' (as Laurence Olivier famously explained to the young Dustin Hoffman)?

Culture and the arts, like so much else, came increasingly to be regarded through a partly political lens. With the Coronavirus pandemic and the closure of most of Britain's great cultural and entertainment centres, many thousands of musicians and dancers, actors, artists, academics and others found themselves without work while their traditional audiences were reduced to watching, if at all, from home online. Simply protesting about the poor jobless artists was no answer. Yes, there should be money to help sustain good museums and theatres in Sheffield, Leeds and Leicester. But taking it from the (diminishing) subsidies to such international institutions of excellence as the London-based Royal Opera or National Theatre was hardly an answer. Increasingly, attitudes towards education, culture and the arts seemed based on social criteria rather than those of excellence. Thus, it was evidently politically safer for money to be allotted to an institution that could demonstrate its concern with its local community, and with such factors as diversity and access, than to one appealing for an increase in funding purely based on the high quality of the work it aspired to achieve. After all, who is to say that your view of what is 'high quality' is more valid than mine?

* * *

With the unanticipated prolongation of the 2020 pandemic, I sensed a nascent confrontation between – and perhaps within – two fundamental values of western democracy: Liberty and Equality. I subscribed to both, of course, and had benefited from both throughout my life. But to each there had to be limits. The debate went back a long way. Among the most famous documents in American political history is the 10th '*Federalist Paper*' by James Madison. Madison, contemplating the potential US Constitution back in the 1780s, had considered the political implications – and dangers – of a democracy in which all were free to vote in elections, with policy following the views of the majority without also having to take account of those of smaller factions. John Stuart Mill similarly, in his 1859 essay *On Liberty*, considered the dangers of what he called the 'tyranny of the majority' while, in more recent times, major figures from Franklin D Roosevelt to Isaiah Berlin had famously defined and distinguished between what they saw as various forms of liberty.

Freedom, all agreed, was an essential element of democracy. But it should never be absolute. Where then should its limits be drawn – regarding freedom of speech and action, for example? There had to be laws banning the advocacy of murder or violent crime. But what about language and actions that many found deeply (and perhaps dangerously) offensive? In London, at the height of the Covid-19 pandemic, public rallies took place at which unmasked speakers addressed enthusiastic, non-distanced crowds and demanded the right *not* to obey the political rules – in the name of 'freedom'. And with the arrival of an anti-virus vaccine, its potential benefits were undermined across the social media by conspiracy theorists asserting that the vaccine was the creation of a lying group of money-makers. Should such views be banned? And, if so, how? Should the police arrest people enjoying themselves at a rowdy, non-self-distanced New Year's Eve or wedding party at the height of the pandemic? What about members of Extinction Rebellion blocking the London traffic in their earnest attempt to bring to everyone's attention the vastly greater dangers of climate change?

I began drafting this in the aftermath of the mass invasion of the United States Congress on 6 January 2021 by thuggish followers of President Trump, egged on by his crudely encouraging tweets. Soon afterwards, Trump's accounts were taken down by Twitter and Facebook, but that only gave rise to complaints of censorship by his followers. After all, the First Amendment to the US Constitution prohibits the abridgement of the freedom of speech, or the right of the people peaceably to assemble and to petition the Government for a redress of grievances. How could a President of the United States be denied the freedom to express his views?

'Equality' too was a fundamental value to which, in general, I subscribed. But with limits. In the emerging digital world of the 21st century an almost aggressive egalitarianism came to hold sway. 'We want to know what you think,' trumpeted the media; 'join the debate!' And the radio phone-in programmes, the tweets and the Facebook entries brimmed over with strongly held opinions by people who had no more than an anecdote or two with which to reinforce their supposed arguments. All and any messages, from whatever provenance or authority, had an equal chance of becoming predominant. Or, to use the jargon of the day, of 'going viral'. To me (as in those BBC programmes I had produced long before with John Vaizey) it was important to distinguish between equality of 'opportunity' and of 'condition'.

I was a passionate advocate of equality of opportunity. Almost Marxist indeed, believing that any honourable government should impose taxation upon all who could pay in order to create a budget capable of giving all its citizens equal access to the finest health care, education, transport, police and general welfare a civilised society was capable of providing. But I was equally adamant in opposing any form of enforced equality of condition: a veritable right-winger, some would say, as I argued against enabling proportionate numbers of men and women or of ethnic minorities or people educated in this or that kind of school necessarily to be represented on the boards of top businesses or in leading universities or in parliament, for example, independent of their personal abilities and qualifications. Everybody should start off with equal opportunities for advancement through life. But if I go to the opera I simply want to see and hear the finest performers the world is capable of assembling, while the England football or cricket team has surely to include the eleven best players the nation can provide regardless of their background or colour.

* * *

On 1st January 2021, the people of Britain woke up to a nation no longer part of the European Union. The UK government had finally signed a somewhat flimsy 'deal' with the EU thereby just managing to leave the bloc by the time they were legally obliged to do so. At least a bad deal was better than what had ominously threatened to be 'no deal', many felt. Meanwhile, the danger of Coronavirus was evidently spreading (perhaps in part due to people socialising, often maskless, over Christmas and New Year) while new 'Variants' of the pandemic, emanating from South Africa and Brazil, helped render the threat ever greater.

Then, on 6th January, while the US Congress voted to certify the results of the 2020 presidential election (which President Trump continued to proclaim had been 'rigged' by the victorious Democrats), pro-Trump protesters stormed the US Capitol resulting in chambers being vandalized and several deaths. This appalling invasion of the home of US democracy sent both lawmakers and members of the press scrambling for safety. Some hid under the table in their offices or found discreet paths out of the building, while others took shelter in the tunnels beneath the Capitol. The event, which Trump had (to put it mildly) done nothing to prevent, led to the lame-duck president being impeached the following day by a shocked

ABOVE *(inset) US Capitol being constructed, 1861.*
ABOVE *US Capitol under attack, 6 January 2021.*

BELOW *President Joe Biden (centre) and Vice-President Kamala Harris (right) following their inauguration, 20 January, 2021.*

and outraged House of Representatives, becoming the only President in American history to have been impeached twice.

* * *

Thus, the world through which I was passing in 2021, and the little bit of it that I inhabited, faced a multitude of problems. But ultimately, I sensed, there was a link between them: the dangerously shifting relationship between the world's population and its life-sustaining resources. In 1800, there had been an estimated population of a little under one billion and, a century later, around the time my grandparents were reaching adulthood, about a billion and a half. By now it had shot up to well over seven billion and by the time my children are elderly it could well have risen to the region of 12-15 billion (barring mass starvation, nuclear war or further fatal pandemics etc). In my lifetime the population of the UK alone has risen from around 45 million to over 65 million and that of the USA from 130m to a colossal 330m. Overall, such exponential growth in the world's population, and its use and abuse of the planet's limited environmental resources, was having and would continue to have a massive and increasingly detrimental impact on the quality of life available to its inhabitants. It was hardly surprising to note that ever-greater numbers of people from the poorer, overheated and increasingly war-torn parts of the world were trying to migrate to places known to be healthier, wealthier, cooler and more peaceful.

I have written above, at the end of the section about 'Cold Places' (Chapter 40), about the long-term threat and dangers of global warming, something that gradually came to be acknowledged by most world leaders (with a few exceptions, notably Donald Trump). But there was very little substantive progress in attempts by the international community to stem, let alone reverse, this deadly process. Some reduction in coal or oil consumption here, a bit of self-sustaining and renewable green energy there and, perhaps, a move in some countries to encourage people to eat less meat. But such developments were mere tinkering at the outer edges of an inexorable process that was already raising sea levels, causing unprecedented forest fires, reducing huge land areas to desert status and polluting some of the most densely populated cities to a point where the mere breathing of the air could prove fatal. In such a world, the increasing competition for clean food and water could lead to war. Most wars historically have been ostensibly for control over the other person's territory. Was it fanciful to suggest that the same might apply today – and tomorrow? If the Tigris and Euphrates, the Nile, the Jordan, the Niger and the Congo, the Yamuna, Ganges and the Brahmaputra rivers were all flowing full, free, fresh and navigable, their extended banks rich in agriculturally productive soil, would the same warlike and terroristic tensions threaten some of their adjacent peoples?

Add to this the socioeconomic tensions augmented in rich countries by people like me: old men and women, no longer of working age, who expected various authorities (the state, pension funds etc.) to provide them with all the services they required in order to be able to live even longer, ever more comfortable lives, the wherewithal provided by a proportionately ever-diminishing younger workforce. I am sometimes inclined to think, in semi-serious Malthusian mode, that the best way to solve the world's problems would be if everyone were shot on attaining their optimal biblical age of threescore and ten!

* * *

As I draw this book towards its end, times have not been easy: for the world, for Britain and for myself. The advent of Coronavirus and subsequent 'lockdowns' put an end to many of the activities to which I had long been accustomed: attending and contributing to events at the Institute of Historical Research, visiting museums and galleries, opera, concerts and the theatre, enjoying lunches and dinners with friends (and holding an annual summer garden party) and travelling around the country and abroad giving talks and lectures to welcoming, intelligent audiences. Would any of this ever return? What kind of intellectual and cultural world awaits my grandchildren? Will they and their contemporaries and successors come to know and value the works of Shakespeare, Goethe, Bach and Beethoven, Dickens and Dostoyevsky or Raphael, Rembrandt and Renoir? Or will these simply sink into becoming the vaguely familiar names of dead, white European males ('DWEMs'), long-since replaced by the latest digitally communicated trends emanating, perhaps, from the ever-growing cultural and commercial impact of the Chinese and Islamic worlds?

I don't know. We historians, supposedly expert at explaining all that has happened in the past, are pretty useless at predicting the future. You want to know the causes of the French or Russian Revolutions? Just ask. But who was able to predict the downfall of Soviet communism? Or the result of Britain's 2016 Brexit referendum? As I write, Britain's Prince Philip has recently died, the most memorable image from his funeral being that of the now widowed Queen Elizabeth II sitting alone and masked. Meanwhile, political ructions in Scotland have led to ever wider demands for a further referendum concerning the possibility of Scottish independence, while in Northern Ireland too it seems that disruptions arising from Brexit have led some on both sides of the political divide, unionists and nationalists alike, to question the Good Friday Agreement of 1998 and call for a referendum on the future of their country. Today, our so-called 'United' 'Kingdom' is still both of those things. For how long? Time will tell.

Looking back at the recurrent delays and failures in Britain's negotiations with the EU, these were widely blamed on the malevolence of the French and their continental partners, while many in Britain took comfort from the decision to station gun boats in the Channel (paid for by reducing the budget for overseas aid) in order to prevent Europeans from fishing in British waters. Rule, Britannia! As for Covid-19, the popular press was exultant when Britain administered the first anti-virus vaccine (one of its earliest recipients being a much-publicised patient named William Shakespeare), some proclaiming this to have been 'V-Day!' Maybe I should have given this book a more celebratory title: *From VE Day to V Day!*

* * *

Of one developing trend, still in its infancy, we can be pretty certain. It is already clear that many of our opinions and habits, as registered by social media, are influenced, subverted perhaps, by the subtle impact of electronic algorithms of which, consciously at least, we tend to remain largely oblivious. We may be vaguely aware of the ways these digital messages supposedly affect our shopping preferences or our voting patterns (the latter, in part perhaps, via the Kremlin or Cambridge Analytica). And, more broadly, whom or what we are inclined to admire, follow, reject or hate. But the impact could, and perhaps does, go far deeper. Into our very being, our bodies as well as our minds. Every 'decision' we make, including whether to scratch our nose, laugh at a joke or cross the road, might in the not-too-distant future be instantly registered and assessed as part of our overall digital profile, with the messages coming our way adjusted accordingly. The very idea that we humans have a degree of free will or the capacity to decide could thereby in effect be rendered obsolete.

My natural instincts deny all this, of course. I make my own decisions, *n'est-ce pas*! But intellectuals such as the Israeli historian Yuval Noah Harari have argued that humanity is on the edge of two major revolutions: one technological and the other biological. Between them, says Harari, infotech and biotech look ready to hand power to remotely controlled digital algorithms capable of manipulating human beings (or human clones?) into holding pre-programmed opinions, a world in which disembodied robotic powers invested with Artificial Intelligence (AI) will likely replace mere humans as Masters of the Universe. All this at a time when humanity faces genuine existential dangers such as possible nuclear elimination and a planet rendered incapable of supporting human life as a result of global warming and the savage onset of a worldwide pandemic. Could humanity finally come together, work together and find viable ways of dealing with supreme challenges such as these? I took some relief from the knowledge that I would not be here to find out. As future historians (if there are any) look back upon the period and place of my lucky life, I have increasingly come to reflect, they will reckon that I timed it well. Now, *there's* a reason, I thought during my early 80s, to look forward with something of a Voltairean smile after all!

Chapter 57

Just Passing Through

'From the War to the Virus'

I do not want to end this book on a negative note. Yes, I could see a broad thread of continuity from the War to the Virus, from a childhood during arguably the most brutal and destructive conflict in history to a global pandemic across an overpopulated world afflicted by catastrophic climate change, with its widespread desertification, fires and floods. Was I in old age just a typical 'angry old man', discriminated against for happening to be a frail, pale, male Oxbridge-educated representative of the much-despised 'metropolitan elite'? I could easily portray myself as such, pompously spouting that everything I was able to experience and enjoy throughout my earlier life – from school and university to job opportunities, people queuing to get on buses, opportunities for international travel, the quality of films and broadcasts, of books and publishers, opera and theatre and much else – was superior to what they had latterly become.

But this of course was nonsense. When I went to Cambridge, only a tiny fraction of late-teenage youngsters in Britain had the opportunity of benefiting from higher education, a proportion vastly increased since then, while the digital revolution had revolutionised worldwide access to a multiplicity of beneficial activities and opportunities that, in earlier form, had largely been limited to small and well-connected elites.

As for Covid-19 and climate change, or the political legacy of Brexit, Trump and the angry populism around much of the world, these may have caused me profound intellectual concern but they were issues from which, at an immediately personal level, I was largely immured – just as I had been as a baby during the War.

I tried to distract myself from the problems around me, partly by being busy with a variety of time-consuming projects - not least drafting the final sections of this memoir. Meanwhile, I received a succession of new books to read and review and had a growing number of lectures to prepare.

* * *

All the lectures I presented during the prolonged virus of 2020/21 had to be done from home via Zoom or Teams, forms of communication I had never even heard of at the start of 2020. Several were about the Hitler émigrés, many of them part of the online continuation of the *Insiders/Outsiders* project. I also gave a more academic paper to the Junior Research Fellows of the IHR as well as a range of illustrated talks focusing on the history of opera for various audiences (including a student group in China). And in early 2021 I began work on a major new lecture course for the V&A, this time on the arts and culture of Victorian Britain, which I had agreed to present a few months later. I enjoyed being busy, especially if it led me to concentrate on aspects of the past rather than the unnerving present.

Addressing a 'virtual' audience online from my office, however, was hardly the same as talking to a live audience with whom one could socialise afterwards. And the reduction in the fees normally paid for lecture appearances in the past ate substantially into domestic finances. But then, life during the virus was a lot cheaper: travel expenses largely disappeared and, while it was sad that Lucie and I were not able to indulge in luxurious, hotel-based holidays in some of the remoter parts of Britain or abroad, it was fun (and far less expensive) sitting out in our beautiful garden for much of the day during the long sunny summer, or indoors doing jigsaw puzzles or playing ping pong on the dining table. And later, after drinks and dinner, revisiting countless old films on TV.

Throughout the extended and depressing period of Covid-19 I remained in pretty good physical and mental health. As a 'vulnerable' oldie with a heart pacemaker I was treated well by Britain's hard-pressed authorities. The BBC and the government continued to provide my regular monthly pension payments, and I was called by the NHS in early January 2021 to report for an anti-Virus vaccination (which had only just become available). Not, to my innocent surprise, at my local health clinic but at a venue I had revered since first being taken there by my father as a kid: Lord's cricket ground. I had my first jab on 8th January; the following day the Queen and Prince Philip, 'locked down' at Windsor, were given theirs.

Elsewhere too there were small signs of hope. In November 2020, Joe Biden and Kamala Harris were elected in the USA to replace the Trump presidency. Following the election, despite Trump's repeated denial of the result, the invasion of the US Capitol by his followers and Trump's second impeachment, Biden continued to speak with quiet dignity about how his intention as President was to try and re-unite a dangerously dis-United States (the theme of his impressive Inaugural address on 20 January 2021). And to mobilise his government to defeat the dangers of Coronavirus and to reinstate US membership of the Paris climate agreement and the hitherto abandoned treaty with Iran while also installing more long-term, humanitarian policies concerning healthcare, immigration and much else.

Around the world it seemed there were a number of prominent leaders, in addition to Biden and his colleagues, who in their own way embodied genuinely humane views and tried to act upon them: the venerable Argentine Pope Francis, for example, or the Portuguese-born Secretary General of the United Nations, António Guterres. And influential individuals, from the teenage Greta Thunberg to the nonagenarian David Attenborough, proclaiming the supreme importance of governments and populations coming together to alleviate, delay or avoid imminent climate catastrophe. At a more local level, it was good to note in early January 2021, while Trump was still President, that the runoff election in Georgia for the US Senate was won by the two Democratic candidates, neither of whom would remotely have had a chance of victory in earlier times: the 33-year-old Jon Ossoff (from a Jewish family) and the senior pastor of the Ebenezer Baptist Church in Atlanta where Martin Luther King had once been co-pastor, Raphael Warnock. When I think back to the vicious, mindless racism I saw in Atlanta sixty years earlier (see Chapter 21), this turnaround was truly spectacular.

As I complete this Memoir, I have no Pangloss-like illusions that our pained little planet might eventually become the best of all possible worlds, a kind of global nirvana. But I have always harboured the hope that, somehow, humanity might find a way of coming together, of collaborating more closely, that 'Alle Menschen werden Brüder!' as I sang joyously in countless performances of Beethoven's 9th Symphony. And, if I may quote another of my favourite musical works, *South Pacific*, I've always been something of a 'cock-eyed optimist' looking out for the better things life has to offer. For all the horrors of the Covid-19 pandemic, I continued to enjoy our comfortable home and lovely garden and, when permissible, seeing friends and neighbours (from a social distance). As I found myself 'passing through', I could only rejoice in the long and fulfilling life I had been fortunate enough to lead and continued to lead. And I prayed and hoped that my children and grandchildren (Ben and his daughter Georgia, and Anna with her adorably energetic little Jude and newly-born daughter

In the garden.

Emmeline) – and their contemporaries and successors – might all be destined for something broadly similar.

* * *

In April 2006, after another extensive lecture tour of Australia and New Zealand, I took a long, tedious overnight flight from Auckland across the Pacific and the international date line (and Equator) to Los Angeles. During the lecture tour, several people had suggested I rewrite the personal profile on my website and, to pass the time on the flight to LA, I found myself starting to draft what I mischievously thought of as a kind of third-person 'obituary'. Every now and then over the years that followed I added brief updates, the last version ending as follows:

> By the time he entered his 80s, Snowman at his curmudgeonly worst would fulminate against the historical and cultural shallowness of the world and its leaders, not to mention electorates capable of opting for 'Brexit' and President Trump. But when in more benign mode, which was most of the time, he remained an engaging conversationalist, peppering his thoughts with insights garnered from a rich and varied life that had enabled him, more than most, to enter the spirit of other people, places and times and find links between them. Although a long-term pessimist (convinced that human life on earth would eventually succumb to the interactions between population increase, global epidemics and climate change), Snowman generally seemed to possess a fundamentally placid temperament, a legacy perhaps of a secure childhood. And, as he readily acknowledged, he was a member of the 'Lucky Generation', born in the right time and place to have enjoyed the best that life had to offer while avoiding the privations of war and want. Like many who enjoy excellent health, Snowman always claimed to be unselfconscious about ageing and unafraid of death (so long as it was reasonably painless). He knew he had had a good innings.

Index

Pages in ***bold italic*** refer to illustrations

Afterword

This book was written over the course of many years, some of the earlier sections drafted as long ago as the 1970s. I came across the existing text when moving home during the mid-2010s, added and edited sections from time to time and then, during the Coronavirus-enforced 'lockdown' of 2020/21, decided to update, edit and conclude the book with a view to publication.

All I have written above is based on personal memory: mainly my own, but occasionally where indicated on that of others who were directly involved. I have also worked my way through a large amount of documentation, starting with the impeccably detailed 'Record Book' my mother kept of my childhood and upbringing. This, alongside a large body of photographs, various surviving objects and many letters to and from my parents, grandparents and early friends and acquaintances, all helped evoke memories and authenticate facts and dates, as did my searches through newspapers of the time.

As I grew into my mid-teens and beyond, I became an almost obsessive letter writer, often sending my parents lengthy and detailed accounts of early visits abroad and the people and places I encountered, and from my mid-20s I also started publishing articles arising from some of these and subsequent experiences. Much of this material has survived and I have made extensive use of it (and sometimes quoted from it) in the course of this memoir. Later articles, reviews and books, as well as the work for countless lectures and broadcasts, have all helped revive detailed memories and all have played their part; without them I would never have been able to write this book. All due diligence has been exercised in ensuring that every word in the memoir is my copyright (except for occasional, brief and clearly identified quotations from other authors). The same applies to the illustrations, almost all of which are from my own collections except where another source is acknowledged or the source is unknown, unobtainable or, to my knowledge, copyright free. In the unlikely event that any copyright material has inadvertently been used, the author and publishers trust this will be drawn to their attention in the hope that formal permission may be obtained and acknowledged in future editions.